# CHOOSE COSTA RICA
## FOR RETIREMENT

# HELP US KEEP
# THIS GUIDE UP TO DATE

Every effort has been made by the author and editors to make this guide as accurate and useful as possible. However, many things can change after a guide is published—establishments close, phone numbers change, facilities come under new management, etc.

We would love to hear from you concerning your experiences with this guide and how you feel it could be improved and be kept up to date. While we may not be able to respond to all comments and suggestions, we'll take them to heart, and we'll also make certain to share them with the author. Please send your comments and suggestions to the following address:

The Globe Pequot Press
Reader Response/Editorial Department
P.O. Box 480
Guilford, CT 06437

Or you may e-mail us at:
editorial@GlobePequot.com

Thanks for your input, and happy travels!

NINTH EDITION

# CHOOSE COSTA RICA

## FOR RETIREMENT

Retirement, Travel, and Business Opportunities
for a New Beginning

JOHN HOWELLS

travel

Guilford, Connecticut

The prices and rates listed in this book were confirmed at press time. We recommend, however, that you call before traveling to obtain current information.

To buy books in quantity for corporate use
or incentives, call **(800) 962-0973**
or e-mail **premiums@GlobePequot.com**.

Text design: Linda R. Loiewski
Map design: Overview by Stephen Stringall, all others by Lisa Reneson; © Morris Book Publishing, LLC

Spot photography throughout © Photodisc or © Shutterstock

ISSN: 1543-6411
ISBN: 978-0-7627-4884-6

Printed in the United States of America
10 9 8 7 6 5 4 3 2 1

# CONTENTS

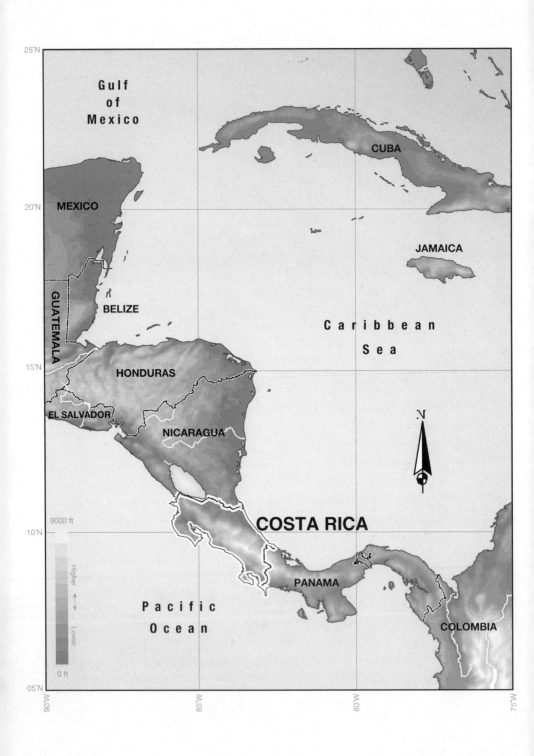

# INTRODUCTION

My love affair with Latin America began when I was sixteen years old, when my family moved to Mexico City. My father, a veterinarian, accepted a position with the U.S. Department of Agriculture on a project to eradicate hoof-and-mouth disease in the Mexican countryside. The job ended after a couple of years, but my family's involvement with Mexico endured for another thirty. My siblings and I attended high school and college in Mexico as we enjoyed the unique experience of being American expatriates in an exotic foreign country. Our family became active in Mexico's sizable British/American expatriate community of that time. All of this provided an insider's view of our fellow countrymen and their lifestyles in a Latin American cultural milieu. Later on in life, this influenced me as a travel writer; I specialized in covering topics on Mexico and Central and South America.

After our children were raised, my wife and I enjoyed taking time-outs from work obligations to experiment with living in Latin America rather than simply traveling. We would spend two or three months in rented apartments or houses in various parts of Mexico, Guatemala, Costa Rica, and Argentina. We enjoyed making friends with expatriate neighbors as well as with native residents. My fluency in Spanish (acquired as a youth in Mexico) as well as the fact that my wife majored in Spanish in college helped to facilitate friendships with our Spanish-speaking neighbors.

As we tested various living situations, we became acquainted with expatriate neighbors, making friends wherever we went. We kept asking, "Who are you, and why do you choose to live here? What's so special about where you live, and what are the drawbacks? What does it cost to live here?" The questions were endless, the answers fascinating.

After one exceptionally long visit—five months spent living in several Mexican towns and villages—an idea began to take shape. Instead of a series of travel articles, why not a guidebook? A guide to retirement in a foreign country?

About that time, we had the good fortune to meet Don and Judy Merwin in San Miguel de Allende. Don was also a writer and had worked for Edward R. Murrow at one time. We teamed up to coauthor a guidebook on living abroad. Our first book, *Choose Mexico for Retirement,* sold 50,000 copies the first year of publication!

Of all the countries my wife and I had visited, Costa Rica was our absolute favorite, so the next question became: Why not a guidebook on Costa Rica? Our first visit there took place way back in 1972 while researching Central America for travel article topics. My wife and I had heard stories of North Americans enjoying retirement in a tropical paradise. We traveled the length and breadth of the country, asking questions, making friends, discovering their "best-kept secrets." We enjoyed our visit and our new friends so much that we vowed to join them at our first opportunity. That opportunity came a few years later when we bought a condo in the San José area. Later we built a home in a delightful little Pacific beach community.

Understand that we are not full-time residents of Costa Rica, or anywhere else for that matter. We feel that life is too short to put down deep roots, not when there are so many wonderful places in the world to be enjoyed. We have a home in California and share time between there, Costa Rica, and traveling wherever our fancy dictates. We spend time in Mexico, sometimes several times in a year. Both our Costa Rica and California homes are popular with home-exchange enthusiasts, so we have no problem trading residences with people in foreign countries.

Our last home exchange was six weeks in the south of France.

This ninth edition of *Choose Costa Rica* is the direct result of our years of research and our insights to beginning life anew in Costa Rica. The book is a how-to-do-it guide to living in our favorite country, whether for retirement, business, volunteering, or simply enjoying the ambience. This book is also designed as a guide for those individuals who manage to have part or all of the year free to do exactly what they feel like doing. It's for the professional on sabbatical, the schoolteacher on a summer

vacation, the construction worker with chronic winter unemployment, the employee who can take a leave of absence, the self-employed individual who can trust the businesses to others.

*Choose Costa Rica* is especially oriented toward those who want to seek a "new start," who might wish to invest time and resources into launching a new business career as well as enjoying a fascinating lifestyle in an exotic foreign country. The book also should be useful for the newly widowed or divorced who are casting about for a new social niche, new friends, and a new beginning. Above all, this book is for those who want to enjoy life now instead of waiting for that future "someday" that may never come.

Our bias for Costa Rica comes through quite clearly, but we try to balance the picture by reminding readers that living in a foreign country is definitely not everyone's cup of *café con leche*. (Costa Ricans don't drink tea.) It takes a special type of person to create and enjoy an interesting and challenging life in any foreign setting. Hopefully, this book will help you determine if you are that type of person.

About prices quoted throughout this edition: They are accurate as of the time of writing, based on the current dollar exchange rates in Costa

Rica. In fall 2008 the Costa Rican currency exchange rate was slightly more than 550 colones to the dollar. More about money exchange rates later on.

> *NOTE:* Unless otherwise stated, all phone and fax numbers in this book are in Costa Rica, and to connect, you must dial the proper access and country codes. Within the country, there are no area codes. See the "Dialing in Costa Rica" section in chapter 5.

# THE SWITZERLAND
## OF THE AMERICAS

Just about every Costa Rica guidebook feels obligated to describe Costa Rica as "The Switzerland of the Americas." Never mind that Costa Rica is as much like Switzerland as a Chihuahua is like a Pomeranian. (They're both small.) So I suppose this book is obliged to make the same comparison. At first glance, the one thing Costa Rica and Switzerland have in common is that they are both small countries. Actually, Switzerland is a little smaller than Costa Rica—one of the few countries with that distinction.

Costa Rica is lushly tropical and continuously swathed in luxurious green vegetation. A place where coffee, sugarcane, and mangoes thrive, and where snow never falls. The exact opposite is Switzerland's snowcapped peaks with high meadows and rugged mountain terrain. Yet the more one travels in Costa Rica, the more apparent certain parallels with Switzerland become. Both are peaceful, progressive countries where democracy and stability are hallmarks. Although Costa Rica's tropical beaches are incongruent with Swiss landscapes, Costa Rica's mountains, in their own tropical way, rival the beauty of the Alps.

Even closer similarities between the two countries appear in their political philosophy and economic structure. Both countries are places of small farms and small businesses, with an air of prosperity and a feeling of equality among citizens. Both countries have renounced aggressive militarism, diverting resources instead toward education, medical care, and other services that benefit society in general. In short, both places are affluent, happy, and tranquil. Both are locations where North Americans can feel at home, safe, and welcome.

There are differences, of course. Costa Rica is nearer to the United States and Canada, making it somewhat more accessible for North Americans than Europe. Costa Rica also enjoys a dramatically lower cost of living than Switzerland. And best of all, Costa Rica has a climate that can be enjoyed year-round by those of us who hate wearing snow boots and earmuffs. Costa Rica's higher elevations (commonly known as the Valle Central, the Meseta Central, or the Central Valley) enjoy springlike temperatures year-round. Brightly colored flowers seem to glow in the crystal-clear atmosphere. The countryside is so fertile that fence posts sprout and become trees despite all the farmers' best efforts. Crossing over the mountains, you drop down to tropical lowlands where some North Americans own plantations of coffee, macadamia nuts, black pepper, and other exotic crops for export. (Macadamia-nut plantations are exceedingly rare in Switzerland.) Beaches flank either side of Costa Rica, dotted with small communities where North Americans and Europeans live in communion with surf and jungle.

## A UNIQUE **HISTORY**

Costa Rica stands out in this hemisphere in many ways, but its biggest contrast is with its Central American neighbors. When you drive across the border into Costa Rica or when you step off an airplane arriving from another Central American country, you know immediately that Costa Rica is a special place. Relative affluence stands out in contrast to the grinding poverty of other Central American locations. Income, wages, and standard of living are the highest of any of the countries in the Northern Hemisphere, with the exception of the United States and Canada.

Citizens of neighboring countries envy Costa Rica's benevolent and democratic government. They point to Costa Rica as an ideal goal. I recall being in Nicaragua in early January 1977, several weeks before the uprising that eventually overthrew the Somoza dictatorship. When a group

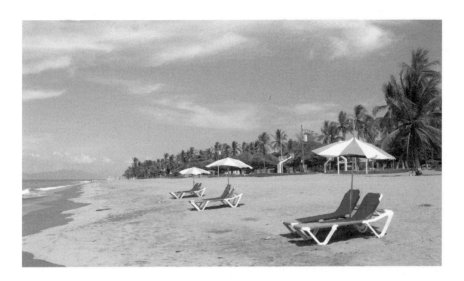

of students in Managua discovered that I was a writer, they surrounded my wife and me, begging that I write something about their upcoming revolution. One student said, "Tell Americans that we are not against the United States! On the contrary, we want to be just like the United States! Look, if Costa Rica can be prosperous, democratic, and free, why can't Nicaragua be the same?"

The students had hoped to start the uprising to coincide with Jimmy Carter's inauguration. When I asked why, they explained, "Because, when Presidente Carter was running for election, he promised he would never deal with brutal dictators. Since our Somoza is a brutal dictator, Presidente Carter will no doubt send U.S. marines to help us."

I tried to explain to the students that although Somoza was indeed a dictator, the U.S. government considered Somoza to be *our* dictator, which made him okay. That idea was dismissed by the students. The rest is history. Jimmy Carter supported Somoza until the dictator finally fled for his life to South America.

Clearly, there's a world of difference between Costa Rica and other Central American countries. How did this happen? Why does Costa Rica have so much less poverty and so large a middle class in comparison with neighboring countries? Answers to these questions can be found in a series of historic events—some accidental, some planned. Let us review:

In 1502, when Columbus happened upon Costa Rica during his last voyage to this hemisphere, he anchored somewhere near the present-day city of Limón and dispatched an expedition ashore. Thinking he had found an island, Columbus waited on the ship for a report from his landing party. His explorers returned with news of an inhospitable jungle and impossible swamps, plus ferocious natives who owned but a few paltry ornaments of thinly pounded gold, probably trade goods from Panamá. In short, the Caribbean Coast offered little to excite the imagination of these avaricious explorers.

According to legend, Columbus gave his new discovery the name *Costa Rica* ("rich coast") to impress the king of Spain. The explorers sailed away as soon as the ships were repaired, without any thought of colonization. The Caribbean Coast was left virtually ignored by Europeans for several centuries. In contrast with the rapid colonization and development of other parts of the Americas, Costa Rica grew very slowly.

It was the custom for the Spanish Crown to grant huge tracts of land to the conquistadores as a reward for their services. Indians were considered a part of the land, and although not exactly slaves, they essentially belonged to the enormous haciendas: They were forced to work as peons for the aristocratic conquerors. In places like Peru, Mexico, and Guatemala, the Indians meekly accepted their new rulers and continued working the same lands as before, paying tribute to new overlords.

However, the Indians of Costa Rica (like their cousins in North America) proved to be determined, fierce fighters who resisted the idea of accepting subjugation. Experts in defending their heavily forested territory, the natives simply withdrew farther into the jungle when defeated. They clearly weren't interested in tilling fields for the pink-faced, bearded intruders. Archaeological evidence suggests that at least some tribes might have been headhunters, similar to the Jívaro tribes in Ecuador, whose warriors dangled their enemies' shrunken heads around their necks as ornaments. In short, these people were unlikely candidates to willingly become docile servants and field laborers.

This left the newcomers in a position they hadn't counted on. Instead of being lords over huge estates and overseeing gangs of laboring peons, the Spanish conquistadores were forced to work the land for themselves. A disappointment, to say the least. The colonists had to resort to manual labor in order to eke out a marginal existence from small, family-run farms. From the beginning, all were equal in their struggle for existence. Even the royal viceroy had to raise chickens and tend his own garden to avoid starvation. Small wonder that many early settlers and would-be exploiters moved on to easier pickings.

Over the ensuing centuries, Costa Rica remained a backwater of Spanish colonization, all but forgotten. Undisturbed, the colony grew in its own way, ignoring the ineffective Spanish governors sent by the royal court of Madrid. Costa Ricans lived quiet and simple lives, isolated and unaffected by events in other colonies. In fact, when Spain granted independence to the Spanish colonies in 1821, Costa Rica was the last to know (and probably cared the least). For all practical purposes, the region had always been on its own. Independence was no novelty.

**COFFEE ECONOMY** Fortunately, Costa Rica's first president turned out to be a progressive thinker, a visionary who wanted to see the country develop socially and economically. He was convinced that growing coffee for export could be a major economic breakthrough, a key to modernization. Coffee profits could build roads, schools, and cities.

Since the country was scantily populated, however, more people were needed to grow coffee in order to fulfill the president's dream. Consequently, free land was offered to anyone willing to plant coffee trees. Since coffee production is ideally suited to small, family-operated farms, European families began immigrating to take advantage of Costa Rica's opportunities. They came from Italy and France as well as Spain. Instead of huge plantations owned by a few wealthy families, as in other Central American republics, hundreds of small farms sprang up, selling coffee beans to merchants who processed and exported the product. This created a tradition of independence and equality, with a preponderance of middle-class farmers and a few moderately wealthy, coffee-exporting families. The spread between rich, middle class, and poor was much narrower than anywhere else in the hemisphere and remains so to this day.

Troubled times in Europe during the last half of the nineteenth century sent new waves of economic and political refugees to the Americas. This was their chance for a new beginning. The standing offer of free land to grow coffee was irresistible. These refugees, instilled with contemporary Europe's liberal intellectual and political philosophy, contributed substantially to the notions of freedom, equality, and individual rights that were already in place.

This is not to say that Costa Rica didn't develop a wealthy oligarchy of elite families whose positions rested upon their control of coffee exports. But because of their tradition of being "self-made" families and their respect for hard work, their mentality was different from that of the arrogant Spanish conquistadores who worshiped royalty and privilege, and who considered manual labor to be beneath their dignity.

Free and compulsory education was an early development, starting in 1869. This established a tradition of literacy that ranks Costa Rica high among other countries of the world. A university was founded in 1844, staffed in part by intellectuals who fled Europe's political and economic maelstrom of that era. These and other modern European traditions developed in Costa Rica in stark contrast with the medieval, feudal heritage of Mexico and other Central American countries.

**DISMANTLING THE MILITARY** A truly significant event that totally separated Costa Rica from the ranks of other Latin American nations occurred in 1948. The ruling party decided not to recognize the results of an election by refusing to give up power. The defeated president ordered new elections because of the closeness of the vote and accusations of fraud. A crisis of democracy threatened. Pepe Figueres, a charismatic member of one of the wealthy families, stepped forward to lead an uprising against the government and its illegal attempt to use the army to hold on to power. The result of this successful revolution (the first and only in Costa Rican history) was a decision to abolish the army and replace it with the Guardia Civil, a civilian-controlled police force that augments the local police. In many smaller towns the Guardia Civil is the only police force.

This was a brilliant and bold step. Barracks were turned into schools. Ex-soldiers were given jobs building roads. Money that would normally be absorbed by military corruption and graft was devoted to highways, education, and medical care. Today a huge percentage of the national budget goes to education and culture. Public money pays for four universities, three symphony orchestras, and five autonomous state publishing houses. Of the gross national product, about 10 percent is spent on medical care. Costa Rica has an average of one physician for every 700 inhabitants.

Some North Americans shake their heads in dismay at the lack of a standing army. They ask, "Without a military, how can you defend your country from aggression?" The answer is simple: The function of a Central

American military has never been to deter aggression. The military's duty is to protect the country's politicians from irate citizens. Soldiers are there to keep people in line, to maintain privileges for the military and the country's financial elite. Democracy doesn't stand a chance when army officers nominate candidates, and armed soldiers threaten voters, conduct elections, and then count the ballots. Are we surprised when generals are elected president?

Throughout this book you will see Costa Ricans referred to as *ticos* and North Americans as *gringos*. These terms are commonly used in Costa Rica and are not meant to be disrespectful (this will be explained later on). These nicknames actually carry an affectionate connotation, since both groups like and respect each other.

## A WELCOMING **DEMOCRACY**

Many North American expatriates will tell you they decided on Costa Rica for a new beginning in life because they feel at home here. We find it easy to make friends among the sizable community of fellow countrymen who have planted roots in Costa Rica. It's a place where North Americans feel comfortable living in ordinary middle-class neighborhoods instead of being forced to huddle together in enclaves of other expatriates for mutual support. That's not to say Costa Rica is crime-free (is there such a place?). Yet compared with other foreign retirement destinations in this world, Costa Rica gives most people a sense of well-being and safety. More about this later.

Costa Rica is a country where your conscience isn't continually assaulted by grinding poverty, malnourished children begging in the streets, or social injustice. Juvenile gangs and graffiti are the exception, not the rule. It's a country of full employment; anyone who wants a job can find one, and wages are the highest of any country between the Panama Canal and the U.S. border.

The Costa Rican personality resembles that of North Americans in many ways: how they view the world, their social behavior, and their value systems. *Ticos*—as they call themselves—are open, friendly, and egalitarian. Most North Americans feel right at home in Costa Rica. (The only other Latin country where I truly feel this way is Argentina.)

Because of these ingrained attitudes, Costa Rica has avoided the problems that have mired other Central American republics in quicksands of turmoil and tragedy. Costa Rica's devotion to democracy and peaceful cooperation with its neighbors has enabled the country to retain its enviable position as a showcase of prosperity, respect for law, and personal freedoms.

**HONEST ELECTIONS** More than a century-and-a-half tradition of free and honest elections forms the basis for today's political life. Instead of frequent military takeovers so common in Latin American countries, Costa Ricans change their government via the ballot box. Although members of the same affluent families often compete in the elections, they are civilians, intellectuals, and, for the most part, working for the good of the country as a whole, not just for one particular class.

Election Day is Costa Rica's most important holiday. It's a riotous celebration with a joyous spirit that goes far beyond mere politics. Voting is mandatory—nonvoters are supposed to pay a token fine—but few citizens would think of passing up the fun and excitement of an election. (Actually, about 60 percent of eligible voters cast ballots, but that's probably double the percentage in the United States.)

Weeks prior to Election Day, all parties campaign vigorously. Homes everywhere display the flag of their preferred party. People proudly pin political flags to their clothing. When an automobile drives by flying a political flag, people either cheer enthusiastically or boo good-naturedly, depending on the flag's colors. On election day, many stores and businesses, and all bars, are closed. Liquor and beer cannot be sold on election day, the day before, or the day after. Oddly enough, wine can be sold. Because it's served with meals, wine appears to be classified as food. (As well it should.) Traditionally, public transportation is supposed to be free on election day. Buses, taxis, and even private cars are expected to stop when someone indicates he or she needs a ride to a polling booth. This is in theory, however; in practice, many autos will stop for anyone who waves and asks for a ride in whichever direction the auto is headed. After all, this is a fiesta!

It's interesting to note that many Costa Ricans, when they move from their hometowns to another part of the country, do not change their voting registration to their new address. Elections are considered an opportunity to return to their hometowns to vote, to visit friends and family, and to party at the same time. Reunions and celebrations are a vital part of Election Day.

Voters must dunk their thumbs into indelible ink to prove they've voted (and cannot vote again). This purple digit is worn as a proud badge of civic duty. Automobile drivers honk their horns and wave their discolored thumbs in the air as they drive along the streets, to show everyone that they have voted, while shouting, "Have you voted yet?" Sometimes there are so many horns blowing on Election Day that it sounds like New Year's Eve at midnight.

As a result, Costa Rica is a country intensely dedicated to principles of equality and democracy. All segments of the political spectrum, from extreme right to far-out left, are represented—any and all parties are totally legal. The crucial point is this: The electorate has a free choice, even though fringe parties rarely garner more than a small percentage of the vote. Voters can vote right, left, or center, choosing whichever party presents the best ideas. Because citizens can change their government at will, Costa Rica is virtually revolution-proof.

The end result is a free, prosperous, and peaceful country.

**HIGH STANDARD OF LIVING** Please don't misunderstand: I'm not implying that Costa Rica has no poverty or that Costa Rican workers are highly paid compared with industrialized countries. Yet compared with Mexico and Central America, workers here enjoy excellent working conditions, living wages, and government guarantees of fair treatment from

You'll see few if any street people, panhandlers, or beggars on Costa Rican streets. Children never beg. You cannot visit some Latin American countries without a flock of hungry-looking kids trailing you. As a friend observed, "Among the world's poor, Costa Rica's poor are probably the world's most affluent."

employers. Even those at the poverty level live far better than in most other third-world countries and better, in my opinion, than millions of people living at the poverty level in the United States.

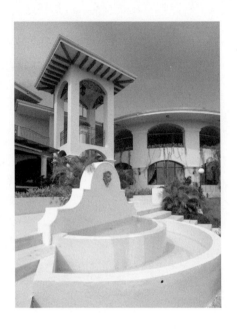

Welfare is an unknown concept in Costa Rica because family and friends are always there for backup in case of disaster. Jobs are plentiful and unemployment a fraction of that in most highly developed countries. Food is abundant; medical care and education are free. Agriculture here depends on illegal aliens from Nicaragua to harvest crops and tend banana plantations; Costa Rican workers prefer not to do this kind of backbreaking work. (Does this sound familiar to Californians and Texans who depend on illegal Mexican immigrants for their crops?) Open-air markets have a tradition of giving food to the poor, with vendors handing out surplus to those in need.

Although wages are higher here than in neighboring countries, they appear to be extraordinarily low to us *Norteamericanos*. How can workers be expected to survive on as little as $70 a week? The answer is that even though the cash salary is small, fringe benefits connected with the job make a big difference. In addition to their cash salaries, workers are guaranteed benefits such as sick leave—at the rate of 50 percent of their salary—from the first day of illness up to a lifetime of disability. Workers receive a month's pay as *aguinaldo*, or Christmas bonus, every year and a minimum of two weeks' paid vacation every year. Medical care is free. Women receive six weeks' maternity leave (at full salary), and all receive a Social Security pension upon retirement. It isn't necessary to put aside money for the children's college tuition, because education is virtually free, a basic right provided by the government. Since medical care is free, a worker can spend his or her entire salary on living expenses without having to put a portion aside for inevitable medical emergencies or illnesses.

All these benefits are guaranteed by law, and all Costa Ricans know exactly what their rights are. Since there's usually a shortage of help in many regions of the country, anyone who really wants to work can find a job. As a result, many employers pay above the minimum wage in order to attract competent workers. This is in contrast with other Latin American countries, where the minimum wage and the maximum wage are considered one and the same.

When you measure these benefits and put a cash value on them, you'll agree that Costa Rican workers are ahead of many North Americans. In the United States a woefully inadequate medical-insurance monthly premium can cost a family as much as a typical Costa Rican worker earns in two months! Since few low-paid U.S. workers can afford medical insurance, one short visit to a hospital can push them over the financial edge. Sick leave? In the United States only large, affluent companies can afford such extravagance. Paid vacations are not mandatory in the United States; they're granted at the discretion of an employer. In Costa Rica, paid vacations are the law.

I'm always amused when I hear ultraconservatives point to Costa Rica's health-care system as evidence that the government is socialist. They overlook the fact that if universal health care makes a country socialist, the United States would be one of the few nonsocialist countries in the world. So where does the money come from for Costa Rica's health care, pensions, sick leave, and such? It comes out of workers' wages in the form of Social Security contributions and matching funds paid by employers as part of the wage package.

## LARGE NUMBER **OF EXPATRIATES**

Costa Rica has a high percentage of North Americans (and foreigners in general) who are "starting over" or living part-time in this exotic semi-paradise. You'll find these newcomers scattered all around the country—almost every nook and cranny has a few of us living there—instead of everyone concentrated in enclaves or colonies, as is the case in many other foreign countries.

Most reliable sources estimate between 20,000 and 30,000 North American citizens reside in Costa Rica—some full-time, others making their homes here seasonally. Exact figures are impossible to come by because the U.S. embassy doesn't keep track of its citizens in the country. Canada does register citizens living abroad, but most Canadians are hesitant to stay out of Canada more than six months at a time because they can lose Canadian health-care benefits. The percentage of Canadian versus U.S. citizens is difficult to state with precision, but you can be confident that plenty of Canadians are represented.

A few North Americans live in other Central American countries—Guatemala, Honduras, Belize, and even El Salvador and Nicaragua—but their ranks are scanty compared with those in Costa Rica.

Costa Rica graciously welcomes seasonal residents, retirees, and business investors, placing fewer restrictions on newcomers than most other foreign countries. Government rules and laws make it easy to own property or start a business. In fact, you can do both, even as a tourist or part-time resident. To live in Costa Rica permanently as a *pensionado* (retiree), you need only have proof of $600-a-month retirement income from Social Security or other guaranteed retirement income benefit. You should be aware that the national legislature is continually talking about increasing this amount, but in my opinion this isn't going to happen anytime soon.

Although living on $600 a month is possible, at least on a basic level, it isn't recommended. Even though $600 is almost twice what a skilled Costa Rican worker earns in a month, the average U.S. or Canadian retiree would need to acquire an enthusiastic appetite for beans and tortillas and be willing to trade his or her automobile for a bicycle.

Those too young to receive a guaranteed company pension or Social Security can still qualify for permanent residency in Costa Rica by showing they have enough income to prove they aren't indigent. The amount required is $1,000 a month, plus an additional $1,000 a month for a spouse. (Details are discussed in chapter 17.)   You can check on the status of any changes in retirement regulations at my Web site, www .discoverypress.com/update.

Because of Costa Rica's affordable cost of living, a retired couple can easily cover basic living expenses on an average U.S. Social Security check: around $1,500 for a couple. On that amount you should be able to afford a part-time housekeeper and gardener, and travel when you feel like it. Just consider the lifestyle you would lead in the United States on that amount! You might be looking for part-time work to make ends meet. I personally know people who manage to get by in Costa Rica on less than $800 a month—and others who spend $3,000 and feel they are economizing.

Salaries in Costa Rica are traditionally adjusted twice a year to compensate for inflation. In January of 2008, the adjustment to Costa Rica's minimum wage structure resulted in a 5.1 percent increase. However, for the first time in recent memory, the increase not only reflected the economy's inflation, but also the devaluation of the U.S. dollar on the world market. The dollar's value dropped from 522 colones to about 490. In July of 2008, when the government declared an additional 6.7 percent increase in wages, the dollar regained much of its value, selling for over 550 colones.

Two other conditions make Costa Rica special as a destination for part-time or full-time living. The first is the almost perfect weather. Being located relatively close to the equator, Costa Rica's temperatures remain constant year-round. (Contrary to popular belief, the weather does not become hotter as you near the equator. It simply levels out, with less extremes in high and low temperatures.) At these latitudes, climate is determined by elevation. That is, at sea level the climate is perpetual summer. Daily highs are in the mid-80s to occasional low 90s. (Although I'm sure it happens, I've never seen the thermometer hit 100 degrees here.) Nighttime lows are usually in the low 70s, just right for sleeping under one sheet.

At altitudes over 3,000 feet, you enter a climate of perpetual spring. Daytime highs are in the mid-70s to the low 80s, while evening temperatures usually drop into the upper 60s. Sweaters often feel comfortable after sundown. Yes, this is in the tropics, and yes, these temperatures are year-round!

The second favorable condition is Costa Rica's exciting investment climate. Instead of placing barriers to prevent foreigners from going into business, as do most other countries in the world, Costa Rica encourages foreign investment. To lure investors, the government offers tax incentives and duty-free imports. Again, you don't have to be a citizen or even a legal resident to own property or conduct a business. You can even own a business on a tourist visa! Not many desirable countries permit you to do this. As a nonresident, however, you are restricted to management chores. It is preferred that tourist-owners not tend bar, wait tables, or make beds in their bed-and-breakfasts. Anyway, who would want to do this when hiring employees is so economical? More about this later.

## PLANNING YOUR **VISIT TO COSTA RICA**

One publication I strongly recommend for anyone considering Costa Rica for anything more than a short vacation is San José's English-language newspaper, the *Tico Times*. If you read every issue from front to back, including the advertisements, by the time you actually get to Costa Rica, you will know so much about the place that you will feel as though you are returning home. The classified ads keep you up to date on rental costs, housing prices, and what secondhand furniture and appliances sell for. Display ads tell you what you should pay for a hotel room or a bed-and-breakfast. You'll find the best places to dine as well as where to go for a beach excursion. The news columns are well written, with complete and unbiased news of what's happening in Costa Rica as well as in neighboring countries—news not available in U.S. or Canadian newspapers. Featured are articles relating to foreign residents, governmental actions, or changes in law that may affect them, as well as news of social activities and club events. An extensive letters-to-the-editor section prints opinions of tourists and residents alike, telling of exceptionally nice places to go and which places are rip-offs, giving opinions about the country, kudos and complaints, political views, and just about anything else you can imagine. By all means, start your subscription several months before you leave. An interesting innovation is that you can subscribe online. That way, you can receive the paper every week and also store a copy on your computer for future reference (in Adobe Acrobat format). Go to www .ticotimes.net to subscribe.

A second essential for your first visit is a good travel guide: *Choose Costa Rica* is not intended to be a travel book. This is a guide to retirement, long-term living, and investment in Costa Rica. United States and Canadian bookstores are loaded with excellent travel guidebooks packed with information about obligatory places to visit, detailed descriptions of the locations, and what to do when you get there. Here again, the *Tico Times* comes to our rescue. Every year the newspaper publishes a new edition of *Exploring Costa Rica,* a most detailed and comprehensive listing of accommodations and restaurants in almost every community you'd care to visit. The book is free with a subscription or can be ordered by mail.

A final essential for your trip is a sense of adventure and an ability to go with the flow. Things are going to be very different in Costa Rica, as you will learn by reading this book. Folks who love Costa Rica are those who savor the differences, those who find inconveniences amusing, or at least tolerable. Those who can't stand Costa Rica are those who are disappointed because everything isn't exactly as it was back home.

**EASY ACCESS** To enter Costa Rica, you simply show your passport and are automatically granted a ninety-day visa. It couldn't be easier. Your passport must have at least three months to go before the expiration date. You can no longer enter with a driver's license or a birth certificate.

Technically, you are supposed to carry your passport with you at all times, but it's okay to carry a photocopy of the page with your photo and another copy of the page with your entry stamp, so it can be determined when you entered the country. Be aware that although a copy is acceptable, the police have the right to accompany you to your hotel to see the original. (This only happens when someone is suspected of wrongdoing or of using a touched-up photocopy.) Be careful not to lose your passport—it's a bummer to have to go to the embassy and apply for a replacement before you can return home. I would highly recommend carrying your original passport when driving a vehicle, in case you do get stopped.

It's possible to apply for a ninety-day visa extension through the Department of Immigration (some travel agencies claim to be able to do this for you). However, many people take the option of leaving the country for seventy-two hours, visiting the beaches of Nicaragua or the islands of Panamá for a three-day vacation. When they reenter the country, they are granted another ninety-day visa. This makes a stay of six months possible, allowing plenty of time to investigate and tour all the nooks and corners of Costa Rica to see whether it would be an appropriate place to retire or go into business.

Theoretically, this "seventy-two-hour turnaround" is allowed once in a six-month period; that is, after the second visa you should remain out of the country for three months before reentering the country. Although still on the books, this rule hasn't been enforced for years. Many foreigners have lived in Costa Rica for years, leaving the country every three months. However, you should be aware that there could come a time when the law is enforced. At that point you might consider applying for residency, especially if you own property; it would be tragic to be barred from entering the country to visit your home! The government refers to these people as "perpetual tourists." Occasionally, the ministry of tourism threatens to crack down on perpetual tourists but rarely takes action, except in the case of a few undesirables. Of course, being in the country with an expired visa, over ninety days, could get you into trouble. You should take this rule seriously.

Don't misunderstand, I am not encouraging anyone to violate immigration rules; I am merely reporting how the laws have been enforced over many years, probably many decades. My personal opinion is that the government recognizes this group of North Americans as law-abiding, peaceful residents who benefit the economy by spending millions of dollars here. However, the governmen's attitude is always subject to change, just as the government itself is subject to change every four years. Therefore, I encourage anyone who intends to live in Costa Rica for long periods of time to apply for permanent residence. (See chapter 17 for details.)

Finally, I urge that you make no decisions about permanent moves or business investments without spending several months "on location," getting to know the country and the community, meeting your neighbors, and learning what Costa Rica is all about. Before making any financial moves, find a good lawyer, one recommended by residents in the North American community. Above all, don't hand your money to someone simply because he or she comes from Akron or Atlanta and has an honest face. Honest faces and firm handshakes are the marks of successful swindlers! Costa Rica has suffered its fair share of sweet-talking gringos with designs on your pocketbooks. There's something about a foreign country that tends to bring out latent larceny in some people. Later on in this book, we'll discuss ways to protect yourself from being swindled.

**RETIREMENT TOURS** Although travel in Costa Rica is easy and plans can be very casual, some folks prefer to take a guided tour to the more popular areas for relocation. An organized tour is more efficient and saves time because the tour guide knows exactly where the expatriates prefer to live, and the guide will be able to introduce you to North Americans who have made the move to Costa Rica.

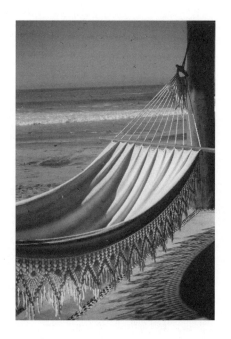

One tour that comes highly recommended is conducted by Christopher Howard, who has been a resident of Costa Rica since 1980, appeared on the *Today* show, and authored several guidebooks about living and retiring here. His in-depth tours take you to the Central Valley and the central and southern Pacific regions of the country. All tours include a two-day seminar on every subject related to moving here. Visit his Web site and blog at www.liveincostarica.com.

Another Costa Rica tour operator, George Lundquist, features a retirement tour called "Expose Me to Life for the Non-Rich in Costa Rica." His four-day tours take guests to some nontraditional retirement locations as well as some of the standard places. He places an emphasis on retiring on Social Security checks. George's Web site is www.costa ricaretireonss.com.

**INTERNET RESEARCH** An invaluable planning tool is the Internet. If you are one of those anti-technology holdouts living in the dark ages without a computer and Internet connection, allow me to strongly recommend that you get one right away. With today's simplified Web browsers, anyone can learn to tap in to this information with an hour or so of instruction. The amount of Costa Rica information available on the Internet is almost unbelievable, and it grows even more comprehensive by the day.

Many expats in Costa Rica don't use answering machines; if friends or family up north call when nobody is home, long-distance charges apply when the answering machine kicks in. An e-mail message serves the same purpose. Not only that, it's a great way to keep in touch with family in the States or friends in Scotland without expensive long-distance charges.

I recommend taking a laptop, since you can carry it on the plane and keep it with you as you travel about the country. If you don't have a laptop, a regular desktop computer can be purchased in Costa Rica for about what you would pay back home. The government places low or no import duties on computer products. Prices are similar to what you would pay in the States.

A Google search will return scads of Web pages with regional descriptions of Costa Rica, real estate for sale, homes for rent, and online expatriate groups. If you want to correspond directly with folks living in Costa Rica or others who are considering moving there, you'll find forums and bulletin boards where they post their e-mail addresses. You should try to make some Costa Rica friends before you ever leave for the airport.

Our favorite bulletin board is Costa Rica Living, a very popular expatriate Web site. The forum allows expatriates living in the country to keep in touch with each other socially, with news of expat gatherings, luncheons, and other events, both scheduled and impromptu. They exchange information about where to find hard-to-find items and are generous when answering questions from those wanting to know more about Costa Rica. The site is www.groups.yahoo.com/group/costaricaliving.

Another valuable resource is the Web site of the Association of Residents of Costa Rica (ARCR). We highly recommend ARCR as the place to apply for residency and buy group health insurance, and for newcomers as well as residents to solve problems. The bulletin board has extensive archives of past messages. The Web site is www.arcr.net.

To keep you informed about important changes in laws or conditions since the publication of this edition of *Choose Costa Rica*, I maintain an "update" Web page at www.discoverypress.com/update.

# WHAT'S
# COSTA RICA LIKE?

Costa Rica is the second-smallest country in Central America, comprising around 20,000 square miles. Many sections are almost unpopulated, mantled with rain forest, dense jungle, and rugged mountain landscapes. Costa Rica is so small that you can have breakfast at a restaurant on a Pacific Ocean beach and drive leisurely across the country in time to have an early dinner at a restaurant on an Atlantic beach. At its widest point, Costa Rica is 174 miles wide; at the narrowest, only 100 miles.

Yet the country doesn't appear small. Certainly not from the viewpoint of tourists driving rental cars over slow roads, winding uphill and down. Every turn in the road brings a new vista, another scene to contemplate, another curve to watch out for cattle on the road and traffic cops armed with radar guns.

Travel articles and guidebooks traditionally describe Costa Rica as being the size of West Virginia. We can also say that Costa Rica is about half the size of Kentucky. If these figures make the country sound small and insignificant, we can balance the equation by pointing out that Costa Rica is twice as large as Israel and Albania. It's also larger than Belgium, Holland, or Switzerland, plus many countries you and I can't even pronounce.

Few countries of any size offer such a diversity of scenery and climate or such a wide variety of flora and fauna. Probably no other country in the world devotes as large a percentage of its territory to national parks and wildlife refuges. About 27 percent of Costa Rica's land is thus protected. These preserves range from cloud forests to tropical beaches, from volcanic craters to jungle swamps and inland waterways. The national park system is a major attraction for tourism.

When you hear friends remark that they were disappointed in Costa Rica, there's a good chance their visit was a one-day stopover on a cruise ship. Cruise ships here disembark at one of two shipping ports, where major scenic attractions are industrial warehouses, tank trucks, and storage sheds. This doesn't usually leave a favorable first impression. So the cruise director loads passengers onto buses and zips them away to the city of San José for a short visit and then back to the ship in time for dinner. Small wonder cruise-ship visitors cannot understand why people praise Costa Rica.

Costa Rica's bewildering assortment of wildlife includes 850 species of birds—more than in all of the continent north of Mexico. Representative mammals are monkeys, coatis, jaguars, and ocelots, as well as sloths, tapirs, and agoutis. One evening down on the Pacific Coast, a large anteater ambled in front of our car, its long snout almost touching the ground in front and an equally heavy tail drooping behind, looking very prehistoric. Turtles, colorful frogs, and toads of all descriptions abound, as do crocodiles and iguanas. Snakes? Of course. They range from huge boa constrictors to tiny coral snakes. Experts say there are more varieties of butterflies in Costa Rica than in all the African continent; more than 2,000 species have been collected so far, and more are being discovered. The number of orchids and bromeliads boggles the mind. This is truly a naturalist's paradise.

Many tropical countries offer beaches and vacation accommodations, but nowhere else in the world can a tourist find such a combination of beaches, mountains, friendliness, and tropical wonder that's accessible year-round.

The Costa Rican government recognizes these unique assets and actively involves its citizens in both the preservation and the exploitation of nature at the same time. How do you protect as well as exploit the environment? Just one example: By hiring local people to guard and preserve endangered-turtle-nesting beaches, jobs are created. Beach villages then become tourist attractions, complete with motels, restaurants, and shops, thus creating even more jobs. Visitors from all over the world can now visit cloud forests, turtle-nesting beaches, and nature preserves—in comfort. In the process, tourists leave much-appreciated foreign currency with Costa Rican businesses and banks.

North Americans and Europeans are scrambling to join this bandwagon and, with government encouragement, are investing heavily in tourist businesses, particularly in motels, restaurants, and endeavors of a like nature. Some enterprises become instant successes, with full bookings and plenty of business. Despite occasional slow spells, Costa Rica's commerce and tourism have forged ahead through the past decade and continue to be healthy and grow into the new century. (Details about starting and operating a business in Costa Rica are presented in chapter 11.)

## A COUNTRY **OF CONTRADICTIONS**

Before readers are left with the impression that everything is perfect in paradise and that Costa Rica is the best of all worlds, let's examine some contradictions.

The first contradiction: Even though the Costa Rican government is totally committed to preserving the environment and tries to control illegal deforestation, it also permits foreign companies to bulldoze forests in order to make more banana plantations and tourist resorts. The government puts large tracts of land into biological and wildlife reserves, forest reserves, national parks, and Indian reservations, yet at the same time, farmers and agribusinesses cut down forests on private tracts almost at will. The economy destroys in the name of progress, while the government tries to preserve in the name of conservation. But at least the government does try, and its efforts are improving.

Another contradiction: The growth of ecotourism in Costa Rica brings hundreds of thousands of visitors to enjoy the ecological wonderlands. But large numbers of visitors tramping through delicately balanced wilderness systems threaten to destroy the very ecological treasures that lure them to Costa Rica in the first place. The government raised admission fees to national parks in an effort to cut traffic to some extent. Some say the increase was merely to bring in more revenue, which may well be true, but it did indeed lower the number of visitors and traffic in national parks. The fee increase had a beneficial side effect in directing more business toward private ecological parks and developments.

Yet another contradiction in Costa Rica is the high incidence of petty crime among such a peaceful population, particularly in larger cities. In fact, a major criticism this book has received in the past was that it did not place proper emphasis on the crime rates. I have to admit that I've had a tendency to overlook this issue, in part because I feel that the problem is lightweight compared with the crime situation in other Latin countries. Violent crime in Costa Rica is almost insignificant when matched with the crime rate in most U.S. communities of similar size. We'll discuss crime in more detail in chapter 5.

Some will disagree, but I feel that Costa Rica's substandard roads, congested traffic in some areas, and serious potholes are a bigger annoyance than petty crime. I must admit, the government is trying its best to upgrade the roads and fill in potholes. A chronic shortage of funds, ever-increasing traffic, heavy trucks, and occasional intense rainfall, however, all make road maintenance difficult.

The problems of potholes in the highways and heavy traffic in the city will always be another of those fly-in-the-ointment nuisances you'll have to accept if you want to live in paradise. Nothing's perfect. The farther you get from downtown San José, the less the annoyance. When you are really deep into rural areas, your biggest obstacle to driving might be a herd of cattle being driven down the road or a sow and litter of piglets ambling across the way.

Another contradiction is the attitude toward foreigners buying prime coastal land now that the foreign population is increasing. Even though the Costa Rican people are friendly, gentle, and welcoming, you might assume they feel some level of resentment as they see foreigners bidding up the price of choice property until it is out of their price range. When they sell their agricultural properties, they are forced to move into local villages and accept employment from the newcomers. The big-money players are heavily represented by North American, German, Swiss, and

Italian buyers (more or less in that order). However, this resentment, when evidenced, is low and balanced by an appreciation of how foreign investment creates jobs and bolsters the economy.

Where my wife and I own property, local people tell us they'd much rather see foreigners own the land, because *ticos* tend to clear-cut the forest to make room for cattle. From the cattle ranchers' viewpoint, trees don't make money until they are chopped down, but pastures with fattening cattle are renewable resources. *Tico* workers are well aware that

cattle ranches create few jobs other than mending fences, while businesses, construction, and working for foreign residents mean full employment and prosperity to all. So the bottom line is that there isn't nearly the resentment toward developers that one might expect.

Visitors and foreign residents can do little to resolve these contradictions, but they need to be aware that problems do exist and may crop up in the future. The best we can do is try to minimize our impact upon the natural resources of the country. None of these problems have gotten out of hand, and solutions are constantly being sought by the Costa Rican government. But in any democracy, the going is slow and cumbersome. Just be aware that not everything is perfect in paradise—but for our money, Costa Rica is still paradise!

## MENU OF **CLIMATES**

For such a small country, Costa Rica has an astonishing variety of climates. From the misty mountaintops of Talamanca and Monteverde to the dry northern Guanacaste province, from the permanent spring weather of the Arenal area to the jungle lushness of the Caribbean Coast, Costa Rica has every kind of climate one might desire. Well, except frozen snow and bitter cold; but you don't want that anyway. Yes, there are seasons, but the differences between them are measured in differences in rainfall rather than in temperature variation. Therefore, unlike many other choice world vacation spots, Costa Rica isn't a one-season destination. Almost any time of the year can be a perfect time to visit. September and October are probably the least popular months, because these are the rainiest. (Conversely, many expat residents prefer these months because there are fewer tourists.)

Costa Rican people transpose the meanings of winter and summer. To them, "summer" months are December, January, and February—the dry season. This is when children take their "summer vacation" from school. To Costa Ricans, "winter" is June, July, and August! Conversations can become confusing when Costa Ricans and North Americans discuss the seasons, with summer and winter having opposite meanings for each. To avoid misunderstandings, I generally say, "June, July, and August" instead of "winter," or better yet, I'll say "dry season" or "rainy season" so that everybody knows what I mean.

The dry season, which begins around the end of November and lasts until May in many parts of the country, isn't parched and arid, as the name might imply. Occasional showers keep plants and lawns pleasantly green and flowers blooming in the higher elevations. Some Pacific coastal areas are truly dry January through April, yet much of the vegetation has adapted to this wet-dry environment and manages to stay green through the yearly drought. On the Caribbean Coast and the northern areas around Lake Arenal, "dry season" is just a figure of speech; rain knows no seasons here.

A common misconception is that "rainy season" means continuous downpours. Typically, even in the most rainy parts of the country, the day begins with glorious sunshine. Blossoms seem to glow in the sparkling-clean air; birds sing happily. Then clouds roll in after lunch. Rain, sometimes heavy, falls between 2:00 and 4:00 p.m. (In some places you can almost set your clock by it.) The downpour sends people indoors for a couple of hours (an ideal time for a nap). Then sunshine returns, and the world is once again refreshed, ready for another glorious sunset. Rain often returns from 2:00 to 4:00 a.m., followed by a gloriously colored sunrise. Seldom does it rain every single day; several days in a row can be perfectly dry.

# TEMPERATURES AND RAINFALL
## FOR SELECTED COSTA RICAN LOCATIONS

### Alajuela

| AVG. | JAN. | FEB. | MAR. | APR. | MAY | JUN. | JUL. | AUG. | SEPT. | OCT. | NOV. | DEC. | ANNUAL |
|---|---|---|---|---|---|---|---|---|---|---|---|---|---|
| | | | | | (In degrees Fahrenheit and inches) | | | | | | | | |
| HIGHS | 81 | 83 | 85 | 85 | 82 | 81 | 81 | 81 | 80 | 80 | 80 | 81 | 81 |
| LOWS | 62 | 62 | 63 | 63 | 64 | 64 | 64 | 63 | 63 | 63 | 63 | 63 | 63 |
| RAIN | 0.3 | 0.5 | 0.6 | 3 | 11 | 11 | 7 | 10 | 1 | 14 | 20 | 1 | 92 |

### Golfito

| | JAN. | FEB. | MAR. | APR. | MAY | JUN. | JUL. | AUG. | SEPT. | OCT. | NOV. | DEC. | ANNUAL |
|---|---|---|---|---|---|---|---|---|---|---|---|---|---|
| HIGHS | 91 | 92 | 92 | 91 | 90 | 89 | 89 | 90 | 89 | 89 | 89 | 90 | 90 |
| LOWS | 71 | 72 | 73 | 73 | 73 | 72 | 71 | 71 | 71 | 71 | 71 | 71 | 72 |
| RAIN | 6 | 6 | 8 | 11 | 19 | 18 | 18 | 22 | 28 | 28 | 23 | 12 | 199 |

### Cahuita

| | JAN. | FEB. | MAR. | APR. | MAY | JUN. | JUL. | AUG. | SEPT. | OCT. | NOV. | DEC. | ANNUAL |
|---|---|---|---|---|---|---|---|---|---|---|---|---|---|
| HIGHS | 86 | 86 | 87 | 87 | 87 | 87 | 86 | 86 | 87 | 87 | 86 | 86 | 86 |
| LOWS | 68 | 68 | 69 | 71 | 71 | 71 | 71 | 71 | 71 | 71 | 69 | 69 | 69 |
| RAIN | 13 | 8 | 8 | 11 | 11 | 12 | 17 | 13 | 6 | 8 | 16 | 18 | 141 |

### Nicoya

| | JAN. | FEB. | MAR. | APR. | MAY | JUN. | JUL. | AUG. | SEPT. | OCT. | NOV. | DEC. | ANNUAL |
|---|---|---|---|---|---|---|---|---|---|---|---|---|---|
| HIGHS | 91 | 93 | 95 | 96 | 91 | 89 | 89 | 89 | 87 | 87 | 87 | 89 | 87 |
| LOWS | 69 | 71 | 71 | 73 | 73 | 71 | 71 | 71 | 71 | 71 | 69 | 69 | 71 |
| RAIN | 0.2 | 0.4 | 1 | 3 | 11 | 13 | 10 | 12 | 16 | 16 | 5 | 1 | 89 |

### Manuel Antonio

| | JAN. | FEB. | MAR. | APR. | MAY | JUN. | JUL. | AUG. | SEPT. | OCT. | NOV. | DEC. | ANNUAL |
|---|---|---|---|---|---|---|---|---|---|---|---|---|---|
| HIGHS | 87 | 87 | 89 | 89 | 89 | 87 | 87 | 87 | 86 | 86 | 86 | 86 | 87 |
| LOWS | 69 | 69 | 71 | 71 | 71 | 71 | 69 | 69 | 71 | 71 | 71 | 69 | 71 |
| RAIN | 3 | 1 | 2 | 7 | 16 | 17 | 18 | 19 | 21 | 26 | 16 | 7 | 153 |

### San José

| | JAN. | FEB. | MAR. | APR. | MAY | JUN. | JUL. | AUG. | SEPT. | OCT. | NOV. | DEC. | ANNUAL |
|---|---|---|---|---|---|---|---|---|---|---|---|---|---|
| HIGHS | 73 | 75 | 77 | 78 | 78 | 78 | 77 | 77 | 78 | 77 | 75 | 77 | 77 |
| LOWS | 59 | 59 | 60 | 60 | 62 | 62 | 67 | 62 | 60 | 60 | 60 | 59 | 62 |
| RAIN | 0.4 | 0.2 | 0.5 | 2 | 9 | 12 | 9 | 10 | 13 | 13 | 6 | 2 | 77 |

To further complicate matters, what is true of the mountain valley environment around San José isn't necessarily true on the Caribbean side, which can be flooded with sunshine while the capital is awash in *aguaceros* (rainstorms), and vice versa. The truth is, no matter what time of year you choose to visit, you're guaranteed a serving of sunny weather—and possibly some rain as well.

On the northwestern Pacific side, the dry season is exactly that, with very little rain falling from early December until the beginning of May. The grass turns brown, and many trees lose their leaves, just as they do in North America in the winter. But the reason for leaf loss is to conserve water, not because of frost and freezing weather. Most trees are evergreen, but even some of these lose a portion of their leaves. It isn't as bleak as it sounds, for many of these trees replace leaves with brilliantly colored blossoms, as this is the time of year to attract bees, butterflies, and other pollinating insects.

Because most North Americans customarily think of the tropics as a place to visit during their winter season—to escape the snow and ice of their homelands—they are often surprised to find that the months of June, July, and August are the favorite time of year for many who live in Costa Rica. "You can't really appreciate this country until you've experienced our winter months," says my friend Graham Henshaw, an expatriate from England. "When the rains start in May, the grass and trees change to a bright emerald color. Flowers that bloom only in July and August are absolutely stunning. That is my favorite time of year."

Even on the dry Guanacaste coast, you'll find microcosms of green environments tucked away in the interior valleys, where sporadic rains are coaxed from the westerly Pacific winds. Farther south along the Pacific Coast, the dry-season rainfall is even more frequent, keeping things pleasantly green during the driest months. The weather chart in this chapter provides statistics on the microclimates of Costa Rica. You will find an interesting interactive weather map on the Internet at www.discoverypress.com/weather.

## INSECTS AND **THE TROPICS**

An odd thing about the weather checkerboard of Costa Rica: Contrary to what one might think, the more humid areas are not necessarily the most insect-plagued. Of course, bring your insect repellent, but I'm convinced that you need it less in most places in Costa Rica than you do in the American Midwest, Florida, or most certainly in many Canadian locations. Along the forested Pacific Coast and the Nicoya Peninsula—where the insect varieties are amazingly abundant—mosquitoes and flies pester you far less than in the dry regions of Guanacaste. On the humid Caribbean Coast, where rain can fall almost any time of the year and where bugs can get so large you'd think they'd been taking steroids, household cockroaches and flies are not nearly as plentiful as I've seen in Houston or New Orleans. (We've seen many interesting beetles but surprisingly few ordinary cockroaches in our Costa Rica travel and homemaking.)

In parts of Costa Rica, even in the most tropical locations, insects are so benign that many natives don't bother with screens on their windows. Of course, the rainy season in some areas will make a liar of me, so it would be best to carry repellent. This is particularly advisable when staying in one of the areas where dengue fever has been reported (mostly around the outskirts of Puntarenas and near Liberia). There's a vigorous campaign continually under way to eliminate the mosquito that spreads the flulike ailment. Although it is potentially dangerous for those who contract the ailment more than once, very few deaths have been recorded in Costa Rica from dengue fever.

Why flies and mosquitoes are scarce might seem puzzling. I'm convinced the answer is because the natural environment in Costa Rica is largely intact. Natural enemies of pests such as flies and mosquitoes haven't been eliminated by pesticides, chemicals, and other methods, as they have back home. By day, birds of all descriptions flit back and forth, snacking on insects, keeping them in balance with nature. Many birds consider houseflies to be special treats. By night, squadrons of bats keep up the good work, finishing off mosquitoes before they get a chance to do much damage. According to one naturalist, a small bat can catch about 600 mosquito-size insects per hour, and a large colony of bats will consume thousands of pounds of insects every night. (Costa Rica has more than thirty species of bats, thank you very much.)

Meanwhile, lizards, geckos, and chameleons patrol the walls and corners of houses, cleaning up cockroaches and water bugs before they have a chance to infest the kitchen or make a condominium out of your bathroom. The fearsome-looking praying mantis sometimes prowls about the edges of rooms, snapping up bugs that the lizards miss. Ugly as the mantis is, we love 'em!

**ATTACK OF THE ARMY ANTS** Folks living in the tropical lowlands have additional help in keeping their homes bug-free. From time to time our Costa Rica house is invaded by army ants. Black and about a quarter of an inch long, the ants come marching in broad formation up the concrete columns to our veranda. They spill over the floors in a busy wave of housecleaning, removing moths and other night-flying insects that committed suicide against the porch lights the previous night. They scour the baseboards, corners, and ceilings in search of bugs, beetles, and insect eggs. Scorpions flee in terror; they have no defense against army ants—if they tarry, they are dismantled and served as snacks. Even snakes fear the ants. We simply stay out of their way or prop our feet out of range on a footstool while we read a novel, until their twenty-minute cleaning expedition is finished. We say good-bye and thank them as they continue on their way to their next housecleaning duties.

To our dismay, when our housekeeper sees army ants coming, she runs for the insecticide can and sprays profusely. This stops the wave of ants immediately, and they retreat. She is totally deaf to our protests and won't stop spraying until the ants completely disappear.

Actually, I'm exaggerating somewhat. (My wife has asked me a million times to stop exaggerating. No, *two* million times!) The truth is, these army ant invasions don't happen all that frequently, maybe once a month or so, depending on where you live. If they happen to arrive while you are out shopping, you'll miss them. But they are spectacular.

During a visit to Cahuita, on the Caribbean Coast, I was about to enter my cabin when I encountered an enormous beetle. It was the size of a large teacup, shaped like a giant ladybug, and the color of an olive drab army helmet. Feeling brave, I gingerly picked it up by its back, correctly figuring that its wicked-looking legs couldn't reach around the shell. I carried it to a nearby restaurant and proudly displayed my beetle to the people sitting at the bar, figuring that I'd raise a few eyebrows. The bartender looked at my discovery with a bored expression as he remarked, "Yes, those little ones are females."

It turned out that I was holding a rhinoceros beetle, possibly the largest bug of the entire insect world. They tell me the male, which I never happened to confront, grows to a length of 10 inches, sports enormous golden horns, and is colored in brilliant metallic hues. Harmless, though. According to one source, it feeds on decaying wood in the forest. My fingers were never at risk!

## CENTRAL AMERICAN **EARTHQUAKES**

All along the mountain chains that stretch from the tip of South America to Alaska, you will feel earthquakes. As a Californian, I've become accustomed to them and seldom experience more than a slight feeling of excitement when windows start rattling and my desk sways. We Californians expect to have several minor quakes a year and a big one every twenty years or so.

So it should come as no surprise that Costa Rica has its share of shakes and tremors. Actually, more than its share. The really big ones here are spaced by decades instead of generations. Costa Ricans are just as calm about earthquakes as most Californians are, however. After all, compared with the 700 or so tornadoes that slam the midwestern and eastern parts of North America, claiming eighty to a hundred victims each season, an occasional California or Costa Rican shaker seems relatively mild.

The last big tremor—a whopping 7.4 on the Richter scale—hit the Caribbean Coast near the city of Limón in April 1991. Older structures suffered the most damage, particularly those not constructed to modern-day standards. However, by the beginning of the next tourist season, most of the damage had been repaired, hotels were operating, roads were open to traffic, and tourism was going full blast.

A few months after the big quake, I visited the village of Cahuita, not too far from the epicenter. Expecting to see a lot of damage and hear horror stories, I was delighted to learn that there were no fatalities in the village and that, except for one major building (which had been constructed of nonreinforced cement) and a few flimsy smaller structures, the town came through relatively unscathed. This is understandable since most Carribean construction is of wood, which may shake, rattle, and twist but doesn't usually tumble down.

Throughout the coastal area, this earthquake claimed about forty lives—one of the country's worst ever. Yet compare this earthquake with one in Iran the year before: It was 7.5 on the Richter scale and claimed more than 50,000 victims. A less-powerful 6.9 quake in Armenia in 1989 killed 25,000 people, yet an earthquake in Costa Rica the following year was just as strong, but nobody was killed. Why the difference?

One answer to this question, besides lower population density, is sensible construction methods. Costa Rican homes and businesses are designed with earthquakes in mind. Costa Rica has prohibited the use of adobe in constructing homes for more than eighty years. In fact, this is the only nation in the hemisphere with a ban on adobe, a material with a tendency to collapse and bury earthquake victims. Wood, reinforced concrete block, or stressed cement is infinitely safer. Instead of picturesque tile roofs, which can crush inhabitants under tons of heavy beams and broken tile, most Costa Rican roofs are of ordinary-looking corrugated aluminum, plastic, or sheet metal. These lightweight roofs may slide about during a quake, but they won't collapse and kill people by burying them.

An interesting feature of the 1991 quake was an uplifting of the coastline. The force raised the land as much as 5 feet near the town of Puerto Limón and 11 feet at Puerto Viejo. What once were coral reefs are now dry land at the edge of surf where fishermen once hauled in crab, shrimp, and red snapper. This lifting of the land from the sea is a wonderful example of how the Central American land bridge was formed some two or three million years ago when quake activity began pushing the land ever higher. Geologists find coral fossils on mountaintops now 9,000 feet above sea level.

# WHAT ARE
# COSTA RICANS LIKE?

Most travelers will agree that every country has its own distinct personality. Native citizens of each country have unique ways of behaving and viewing the world. My favorite story to illustrate differences in national personalities is called Traveler's Heaven and Traveler's Hell:

"Traveler's Heaven is when you are greeted by the British, the French do the cooking, Italians plan the fun and games, and Germans keep order. But Traveler's Hell is when you are greeted by the French, the British do the cooking, Italians keep order, and Germans plan the fun and games!"

Americans and Australians, for example, are stereotypically outgoing, friendly, and loud talkers. Russians are pictured as dour and morose, with no sense of humor. British are said to be terrible cooks. Of course these are stereotypes, and we all agree that it isn't fair to apply stereotypes. (Except in the case of the Brits, who tend to boil everything they can't fry.) Yet there is more than a kernel of truth here. The reasons for a nation's personality differences often can be explained by the historical development of each country.

In South America, for example, Argentina has a personality that reflects the heritage of its large Italian immigration, while next-door

Chile was influenced by English and German newcomers who joined the original Spanish settlers. The result is an outgoing, vivacious, and self-confident Argentine personality compared with Chile's more reserved, polite, and introverted temperament.

Costa Rica's distinct personality also is a product of history. In chapter 1 we discussed Costa Rica's isolation during the early Spanish years and how, during the early days of the republic, Costa Rica invited Europeans from all nations to immigrate and start coffee farms. Italians, the French, and refugees from other European countries joined Spaniards in the land rush, each nationality bringing its customs and personalities to blend together into Costa Rica's unique European–Central American culture, thus creating the *tico* personality of today.

One way *ticos* differ from residents of some other Latin American countries is tolerance toward other religions and other points of view. Costa Ricans are predominantly Catholic but without the zeal and rigidity usually found in other countries. This, too, has a historical explanation. In the early days, villages were so isolated that the Church either couldn't or didn't bother to build churches. Priests visited villages on rare occasions, sometimes never. The result was a view of religion as something remote and almost irrelevant (except for the celebration of village saints' days). Even today Catholic churches in many small villages are attended only by visiting priests. This situation creates fertile ground for evangelical denominations to establish churches. Many small villages have evangelical Protestant churches only. An example of Costa Rica religious views: Three-fourths of all couples prefer civil ceremonies, with only one-fourth of young couples tying the knot in church in front of a priest or preacher.

Yet curiously, one of the country's most important celebrations is on August 2, when thousands of Costa Ricans end a pilgrimage walk of several days to pay homage to the *Virgen de los Angeles* statue in Cartago. Throughout the country, Catholics, Protestants, and agnostics alike enthusiastically celebrate their villages' religious fiestas with dances, bullfights, parades, and fund-raising events. It's more like a carnival than a religious observance. By the way, do not miss attending these celebrations! The local people appreciate gringos joining in and will welcome you with enthusiasm. You'll have a great time.

# WHY *TICOS?*

Throughout this book you'll see the term *tico* used when referring to Costa Ricans. This is the appropriate nickname for a Costa Rican citizen, just as *nica* is a Nicaraguan, and *gringo* describes North Americans in general (as well as any foreigner whose natural language is English). Costa Ricans call themselves *ticos* when distinguishing themselves from foreigners, instead of the more cumbersome *Costarricenses*. Personally, I much prefer the term *gringo* over the dictionary-correct *Estadounidense* (which I couldn't spell, even on a bet).

The nickname *tico* comes from an archaic practice of using the sound *-ico* on the end of a word as a diminutive instead of the normal *-ito*. For example, whereas a Mexican would say *momen**tito*** for "just a tiny moment," some Costa Ricans (not all) might say *momen**tico***. Thus, a kitten would be a *ga**tico*** in Costa Rica but a *ga**tito*** in Mexico. Note that not all Costa Ricans use this ending, but enough do to keep the tradition alive.

This isn't something that originated in Costa Rica; the use of *-ico* was common in sixteenth-century Spanish literature. However, it dropped out of style sometime after Costa Rica was settled. The country's limited connection with Spain didn't allow Spanish vernacular to stay current.

# THE *TICO* PSYCHE

An outstanding difference between the psyche of Costa Ricans and other Latinos is the way they view the world and their place in it. Because of a long tradition of democracy and equality, the country has developed an egalitarian society similar to the United States and Canada in terms of social equality. Unlike many other Latin American countries, the spread between Costa Rica's rich, poor, and middle classes is narrow. The middle class is large and relatively prosperous; the upper class is small and only moderately wealthy. This is a country where you can see the president and his wife pushing a grocery cart in a supermarket. People here feel an extraordinary sense of equality: They look you in the eye and shake your hand, fully convinced that everyone is equal.

Because *tico* attitudes are similar to North Americans', we feel comfortable when socializing with our Costa Rican neighbors. However, there are some subtle differences in the *tico* psyche that need to be understood. First of all, it is considered ill-mannered to be loud, brash, argumentative, and overly competitive, as Americans tend to be. (The exception, of course, is when *ticos* are playing soccer or driving a car.) In fact, they dislike confrontation or making someone feel bad so much that they'll do anything to avoid giving you bad news. When your contractor tells you that the transformer for your new home didn't arrive today but might be coming *mañana,* he may be avoiding the bad news that it could be a week, or a month, before you have electricity. Costa Ricans want to tell you what you would like to hear if at all possible. If it's not possible, they avoid talking about it so you won't feel bad.

In line with the hesitation to give bad news is a tendency to avoid saying a definite "no" to a request or business proposal. If saying no might make a *tico* appear rude, or might hurt your feelings, he becomes vague. So when doing business, remember that you can only count on an outright "yes" or "no" as being definitive. A hesitant "yes" or "maybe" could mean anything.

Another interesting trait is the reluctance to accept blame. When our maid drops a plate on the floor, she says, *"Se quebró el plato,"* or "The plate broke itself." I once tried to convince an electrician that he had installed my telephone incorrectly. (The problem was obvious: He had shorted the wires by pounding a staple across the cable shroud.) He insisted that the problem was a temporary glitch at the telephone exchange. "Pretty soon they'll find their mistake and fix it." He installed a new cable at my insistence and according to my directions, after which the phone worked. "You see?" he crowed in triumph. "While I was putting in the new cable, the telephone company found their mistake and fixed it!" I agreed with him so he could save face.

Something I do *not* believe is the often heard claim that *ticos* deliberately mislead you about directions rather than admit that they don't know the answer. For example, some claim that when asked directions, *ticos* might give any response, pointing whichever direction they think you might like. I've often wondered where that notion came from. I have never, in all my years of traveling anywhere in Central America, had anyone do that. (I ought to know, because without street signs, I have to ask for directions frequently.) When *ticos* don't know the answer to a question, they simply say so, like anyone else. On several occasions when the people I asked for directions didn't know, they flagged down passing automobiles to ask. Giving misleading directions would be the height of rudeness and a violation of *tico* etiquette.

The well-known *mañana* attitude of Latin America is present in Costa Rica, but not nearly to the extent as in some other Latino countries—at least in my experience. Our workers are usually always at the job on time and work hard while they are there. (They also quit exactly on time.) The exception to this rule is on Monday mornings after a Sunday fiesta celebration. Nobody expects all of their workers to show up on time or without hangovers on those Monday mornings, or to be really capable of work, for that matter. (They love fiestas!)

Guests to your dinner party will be late anywhere from fifteen minutes to half an hour. Your auto mechanic will be an hour late changing your oil, but seldom a day late.

In several ways, *ticos* are very much like us, except that they speak more softly and seem more stoic about the world's problems than some of their Latin American counterparts. They laugh just as much as we do and share the same sense of humor. The best part of all: They really like North Americans, because our personalities mesh. Most of us who live in Costa Rica reciprocate this instant friendship; we like *ticos*, too.

## COSTA RICAN **SPANISH**

One of the ways to get the most out of living in a foreign country is to learn to speak the language. In Costa Rica, speaking Spanish is neither essential nor necessary because you'll have many English-speaking neighbors, both expats and *ticos*. But learning to communicate will open many doors, and it helps you make Spanish-speaking friends.

I have a couple of suggestions. First, get over the notion that you can "pick up Spanish" just by being exposed to people speaking Spanish. It doesn't work that way. It takes study and hours of conversation with Spanish-speaking people. Stick with it and speak Spanish at every opportunity, and you'll find yourself enjoying the process. Fortunately, just about all *ticos* have studied English in school, so you can build fluency and confidence by throwing in English words when you can't remember or haven't learned the proper word. If you have a background in Spanish, either from high school or college classes, you will have no difficulty with Spanish in Costa Rica.

Nevertheless, there are some differences you should be aware of. Because of Costa Rica's early isolation from mainstream Spanish colonies, the country maintained archaic words and idioms that long ago faded from Spanish spoken in neighboring colonies. Furthermore, within Costa Rica itself, pronunciation and accents developed in isolated parts of the country when communication between regions was severely restricted. For example: Before the railroad was constructed to transport coffee to Limón to be shipped to Europe, an oxcart journey took nearly two weeks. Today it's a two- or three-hour drive. So it isn't surprising that local idioms and accents developed in isolation throughout the country.

These accents vary from being so slight that it takes an expert to distinguish them, to being all but unintelligible to those trying to learn Spanish. The differences are similar to the way words are pronounced in Minneapolis, Minnesota, as compared to the way they're pronounced in Montgomery, Alabama. This is most noticeable in Guanacaste (northwestern Costa Rica). Like the Alabama accent, the Guanacaste accent is the result of dropping consonants and slurring vowels together. This lingo is similar to that spoken in Nicaragua (not surprising since Guanacaste originally was part of Nicaragua). Once you get used to this blending of sounds, it becomes clear.

Don't worry too much if you are just learning Spanish. Almost all people can and will speak "proper Spanish" when they realize you don't understand them. They simply repeat their words with a more careful pronunciation and avoid using local slang—just as they learned to do when they were in grade school. English is mandatory in all grammar schools, by the way, from the second to the sixth grade.

One outstanding difference between *tico* Spanish and standard high school Spanish might puzzle those who have studied the language back home. Instead of using the traditional polite *usted* and informal *tu* forms of Spanish normally taught in our high schools and universities, Costa Ricans use the archaic Spanish *vos* instead of the more common *tu* for the familiar first person singular. Originally, *vos* was the polite form of Spanish first person singular, and *tu* was familiar. Then somewhere in the late sixteenth century, the use of *vuestra merced* ("your grace") became the polite form, later shortened to *usted*. This downgraded the formal pronoun *vos* to informal use, and the pronoun *tu* was used only when speaking to inferiors or animals. Later, the use of *vos* was totally dropped and *tu* once again became standard for informal speech in Spain. However, the first Costa Rican immigrants from Spain arrived before that switch in grammar occurred and therefore retained the old custom. To make things more confusing, the *tu* form is sometimes used as a form of intimacy between lovers.

Verbs have a different declension or word ending when using *vos*. Unfortunately these grammatical verb forms aren't taught in U.S. schools, even though the *voseo* mode is used by several million people in the Western Hemisphere. (Yes, they teach the *vosotros* form, but that is plural and is used mostly by Catholic priests when addressing a congregation.) It takes some time to become comfortable with the *vos* form; in the meantime, play it safe by using *usted*. Look at the chart below and note the differences.

|  | **Usted** Form | **Tu** Form | **Vos** Form |
|---|---|---|---|
| **Do you want?** | *¿Quiere Ud?* | *¿Quieres tu?* | *¿Queréis vos?* |
| **You speak . . .** | *Usted habla* | *Tu hablas* | *Vos hablás* |
| **You are . . .** | *Usted es* | *Tu eres* | *Vos sos* |

You'll also encounter some interesting differences between *tico* expressions and Spanish usage in other countries. Some are quite charming. For example, in most Spanish-speaking countries, the term for "you're welcome" is *por nada* ("it's nothing") or *no hay de que* ("don't mention it"). Costa Ricans feel that those expressions are somewhat impolite. To say "you're welcome," they say *con mucho gusto*, which translates as

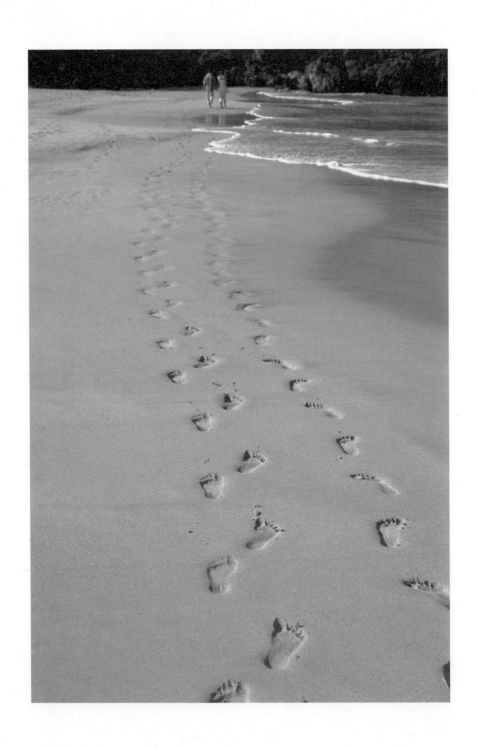

"with much pleasure." (Now, is that polite or what?) Of course, they're used to hearing gringos use the other expressions, so they won't be surprised when you say *de nada.*

Instead of greeting close acquaintances with *¿Como está usted?* ("How are you?") they'll often ask, *¿Como amaneció?* ("How did you wake up this morning?").

Another curious custom: For some reason *ticos* feel that asking for something using the verb *dar* (to give) is impolite. Instead of *Dame una coca, por favor,* meaning "Give me a Coca-Cola, please," they consider it more polite to use the verb *regalame,* which means "give me" but also could mean "make me a gift of . . ." So to be polite in a *tico* sense, you might say, *"Regálame una coca, por favor."* A *tica* friend told of her first visit to Mexico and of ordering a cup of coffee in a restaurant by saying *"Regálame un café con leche, por favor."* The waitress was obviously embarrassed when she said, "I'd love to give you some coffee, but the owner would be angry with me if I did!" My friend giggled about this, saying she hadn't realized that she could be misunderstood.

One uniquely Costa Rican term, solidly ingrained into the language, is *pura vida.* I suppose this would translate as "it's a great life," but in effect it means "okay," "cool," "all right," or sometimes an emphatic "aw-right!" Instead of asking "Would you like anything else?" a clerk in a store might say, *"Pura vida?"* A gas-station attendant might ask, "Is your oil *pura vida,* or should I check it for you?" When you greet someone with *"¿Como está usted?"* the answer is often, *"Pura vida!"*

A couple of strictly Costa Rican expressions initially puzzled me and could be puzzling to those learning the language. This is a tendency to begin sentences with the words *vieras que,* or simply *vieras.* Literally it means something like "You see" or "You know." Also used in the same way is *digamos* ("let's say. . ."). Since the sound *d* is often softened or dropped entirely, it often comes out *"igamos."*

Remember that slang changes over time. Many years ago I ran across a series of tapes with *tico* slang expressions, bought them, and put them away, vowing some day to master *tico* slang. Twenty years later I actually began to study those tapes. Armed with this knowledge of *tico* slang, I ventured forth to display my proficiency and was shocked to see smiles and laughter. Then I realized that over the years, this slang had fallen from favor. I was saying things like "Twenty-three skidoo!" or "Groovy!" or "Far out!"

For those who would like to study Costa Rican slang, a Google search will return several Web sites devoted to this. One can be found at www .discoverypress.com/slang.html. A word of warning: Those who have learned and used Spanish slang in another country should be careful when using it in polite company in Costa Rica. Some expressions that might be clever and inoffensive in Mexico, for example, could mean something obscene or insulting in Costa Rica, and vice versa.

# WHY CHOOSE
# **COSTA RICA?**

Ask the question, "Why did you choose to relocate in Costa Rica?" and you'll receive almost as many different answers as there are expatriates living in Costa Rica. Typically, the process of choosing Costa Rica for a new beginning starts with a vacation visit. People are curious about this small Central American democracy. They've heard of lush rain forests, lofty mountains, marvelous wildlife, and gorgeous beaches. Costa Rica's welcoming expat community and friendly natives make tourists feel at home. Before the vacation is over, the possibility of living in Costa Rica on a permanent vacation begins to look very attractive.

Costa Rica's unique selection of climates is a definite drawing card, with fugitives from bitter-cold winters or suffocating summer heat finding welcome relief from weather extremes. "I grew up in Kansas," one retiree explained, "We had blizzards and frozen ground in the winter, then 110-degree days trapping us indoors in the summer. Where we live now, on the hillside above Escazú, we only need one set of clothing—for spring weather."

Some who succumb to Costa Rica's attractions are much too young to retire, either mentally or physically. Their goals often include some kind of business enterprise they've always wanted to try. This is their chance to do what they want to do rather than what they have to do, or what they are told to do. Later in this book we have a chapter on doing business in Costa Rica and why some make a success of it and others do not.

To most retirees, business sounds like work. Work is exactly why they are retiring in the first place! Yet lying around the swimming pool or hanging out on a beach isn't exactly what they have in mind. An alternative is volunteering in some worthwhile activity. Perhaps at the local library, teaching English to children. Maybe helping preserve turtle nesting grounds, or working with any of the multiple expat social clubs and organizations. The need for volunteers is unlimited. Besides self-satisfaction, you immediately become part of a social group of like-minded compatriots and friends.

Some relocate to Costa Rica simply for the enchanting experience of living in a foreign country: learning a foreign language, making friends in a totally different culture, learning how other people live. This includes creating an active social life among fellow countrymen, with clubs, evening get-togethers, and travels throughout the region. Costa Rica's relative affluence and absence of obvious poverty make retirees feel comfortable while experiencing the stimulation of foreign retirement. The fact that Americans genuinely feel welcome makes it easy for retirees to settle almost anywhere they choose, not necessarily confined to expatriate gated communities.

Most people do a lot of research and spend some time in the country before making a solid decision about moving here. But not all. When asked how she and her husband made the decision to move to Costa Rica, one lady said, "We probably did things differently than most sane people do. We decided to move here without even visiting. We had traveled in Mexico, and everyone we spoke with compared Costa Rica favorably. In fact, some people liked Costa Rica better than Mexico. We decided we could handle Costa Rica without testing the waters first. Our initial plan was to spend a year in Costa Rica, rent furnished homes, learn the language, and take our experiences back home when it was over. However, our children were enjoying school here, so after one year into it, we expect to be here for a long while."

# LOW COST **OF LIVING?**

Sometimes I hesitate to mention this, but one of the benefits of living in Costa Rica is an affordable cost of living. Although prices have risen lately, with inflation in both North America and Costa Rica, and a devaluation of the U.S. dollar, it is still fairly easy to live on a much higher standard here than on the same budget in most parts of the United States or Canada. There are two reasons why I'm reluctant to emphasize Costa Rica as an inexpensive place to live.

The first reason is that some folks will be encouraged to come to Costa Rica simply because it is an inexpensive place to live. Those who do move to Costa Rica for this reason are continually comparing prices and conditions. They complain bitterly and suffer frustration and disappointment when other conditions are substandard in comparison with back home: roads, bureaucracy, the *mañana* syndrome, and so on. They feel cheated to discover some items cost as much here as they do back home—imported goods even more.

The second reason is that since the fall of the U.S. dollar against world currencies, everyday living costs are not the bargain they were a couple of years ago. The devaluation of the dollar is matched by inflation in colón prices in Costa Rica, with workers receiving unprecedented 20 percent wage hikes. This is only fair, since the cost of food in the last half of 2007 rose 18 percent. Similar inflation is going on in the United States, with the highest inflation since 1991. Prices are rising in tandem in North America as well as Central America. Nevertheless, *tico* prices started at a lower level, so the living expenses are still much less than up north.

It's always amusing to hear tourists—and even an occasional resident—complain about high prices in Costa Rica. For some reason people assume that property, goods, and services ought to be dirt cheap in a developing Central American country like Costa Rica. A few months ago my wife and I happened to be dining next to a couple from New England who were first-time visitors to Costa Rica. They expressed disappointment with Costa Rica as a place to retire. When asked why, they replied that they felt that Costa Rica was not the beautiful and interesting place described in magazines and guidebooks. (They didn't know that we were authors of a guidebook.)

Dumbfounded by their answer, I politely inquired how long they had been in Costa Rica and where they had visited. They admitted that they

had just arrived three days earlier and that their travels were limited to taxi rides around the San José area.

"Okay, we realize there must be more to Costa Rica than San José," the husband explained. "But we were under the impression that everything is cheap here. But that's not the case. For example, we see houses advertised in the *Tico Times* priced almost as much as back home." They admitted that they hadn't actually looked at any of the houses. They had expected to find a nice home for around $30,000.

Their concern over high prices amused us. They were enjoying a delicious sea bass dinner priced at $8, including dessert. They were drinking Costa Rican beer priced at $1.50 a bottle. They were staying at a nice bed-and-breakfast for about $40 a night. To be polite, we agreed with the couple; Costa Rica probably wouldn't be the ideal place for them to retire.

Although I have a hard time imagining a quality place in the United States or Canada that makes Costa Rica look expensive, my routine reply to bargain hunters is: "If rock-bottom prices are your priority, look at Mexico, Guatemala, or Nicaragua." Many third-world countries offer cheaper living than Costa Rica. But is the quality of life the same? Is the weather as nice? Are the people as friendly?

The bottom line is: You're in for disappointment if you expect to pay $5-a-day wages for your gardener or maid, or purchase ocean-view property at Texas Panhandle prices. If you anticipate luxurious $10-a-day hotel rooms and lobster dinners for $3, this might be the time to stop reading this book.

**AFFORDABLE, NOT CHEAP** In general, I estimate most Costa Rican prices to be about two-thirds the cost in most North American communities. Of course, imported goods can be much more. The hotels Costa Rica expatriates patronize usually range from $35 to $65 a night, including breakfast. These aren't luxury establishments by any definition, but they clearly offer far more than budget hotels do in the United States or Canada for the same price. Backpackers are delighted to find rooms for $10, since they don't mind sharing the bathroom.

Go to just about any nice restaurant in Costa Rica and check the menu. Few entrees are priced over $9. A juicy steak goes for about $8, pasta Alfredo for $4. If the entree exceeds $13, you're probably ordering lobster or jumbo shrimp. (For some reason, jumbo shrimp is expensive in Costa Rica.) If you're into *tipico* Costa Rican food, you can order a *casado* for about $3—a delicious plate of beans, rice, fried banana and yucca, and salad, with your choice of chicken, fish, or pork chop. My favorite *tico* restaurant serves a delicious butterflied pork chop half the size of a dinner plate for about $3.50.

Let's forget about hotel prices and restaurant costs; they don't figure heavily in most long-term residents' budgets. More important is comparing the cost of everyday living here with the lifestyle the same amount of money provides in the United States or Canada. You would be hard-pressed to find another place with so much to offer for such a reasonable outlay. Without snow, as a bonus.

**CAN YOU LIVE ON SOCIAL SECURITY?** The answer depends on the size of your monthly check. Current U.S. Social Security benefits for a couple average around $1,500 a month. Assuming no extraordinary expenses, most people would have no problem maintaining a comfortable lifestyle on that amount. (After all, this is more than three times the income of a typical Costa Rican family.) Additional income could be banked or saved for emergencies. Yes, you can probably get by back in the United States living on $1,500—provided you lived in an inexpensive part of the country—but it would require some creative budget trimming.

Numerous surveys here show that most expatriate couples report spending between $1,400 to $1,800 in Costa Rica to maintain an acceptable lifestyle. This would involve comfortable living accommodations, an inexpensive auto, a part-time housekeeper and gardener, plus a certain amount of travel around the country. Clearly, the standard of living on budgets like these will be much higher than one could ever hope for in the United States or in Canada for the same outgo. Some people spend a lot more, but their living standards are much higher as well.

Of course, many people draw below-average Social Security benefits, often as low as $600 a month. Even though this is almost twice the average income of a Costa Rican worker, it would require considerable downscaling on the part of most North Americans to get by. I know a few who do, but not at what my wife and I would consider a pleasant lifestyle. More about this later.

One way of economizing is by living in ordinary rather than deluxe housing. In many foreign countries North American residents feel they must live in certain "safe" areas, gated communities for which they pay premium prices. Because Costa Rica is not a highly stratified society, North Americans feel comfortable living in almost any middle-class neighborhood or small villages where there are other expats in residence. This translates into a wide selection of rents and housing prices. While you can pay $1,500 a month to rent in a luxury section of Escazú, you can often find a nice place for $500 a month in a nearby neighborhood. For $350 you can find accommodations in very livable areas such as Alajuela or San Pedro. If you're content with less-sumptuous digs, your rental costs can be even less. I have a friend who lives in a small house near San José that he rents for $250 a month. (Understand, we're not talking about premium beachfront properties with ocean views!)

Utilities, a significant part of most budgets, are very reasonable in Costa Rica compared with the United States or Canada. Our telephone bill is usually between $10 to $20 a month, plus an extra $24 for broadband Internet charges. Homes seldom have air conditioners (much less furnaces) to drain money from budgets. At our Pacific Coast home, electric bills are around $45 a month (with electric dryer and washer). In our particular community, our non-government water-company bills are unusually high (only because our water bills include road maintenance and other services).

Property taxes are almost nothing, at least for North Americans accustomed to forking over big money for taxes. Taxes are supposedly figured at 0.25 percent of the recorded value. Therefore, a property with a recorded value of $100,000 should have an annual assessment of only $250. (Most people pay much less because they routinely understate the recorded value.) According to people I interviewed for this book, an average middle-class home—with three bedrooms and two baths—is taxed at rates varying from $50 to $600 a year. Most U.S. communities collect more taxes than that every month.

Besides affordable housing, utilities, taxes, and food costs, what other bargains does Costa Rica offer? Oh yes: servants. A full-time housekeeper will clean your house and wash and iron clothes for about $250 a month. That includes benefits such as Social Security, paid vacation, and a Christmas bonus. (See chapter 12 for further details.) We pay our gardener-handyman $3 an hour for part-time work, and that's well above minimum wage. We have a friendly cleaning lady who comes in one half-day each week. She washes clothes, changes bed linens, mops and disinfects floors, and waxes the veranda deck—also for $3 an hour. (By the way, what do you pay servants in your hometown?)

Is everything inexpensive in Costa Rica? (Don't we wish!) Gasoline is more expensive, depending on the current world price of crude oil and whether the government needs more tax revenue. Last time I filled my tank, it was almost $5 a gallon. Expensive gasoline makes people think before making an unnecessary trip to the supermarket. Automobiles are heavily taxed, and repair parts can be costly.

High import taxes are a way of life in almost all Latin countries. This makes automobiles very expensive. You'll need to brace yourself before asking the price of a new car. Even a used car. Until a couple of years ago, customs and sales taxes cost as much as 100 percent of appraised value! It's a little better today, running from 40 to 77 percent of the vehicle's value. These tax rates change frequently, but you can be sure that autos in Costa Rica will always be expensive. Calculations for automobile duties are made from something called the Black Book, listing new- and used-car wholesale auction prices—the bible for U.S. car dealers, loan officers, and Costa Rican customs agents.

Fortunately, public transportation is excellent and inexpensive. Depending on where you live, a family car may not be the absolute necessity that it is back home. Buses travel all over the Central Valley, at frequent intervals, for less than $1 for considerable distances. Taxis are plentiful and inexpensive. Even in the country, far from city conveniences, buses and taxis are abundant. Where public transportation is all but non-existent, the custom is for automobiles and trucks to pick up pedestrians. We've made several *tico* and gringo acquaintances that way. Would you consider picking up hitchhikers back home? I wouldn't!

**LOW-BUDGET EXAMPLE** This may sound repetitive, but I feel it's important to emphasize: In no way would I encourage anyone with a limited budget and no backup funds to move to Costa Rica simply because of the relatively low cost of living. That would be an invitation for disaster. At home, low-income people qualify for Medicaid, welfare, food stamps, and other public programs. Safety nets such as these do not exist in Costa Rica. However, if you have sufficient funds to cover emergencies and money to splurge for luxuries on a regular basis, you are encouraged to investigate further.

One of my favorite examples of living in Costa Rica on a restricted budget is our friend Tom Stafford from California. Like several million other U.S. retirees, Tom draws Social Security benefits of less than $700 a month. Although he had accumulated a modest nest egg as a backup, Tom knew he had to live conservatively, preferably within his Social Security income.

Tom says: "The decision to live in Costa Rica was made after my third trip. I began to scout out a piece of land with the idea of building a home. When a friend bought a few acres north of San Ramón, I threw in with him, buying a one-half-acre plot for my house. I decided on a prefabricated Swiss chalet–style log cabin that seemed to fit me like a tailored suit. While only 750 square feet, it has a commodious loft and plenty of beautiful land all around it."

Tom points out: "My transition to 'tico provisional' was not all that smooth. Without the generous help and advice of friends I made along the way, it might not have happened at all. One piece of advice I would give to anyone thinking of coming here is: Meet a lot of people—both expats and ticos—make friends with them, and follow their advice. I know it's a cliché, but there is no sense in reinventing the wheel."

Tom manages to get by just fine on $671 per month (his Social Security check), but only because he owns his home, thus eliminating rent. His monthly expenses, such as electricity, water, and telephone, are very low. Public transportation allows him to get by sans automobile. Tom says, "My budget doesn't leave much for nights out on the town or rollicking good times. But after two years, I'm convinced I made the right decision."

At the conclusion of our visit, Tom said, "I often sit on my upper veranda in the morning—looking out over a vista my friends in California would pay a million dollars for—and I ask myself: 'Tom, what the hell did you do right to deserve this?'"

As we drove away from his charming little home, we couldn't help but wonder: How would Tom be making out in Los Angeles, California (instead of Los Angeles, Costa Rica), in his struggle to survive on $671 a month? Yes, millions of U.S. residents are forced to get by on Social Security as their sole income, but with what level of dignity?

## COSTA RICA **SOCIAL LIFE**

When asked why they decided to live in Costa Rica, most people begin by describing Costa Rica's gorgeous weather and magical tropical surroundings. They'll rave on about favorite beaches, mountain retreats, and cloud forests, and eventually they'll mention the affordable cost of living.

But oddly enough, when you ask people to pinpoint the most important factor in making the decision to relocate to Costa Rica, most people admit that lovely surroundings are only part of it. After a while, pretty, exotic scenery becomes like new wallpaper—you get used to it. When you pin many people down, they'll agree that a most important factor in enjoying Costa Rica is the numerous friends and acquaintances they've made and their active circle of expatriate comrades.

It's interesting to observe how North Americans who live in a foreign country—any foreign country—tend to cling together, to form close social groups. They reach out to draw newly arrived English-speakers into their midst. Since the pool of English-speakers is limited, each addition to their circle of friends is valued. People with almost nothing in common—who wouldn't even nod at each other back home as they passed on the street—become great pals in a foreign setting. In Costa Rica, newcomers are eagerly sought after.

I've found this to be true no matter which foreign country we've researched. Expatriates in Mexico, Spain, Argentina, and Portugal affirm this close camaraderie among fellow English-speakers. Foreign residents usually explain their love for their new surroundings by saying, "Everyone is so friendly here! I have more friends and companions than I ever had in my hometown. There, our closest friends were mostly people we worked with." Almost as an afterthought, they mention the exotic surroundings or affordable living costs.

This doesn't mean that you needn't work at making friends in Costa Rica. You must go halfway. If you wait for expatriates to knock down your door and drag you out to dinner, you may give the impression of wanting to be a hermit. We have those here, too.

**MIXING WITH *TICO* NEIGHBORS** The usual strategy for newcomers is to seek out a place where most neighbors are fellow countrymen who speak English and are available to guide them through the process of fitting into their new surroundings. This is the preferred strategy for most newcomers. It is usually best to become accustomed to the environment and learn at least some Spanish before settling in a *tico* neighborhood with no English-speaking neighbors.

But not everyone feels this way. Before Laura and David Streek of Cambridge left England for Costa Rica with their two young daughters, they decided they wanted their Costa Rica adventure to be something special. Laura said, "We looked forward to integrating into the community and society of a new country where we could lead a simpler, warmer life spent mostly outdoors. We wanted our children to experience a new culture and learn a new language." They discovered a village they liked on the Pacific Coast and decided to try living there.

Instead of joining the foreign community who lived in tasteful and comfortable homes with lovely views of the ocean, the Streek family rented an older *tico*-style house, right in the center of the village. Little stores flanked both sides of the house, and goal posts of the village soccer field were across the street. The grade school where their children attended classes was located near the sidelines of the soccer field.

Their neighbors were mostly *ticos*, with a scattering of North American and European émigrés from Switzerland and Holland, some of whom were operating small businesses in the village. They immediately set about making friends. They found it surprisingly easy. Before long, the family felt comfortable with their surroundings and became acquainted with enough of their neighbors to have a party.

Laura said, "We decided to have an open house one weekend, which begged the question: Where else in the world could you have moved to, not knowing a single soul, and within two weeks have met enough likable people to have a house party? We spent a happy afternoon of flower arranging, stringing fairy lights, and setting up the music system in readiness for the night's festivities.

"Soon after sundown, with the house sparkling in the twilight and music drifting out into the balmy air, people began to arrive. Before long the party was in full swing, with guests bringing pots of chili, dips, tortillas, crates of beer, and gifts. The porch was filled with young *ticos* and gringos alike drinking beers. The living room held the food, and young children danced the salsa with the more-than-willing grown-ups. The kitchen and back rooms bustled with the usual party activities. The garden was the only place one could find to sit under the stars and enjoy a conversation with new friends."

In many countries, something like this could never happen. Class lines are too rigid. But *ticos* have a strong sense of equality and think nothing of joining multicultural celebrations. Instead of meeting foreigners with an awestruck bowing of the head—as is the custom in many Latin American countries—*ticos* look strangers in the eye, shake hands, and sometimes even invite the strangers to visit their homes. That probably wouldn't happen in your hometown, would it?

The Streek family have since returned to England, to their hometown of Cambridge, but I am confident that they will always look back with fondness on their interlude in paradise. They will remember the *tico* and gringo friends they made while in living in the village. The children will always have the advantage of being bilingual, with a Costa Rican accent to their Spanish.

Even if your Spanish is far from fluent in situations like this, communication flows. Most *ticos* have learned about as much English in high school as you learned Spanish in high school. (They have also forgotten as much English as you've forgotten Spanish!) Yet both sides have fun talking, learning new phrases in the other's language, and becoming friends.

Making friends among the *tico* community is a rewarding experience. However, you should resist the temptation of moving to a totally "nongringo" community, far from other English-speaking neighbors. The fact is, most newcomers need a circle of English-speakers to round out their lives. They find that even though communication skills with *ticos* are okay, many common elements of understanding are lacking. After a while there's a craving to talk politics, to discuss movies, or to reminisce over the "good old days." You'll receive blank stares from your *tico* friends when you start speculating about the Chicago Cubs' chances for the pennant or whether Senator Phoghorn can be reelected. In short, the average newcomer to Costa Rica needs both gringo and *tico* friends. Happily, this is possible. Newcomers are attacked with aggressive friendliness.

## CLUBS AND **ACTIVITES**

There's no excuse for being lonely in Costa Rica: too much to do, too many people to meet, too many places to go. Take some Spanish classes, attend a meeting of Republicans Abroad or Democrats Abroad, do some volunteer work, learn to play tennis or bridge. You'll meet more friends than you've dreamed of, and you'll live the rich life you moved to Costa Rica to find.

The biggest mistake some make is not keeping active. Some newcomers will take a drink or two when things get too quiet for them; next thing they know, they're drinking too much. If you haven't already acquired interests to keep you busy in your new location, open the *Tico Times* to the "Club Directory" section and look at the broad range of invitations. (If you can't find a group of friends who are involved in your favorite activity, chances are your favorite activity is illegal, immoral, or boring!) Volunteer work is another satisfying way to make friends and become involved in fun activities; this can be much more satisfying than sitting around a bar until closing time.

An example of a volunteer project, one in which my wife and I worked on, was establishing a library in a village in Guanacaste. Local expatriates contributed funds to purchase several shelves of reference material as well as books that are fun to read for adults and that will enhance the local children's interest in education. When enough money was donated, we expanded the library by renting a building separate from the school and opened the facility to adults as well as children. Within about six years, the library accumulated enough donations to build a beautiful new building on land donated by the village. The library has ten new computers for teaching marketable skills to teenagers and adults, and fiction and nonfiction shelves in both Spanish and English for gringos and *ticos*. Just a slight exposure to worthwhile projects like this increases one's social circle immensely.

## BEING SINGLE **IN COSTA RICA**

As you'll notice, much of the advice, experiences, and examples of living in Costa Rica given in this book seem directed toward married couples. The fact is, you'll find an unusually large number of single people happily residing here. Some have never married, some are widowed, and many are divorced. A single man I interviewed, when asked why he was single in Costa Rica, observed, "I never understood what complete happiness meant until I got married. Then it was too late. So after the divorce, the first thing I thought about was leaving the country! There's something romantic about the name 'Costa Rica,' so I just knew this would be a great adventure."

I've known a dozen or more fellow countrymen who married Costa Rican women. A common explanation goes something like this: "Actually, I planned to stay for only one month, but before I knew it, I met this nice-looking lady, and now I'm married again!" When I asked an ex–New Jerseyite why he married a *tica*, he explained, "The thing is, Costa Rican women are different in many ways. It's not just that they are pretty and maybe younger. That's not what it's all about. We come here looking for something we feel we lost somewhere back along the years. What I found is someone who treats me as if I were special, and as if I were twenty years younger. She doesn't nag or complain because I'm not perfect. She is much more than a wife; she is my best friend."

This is not a one-sided proposition. Having a gringo husband offers advantages for the Costa Rican woman, too. The groom's Social Security check is more than enough to maintain an enviable standard of living. The groom is expected to provide not only for his new wife, but also support the children from her previous marriage. This typically includes paying tuition for private schools and sometimes college in the States. The husband usually finds himself responsible for his new in-laws as well. When Mámi wants a new refrigerator or Pápi needs a new set of dentures, guess who is expected to pay?

Now, having created all these cheery and optimistic scenarios about gringo men marrying *ticas*, let me follow up with a few words of caution. As a friend once pointed out, "My trophy girlfriend was more expensive than I ever dreamed possible." Because she never insisted on marriage, my friend didn't give any thought to legalities and assumed himself to be single. To his dismay, it turns out that when a couple lives together for a length of time, ostensibly three years, the woman acquires all the rights of a legal marriage. So when they broke up, his girlfriend went to court and was awarded the house he had purchased, plus support for her three children (which she had neglected to mention) until they reached the age of eighteen.

I have heard of other situations where a wife claimed spousal abuse (falsely, according to the husband, but who knows?). The wife had her husband permanently barred from entering the home they had bought, and she was granted monthly support payments. Costa Rican judges are reputed to routinely favor the wife's interests over the husband's, and even more so in the case of a gringo husband. (Also, consider that a large number, if not half, of Costa Rican judges are women.) These stories are legend in Costa Rica, although I'm sure that happy arrangements far outnumber the scams.

**GRINGO GULCH** Single gringo males tend to congregate in an area of downtown San José that I call Gringo Gulch—around the odd-numbered *avenidas* and *calles*. A concentration of inexpensive hotels and gringo bars attract a large number of recently arrived single or divorced fugitives from northern climes. They hang out in these bars of sometimes-questionable repute, where they drink Pilsen beer and exchange lies about their romantic conquests, their financial successes, and the injustices of their divorce settlements. Most habitués of Gringo Gulch are transient and ephemeral. Within a few weeks they either move on to discover the real Costa Rica or return home with exaggerated tales of their adventures in Central America.

The majority of these Gringo Gulch habitués are of Social Security age, looking for that one last go-round. Some are hoping to find a woman to become a life partner. Surprisingly enough, some actually find one. The fact is, all women who visit the gringo bars aren't necessarily prostitutes. Sometimes they're simply working women hoping to meet a wealthy

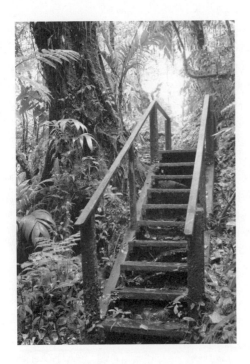

foreigner to marry, someone who will "take me away from all this." (*Wealthy* being defined as someone with a monthly Social Security check. With that income, the woman can quit her job and support her children in style.)

A word of caution to would-be gringo Don Juans: Be careful after dark, and avoid the *zona roja* (red-light zone) as the evening gets late. Some street girls here are rather skilled thieves. Your wallet can disappear quickly while you are basking in sweet talk from one of these women. Often their scam is pretending to be overwhelmed by a man's sex appeal. While several enthusiastic girls hug and caress the delighted gentleman, others are helping themselves to the contents of his pockets. It's almost always a nonviolent robbery; the victim doesn't realize he's been had until he tries to pay for his next drink. (Sorry, I have difficulty feeling sorry for his loss.)

Although an occasional visit to downtown San José bars can be entertaining, it's all too easy to make hanging out there your social life to the exclusion of all else. (Of course, that's a hazard anywhere in the country.)

If you're single and looking for someplace to go and people to meet, simply open the *Tico Times* to the "Calendar" section. You'll find a page and a half of listings: classes, art exhibits, concerts, lectures, dances, theaters, political clubs, sports, and every possible activity you can imagine—great places to meet people and make quality friends. There's no excuse for being bored in Costa Rica.

**SINGLE WOMEN** We know numerous single women and single mothers who are quite happy with their move to Costa Rica. We've also known several single women who tried Costa Rica and found they couldn't stand living here. My observation is that single women (or married, for that matter) tend not to enjoy Costa Rica as much as men.

My wife explains it this way: "Men enjoy sitting in a fishing boat under a blazing sun or surfing from daybreak to sundown. They love to hang around *tico* bars, drinking beer, gossiping, and trading stories—as well as checking out the local babes." (My wife harbors the ridiculous suspicion that female companionship is at the top of the agenda for men traveling alone.)

The fact is, single women socialize differently than single men. Women can easily become bored with the typical macho scene. Single people we know (men and women) who have made successful and happy transitions to living in Costa Rica are those who become actively involved in the social scene from the very beginning. Making friends is the key. Joining special-interest clubs, political or church groups—any situation where you come in contact with other expatriates is the key.

A great way to make friends is through volunteering. One woman explained, "While volunteering I became involved with of a group of like-minded friends. Before long I was invited for cocktails to meet other volunteers, then a dinner party, and other social gatherings. My circle of acquaintances kept widening, until today, I have more friends than I've had in my entire life." Women with children find volunteering at school puts them in social contact with parents of their children's classmates. Almost every community has volunteer opportunities for newcomers.

I have no firm statistics, but I'm firmly convinced that among expats, eligible single men outnumber single women by a large percentage. That's the good news for single women who might want to socialize with men friends as well as women. Of course, just as it was back home, "eligible" bachelors are vastly outnumbered by those who are single for very good reasons. (Their ex-wives could have interesting tales to relate in this regard.) Nevertheless, we've seen many happy and successful marriages among North Americans who met in Costa Rica.

Single women soon discover that many Costa Rican men like to fancy themselves as prototypes of the "Latin lover." A Brazilian friend once explained: "When I was young, my father took me aside to tell me the facts of life. He said, 'My son, in this world you must understand one thing. You *cannot* expect to go to bed with every woman you meet. But, of course, you must *try!*'"

That's the essence of a "Latin lover." The stereotype is a playboy supporting one or more mistresses and continually trolling for more conquests. To a small extent this could be true among the more affluent Costa Rican business types (same as anywhere else in the world), but the average eligible *tico* bachelor, the type most single women will meet, doesn't earn enough to even dream of supporting a mistress. He has a tough time scraping together enough money to keep gasoline in his car's gas tank.

Although we've seen some successful romances develop between foreign women and *tico* men, more often than not, cultures clash and the relationship falls apart. Again, I have no statistics on this, it's just our observation of couples we've known. Typically, the *tico* husband becomes deeply disappointed when his wife will not, or can not, provide enough income for the husband to enjoy the luxurious life to which he had expected to become accustomed. Therefore, no matter how much an expat woman loves her intended, it's important to consult a competent lawyer to ensure that in case of a marriage crash, the groom can't walk away with assets of the bride. Particularly if they plan on investing in property after the marriage, when community property issues can arise.

For a good book about a single woman's experiences in Costa Rica, I recommend *Butterfly in the City* by Jo Stuart. Jo is a friend and a columnist for *AM Costa Rica*. To order, write to jocstuart@gmail.com.

## GAYS IN **COSTA RICA**

We've interviewed several gay couples who have lived in Costa Rica for some time, asking about their acceptance by rank-and-file *ticos* and expatriate neighbors. Most experiences have been positive. There does seem to be a certain amount of disapproval of public displays of affection between gay couples, as if it's okay to be gay, only don't flaunt it. The antigay indignation demonstrated in some other parts of the world is rarely encountered in Costa Rica. In the final analysis, *ticos* seem to view homosexuality as mildly humorous and an inescapable fact of life rather than something that raises hostility.

# LIVING IN
## COSTA RICA

Used to be, we could easily distinguish between "first-world" and "third-world" nations by the standard of living and the type of government. First-world countries enjoyed individual freedom, democracy, and, most important, a viable economy where people lived dignified lives and enjoyed economic security.

Third-world countries were none of the above. More often than not in Latino countries, the ruling elite would be a group of wealthy families with a well-armed military to enforce order, using terror to keep working-class citizens in line. Thankfully, over the past twenty-plus years, conditions have changed for the better in most third-world countries in this hemisphere. Some, such as Argentina and Chile, have achieved living standards not too much different from North America. Costa Rica will probably never progress that far, yet the potential is definitely there.

Costa Rica never went through the repressive conditions described above. It started out as a democracy and has never experienced a military dictatorship. The overall standard of living in Costa Rica is admired and envied by neighboring countries. Costa Rica is different. After all, it's a place where you can drink the water and eat the food without risking your life. Where your conscience isn't continually assaulted by beggars and abject poverty. Furthermore, it's a place where the government isn't run by a bunch of uniformed thugs.

For these reasons, we North Americans find adjusting to Costa Rican living conditions rather easy. Of course, there are differences in lifestyles, but instead of being traumatic, in most instances the variations are charming. Whether you will enjoy living in Costa Rica depends on your approach to life and your expectations. If you expect people to conform to your ideals and you want conditions to be exactly as they were in your hometown, you are bound to be disappointed. Costa Rica is, after all, a foreign country. That's exactly why so many gringos choose to live here. We enjoy living in a foreign country.

In this chapter we'll look at some everyday living conditions that make Costa Rica different.

## COURTESY AND **CUSTOM**

Costa Rican social behavior is a curious mixture of old-world, European formality and a special *tico* style of relaxed interaction. You shake hands politely when being introduced or when meeting an acquaintance on the street, women as well as men. Women may also greet other women friends with a kiss on the cheek; with close friends a woman may do the same with a man, but only if they know each other well. Usually touching cheeks without the kiss is the custom. Exaggerated hugging and kissing, while common in the United States, is not approved of here. Men, when greeting truly close friends, will give an *abrazo*—a quick hug and pat on the back—or perhaps lightly clasp the friend's wrist or forearm instead of shaking hands.

"Getting down to business," as we North Americans are apt to do, without any preliminary greeting and small talk, is considered somewhat rude in Costa Rica, but not terribly so. Costa Ricans know how we North Americans are, so they never make a big deal out of it; they realize that "business" is the custom in our countries. To be polite, you might spend a few moments inquiring about someone's children or spouse, or perhaps give a compliment about the person's clothing, the weather, or anything else you might think to say before talking business. Doing so gets things off to a smoother start.

Costa Ricans have a delightful habit of issuing off-the-cuff invitations to visit them at their homes for dinner or for cocktails, but you should always wait for the invitation and not just drop in. An exception to this is when someone moves into the neighborhood or when you move into a new home. Then it's considered polite to knock on the door and introduce yourself.

A crucial point to remember: In social or business transactions, *ticos* just cannot handle confrontation. Unlike the people of some countries, where arguing, shouting, and mock displays of anger or emotion are the accepted norm,

Costa Ricans are appalled at such behavior. It's considered not only rude but also degrading. Confrontation is foreign to the culture.

I know a New Yorker who lost an excellent gardener when his gringo temper flared momentarily. Chuck's employee had planted some flowers in the wrong place. As usual when making a point, Chuck raised his voice and waved his hands in the air to signify his displeasure: "No, no! Not here! I wanted the flowers over there!" The astonished gardener loaded his tools in his wheelbarrow and left the property, never to return, despite pleas from the homeowner's wife, who tried to explain: "That's just Chuck's way. He doesn't mean anything by shouting."

## LATIN AMERICAN **TIME**

A difficult notion to understand is the way Latin Americans view time. When invited to a social event in the United States or Canada, it's considered ill-mannered to arrive late. Not so in most parts of Latin America. Should you receive an invitation for dinner, say, at 6:00 p.m. and actually arrive at that time, you are likely to embarrass the hosts. She is probably in the shower, and he still at the office. Guests are expected to arrive late. It doesn't matter, because dinner isn't served until 8:00 or 9:00 p.m., anyway.

When keeping appointments with businesspeople, you can arrive at their offices fifteen minutes late without worrying about it. You'll probably have time to catch up with the latest goings-on in the world by reading *Newsweek* and *La Nación* while waiting for your appointment. Most Costa Ricans share this cavalier view of time—not, however, to the extremes found in Mexico or some other Latin countries. Still, after several decades of exposure to Latin American time, I've never understood it and never will. When my contractor says he will be at the house at 8:00 a.m., I sometimes ask, "Is that *tico* time or gringo time?" The reply is usually a sheepish grin and, "Better make that nine o'clock." (I can't really count on nine o'clock either—my contractor doesn't wear a wristwatch.)

On the other hand, my personal experience with Costa Rican employees is that they're usually on time. I'm always surprised to see them arrive at the job a few minutes early, start to work on time, and—after a morning and an afternoon break—go home on time. Maybe this is because I pay higher than the going wage scales, but I am convinced that the Costa Rican work ethic is unusually positive, at least for Latin America.

## HOUSEHOLD **SERVANTS**

The notion of having housemaids and gardeners seems a bit wild for many of us when we first move to Costa Rica. (The last time we hired a cleaning lady in the United States, she charged $16 an hour and wouldn't do windows.) But in Costa Rica servants are affordable. It makes sense to hire a housemaid and a gardener, at least on a part-time basis. *Ticos* are generally hardworking and honest, so if you can afford $2 or $3 an hour for part-time help, you can have someone working around the house who won't complain about doing windows.

Most North Americans report that they pay more than minimum wage; doing so keeps their employees happy and loyal. Although servants are affordable, you must be aware of the laws covering their benefits. By law, not by custom, you are responsible for things like vacations, Christmas bonuses, Social Security, and severance pay. Wages are indexed twice a year, according to inflation. You are responsible for knowing about the benefits and paying them on time. These rules are discussed thoroughly in chapter 12. Don't hire a servant until you've read the rules!

One way to avoid the problem of being legally incorrect when hiring servants is to contract with a property manager. In addition to paying your monthly bills, taxes, and insurance, the property manager sends a housekeeper and/or gardener to your home as often as needed. This way, your domestic workers do not work for you; they work for the manager. Therefore, it is her responsibility to take care of her employees' monthly obligations, such as keeping track of holidays, paying social security, insurance, and pension payments at the proper local office. With your property manager in charge, you needn't worry. However, you should make sure that your manager is actually doing all of this, because if she isn't paying the benefits, you could be liable in case of a problem.

## COSTA RICA **FOOD TREATS**

You'll find every type of restaurant you can think of in Costa Rica, from steak and lobster to Chinese to McDonald's hamburger emporiums. But for really authentic Costa Rican food, you need to go to *tico*-style restaurants where they serve *comida tipica* ("typical dishes"). *Comida tipica* is home-style cooking as found in *tico* homes throughout the country. This cuisine relies on simple ingredients such as rice and beans, free-range chicken, and tasty, lean pork flavored with plenty of garlic. One of my favorites is *aroz con pollo* (chicken with rice) piled high on a dish, steaming with the savor of cilantro and diced peppers. It is often served with shrimp and calamari instead of chicken. Try the *sopa negra* (black-bean soup), topped with chopped green onions, crumbled white cheese, and a fresh egg poached in the thick broth, plus a dollop of natilla (a thick sweet cream).

You might be disappointed with Costa Rican beef steaks, however. They don't exactly come from Black Angus; more likely from one of those large, homely, bony, grass-fed creatures from India, called Brahmas. It's tough and dry, more suitable for hamburgers than steaks. That's not to say you can't find good beef; you just have to go to a good butcher shop or order a rib eye in an expensive restaurant.

In the larger cities, you can find interesting dining places ranging from elegant French restaurants to superb pizzerias. Some excellent Chinese restaurants will surprise you with dishes that are quite different from what you are used to back home. Their style of cooking is a cross between traditional Asian and tropical American. Some terribly mediocre Chinese restaurants are also to be found (ask friends for recommendations).

One very common Costa Rican food—served everywhere for breakfast, sometimes for every meal—is *gallo pinto,* which inexplicably translates as "spotted (or painted) rooster." This is a mixture of cooked rice and black beans—sometimes mixed with cilantro and chopped onions—fried together until the rice turns a purple color. Mixed with eggs and topped with *salsa Inglesa* or *salsa Lizano,* it makes a filling breakfast—nutritious but boring when served every morning.

In small restaurants away from the city, a typical menu item is a *casado:* a large plate with beans, rice, fried *plátano* (a green cooking banana), and some sort of meat, chicken, or egg. (*Casado* means "married man." Why the meal is called this is a mystery.) *Olla de carne* is a tasty meat stew with vegetables such as chayote, squash, yucca, and *plátano.*

Another favorite is empanadas: fried dumplings filled with meat or cheese, sometimes sold by children, who carry them around in galvanized buckets. A *tortilla Española* in Costa Rica is an omelet made with chopped potatoes or yucca root. Mexican-style corn tortillas are popular in the countryside and are simply called tortillas; these are far more common than the egg-and-yucca variety.

**BOCAS** A delightful custom in Costa Rica is the serving of *bocas* (free appetizers) with drinks in bars. The treat could be a small dish of chicken and rice, or perhaps a chicken wing, a piece of fried fish, or *chicharrones* with yucca—whatever the exotic specialty of the house happens to be. *Bocas* aren't served as frequently as they used to be, especially in bars mostly patronized by gringos, since we don't expect them. But *tico* bars often sustain this custom, so when you see someone else being served a treat, don't hesitate to ask. You may have the chance to sample a raw turtle egg—bars are just about the only places where you can legally find them. They are served one to a shot glass, with a little hot sauce. You do a bottoms up and chew it to taste the yolk. Some people love 'em; my wife wouldn't touch one with a pointed stick. *NOTE:* Some bars have *bocas* but no longer give them away. You have to pay a small amount, 50 cents or so, but they are worth it!

*Bocas* aren't just served in bars; they play an essential role when entertaining guests. Informal "*boca* parties" are a popular substitute for more formal dinner parties. Guests are expected to bring their favorite *boca* to share with other guests, thus eliminating the need to cook and serve dinner; people help themselves. When you have no way to make *bocas* (if you are a tourist staying in a bed-and-breakfast, for example), a bottle of Centenario rum or a bottle of good wine is a substitute, or if you prefer, a takeout pizza cut into small pieces. Friends compete for new and unusual recipes for tasty *bocas*.

**GRATUITIES** Restaurants are supposed to add a 10 percent service charge to the bill—then it's up to customers if they care to leave something extra. Some restaurants cheat and don't give tip money to employees, so leaving an extra 5 percent tip on the table after paying the bill ensures that your waitress at least gets something—and guarantees special service next time. Away from the city, many restaurants don't add tips to the bill; it's customary to tip 10 to 15 percent in these cases. Barbershop and beauty-salon personnel expect a 10 to 15 percent tip. My last haircut cost 1,650 colones ($3) and I tipped 400 colones (60 cents).

By law you must give a Christmas bonus to your maid, gardener, and other employees. This bonus is called an *aguinaldo* and consists of one month's pay, prorated on the number of months worked. This Christmas bonus is not a gift or a tip but is required by law. An extra present to special employees is considered thoughtful and generous.

If you are a guest in someone's home where there are servants, it isn't necessary to tip them unless they've done something special for you, such as laundry, ironing, or running errands. If a friend lends you the services of her maid, it's customary to tip and to pay for her taxi or bus fare home. Hotel chambermaids like to be tipped just as they do back home.

# COOKING **AT HOME**

For those staying for longer than a vacation, an apartment or house with a kitchen is a wonderful way of enjoying Costa Rican cooking and experimenting with the unusual tropical ingredients available in the markets. Around the San José area, every neighborhood has at least one super-market, supplemented by weekend *ferias* (open-air markets). Many neighborhoods and most all small villages have *pulperías* (rustic convenience stores), where you can buy items you forgot at the other markets.

Some major supermarket chains are: Auto Mercado, Periféricos, Pali, and Mas X Menos. By the way, the X in Mas X Menos is pronounced as it would be in a mathematical equation: In English we would say "two times two," while Costa Ricans would say *"dos por dos."* Since the Spanish word *por* can also mean "for," the literal meaning of the store's name, *Mas por Menos,* is "more for less." (Yes, I know, it would be less confusing if they simply followed American custom and gave supermarkets names like "Safeway," or "Albertsons," but this is, after all, Costa Rica.)

Open-air markets are held on weekends, the major ones being Saturday in Escazú, on the south side of the main square; Saturday in Pavas, about 5 blocks from the main shopping center; and Sunday in Zapote, next to the Bull Ring. Heredia's farmers' market, also on Saturday, is perhaps the best known of all, with local families selling produce grown in their backyards. Heredia's main market, open daily, is a wonderful place to browse for food, clothing, tools, furniture—anything you can imagine.

Costa Rica's selection of fruits and vegetables is sometimes bewildering for North Americans. In addition to delicious pineapples, strawberries, melons, and other produce we recognize, you'll find chayotes, *pejebayes, palmitos, plátanos,* and other strange-looking items that will soon become standard ingredients of your menu. A common substitute for potatoes, the yucca root, in my opinion, tastes much better than ordinary spuds. Exotic tropical fruits such as *guayabas, tamarindo,* and carambolas are exciting to experiment with and make delicious *refrescos* (blended drinks). One of my favorite *refrescos* is made by blending fresh cacao nuts (the source of chocolate) with *horchata* (a rice-flour and sugar drink). My wife prefers a *batida* of fresh papaya, milk, and ice, whipped to a milk-shake-like consistency.

Some fruits are so exotic they border on fantastic. Sporting shells, spines, and barbs, they look like something from a science-fiction book cover. Especially interesting is the *marañón* fruit, the source of the common cashew nut. The nut itself grows at the end of an edible orange or yellow fruit that can be eaten raw or, more often, made into a *refresco* by blending it with sugar and ice cubes. The cashew nut itself is encased in a rubbery shell that is primed with cyanide. That's right, cyanide, which makes the shell bitter and somewhat poisonous. We have to marvel over the wonderful way nature designed this fruit as an efficient way to disperse its seeds. In the wild, monkeys, parrots, and other creatures pluck the fruit and carry it away to be consumed. When they finish eating the sweet fruit, they drop the bitter-tasting seed on the ground, where it produces another tree.

Costa Rica is a cattle-growing country, and beef is plentiful, although as mentioned earlier, it's not the same quality as we are used to in North America. But the quality of pork and chicken here is excellent, mostly because they are raised differently. Instead of being tightly penned or caged and force-fed to put on weight, the animals usually run loose, foraging for food as well as being fed at the farmhouse, living a natural, albeit sloppy, existence. Pork is lean with a firm texture. Eggs—especially those from free-range hens rather than crowded egg factories—are delicious, having a brighter-colored yolk and a better flavor than we're used to up north.

With an ocean on both sides, Costa Rica, of course, enjoys a wide selection of seafood. Since shipping distances from either ocean involve just a few hours, the sea harvest arrives fresh. Almost any kind of fish and shellfish you can imagine is available, plus some you can't imagine. You might want to try some of the shellfish and conch that thrive only around the Costa Rican shores. My favorite is a shellfish known as *cambute*, similar to conch shellfish found in the Florida Keys. Like abalone, the *cambute* has to be pounded before cooking, and it tastes very much like the almost extinct abalone.

Imported foods can be somewhat expensive. Partly because of shipping costs and partly because of foreign-exchange differentials, North American and European products can be costly. Central American substitutes are often as good and locally grown. For my money, fresh foods are always much better than canned or packaged food.

## GREAT **COFFEE**

Some of the best coffee in the world grows on shaded mountain slopes in Costa Rica. These exceptionally rich-tasting beans are in demand by coffee wholesalers, particularly those who boast that their products are "mountain grown." To substantiate such a claim, at least 60 percent of the coffee has to come from mountain farms in places like Guatemala,

Colombia, or Costa Rica. Curiously, Costa Rican coffee is exceptionally low in caffeine. Retailers blend it with high-caffeine (and less expensive) beans from Brazil and Africa to bring the jolt up to what we coffee drinkers expect. In Costa Rica you have the advantage of brewing coffee from 100 percent Costa Rican beans. If you need more caffeine, drink another cup! We sometimes purchase coffee beans directly from the roaster and take them home while they are still hot. The use of instant coffee (a barbarous practice) hasn't caught on here. A café con leche with just a dash of sugar makes a wonderful starter for breakfast and is great for washing down savory *gallo pinto* and warm tortillas.

Costa Ricans have an interesting way of making coffee that gives a characteristically rich flavor to the brew. Instead of using a percolator or an automatic coffeemaker, *ticos* use a wire or wooden stand holding a cloth strainer bag, shaped like a sock, that hangs over a waiting cup. They place two teaspoons of coffee into the bag and pour boiling water over the grounds, letting it drain into the coffee cup below. For each additional cup of coffee, another teaspoon of ground coffee is added. The result is a flavorful, velvety drink that grows richer with each cup made. The grounds aren't discarded until the sack is full of grounds or until the end of the day, whichever happens first. "The aroma and essence of the coffee is much better if it isn't boiled," explained a *tico* friend. "We call our coffee-making system a *chorreador*. It brings out the flavor without acid bitterness. This method requires more coffee grounds, but since coffee is inexpensive, we use nothing but the best."

## FURNISHING **YOUR HOME**

At one time, when foreign retirees received their residency papers, they had a one-time right to import household goods duty-free, and the right to bring in an automobile every three years and thus avoid enormous customs taxes. This was a valuable consideration, since high import duties in those days made electrical appliances, televisions, video recorders, and the like very expensive in Costa Rica.

To the dismay of future *pensionados,* this benefit was repealed several years ago. However, duty-free imports on household goods aren't nearly as important today as they once were. Supply has caught up with demand; you'll have no problem finding a wide variety of furniture at reasonable prices. The amount of money you'd have to pay just to have that bedroom suite and living-room furniture shipped from Topeka or Toronto would pay for furnishing your home in Costa Rica with brand-new merchandise. Furniture stores have great selections, and you can visit small, family-operated factories and have pieces custom-made for about what you'd expect to pay for retail back home. Also, furniture made here in Costa Rica is designed for a tropical climate, whereas some furnishings made in the United States can be unsuitable or susceptible to mold or insect damage.

Household appliances such as refrigerators, washing machines, and TVs can be purchased from local dealers without waiting for months, as was the situation before. Import taxes on these appliances have dropped dramatically. For example, recently my wife and I built a new home and bought a washer and dryer for almost the same price as they would have cost in California. Our *tico* neighbors, by the way, were astounded that we would waste money on a dryer when we could simply hang the wash on a line and let the sunshine dry it in an hour for free. But being spoiled gringos—too impatient to wait for the sunshine and too often forgetting about the drying clothes until after the next rain shower wet the clothes down again—we felt we couldn't live without an electric dryer.

## TELEVISION AND **OTHER MEDIA**

A few years ago, in order to watch baseball or football games, you had to wait for a videocassette to be mailed from the States. Today there are six cable TV services in the San José area alone, plus satellite dishes throughout the country. Costa Rica's modern television system offers six channels, some of which can be received in remarkably out-of-the-way places. On our San José cable system, we enjoyed abundant programming direct from the United States: two TV stations from Denver, one from Atlanta, and one from Chicago. Several international channels delivered programs coming from South America, France, and Germany as well. We found that watching CNN, CBS, and NBC nightly news on our cable TV made up for not having a daily newspaper delivered to our door.

Note that I describe our TV cable system in the past tense; where we live now, on the Pacific Coast, cable is unavailable and normal reception is confined to a few weak channels. (That's the price you pay for living away from the big city.) The answer for those who need to watch CNN, the World Series, and Home Box Office movies is satellite-driven DIRECTV, with an almost unlimited choice of channels. Reception is as good as it gets, and monthly charges are about what you would pay in the States.

In San José and most of the surrounding cities, you'll find stores selling English-language paperback books and magazines. In addition to the essential *Tico Times*, you can buy daily editions of just about any major U.S. newspaper. These papers are a bit expensive—they arrive by airplane—but at times North Americans become starved for a big-city daily newspaper. However, it's easy to keep up with major newspapers and very likely your hometown newspaper via the Internet. Every morning with my coffee, I read the front pages of the *New York Times*, the *Washington Post*, and the *San Francisco Chronicle* (including the comics). Several Costa Rica daily newspapers are online, so I browse *La Nación*, *Diario Extra*, and the *Tico Times* for Central America news. And they are all free.

## MONEY **MATTERS**

Costa Rica's currency is the colón, which was valued at 550 to the dollar in mid 2008. The exchange rate between the colón and the U.S. dollar varies depending on the world value of the dollar and the inflation rate in

Costa Rica. For example, in 1997 the exchange rate was about 250 colones to the dollar; ten years later, in late 2007, the colón's exchange rate increased steadily to 550 to the dollar, as it was adjusted to reflect rate of inflation. Then, in the beginning of 2008, for the first time in decades, the dollar's exchange rate fell against the Costa Rican colón. This reflected the dollar's devaluation on the world financial markets. The exchange rate suddenly went from 550 to 490 to the dollar. However, by mid-2008 the exchange had risen to 560 to the dollar.

Some people feel uneasy when inflation continually deflates a nation's currency. The important point is whether the exchange rate between Costa Rican colones and U.S. or Canadian dollars is in line with reality and not arbitrarily set by the government (a practice that continually leads to disaster in other Latin American countries). Many people, even some economists, tend to assume that when the exchange rate is stable, inflation is under control and all is well. That's not necessarily so. When exchange rates are steady yet prices of goods and services rise in the host country, your dollar loses value every day. A currency holding its own against the dollar isn't necessarily a sign of a healthy economy. It could be an artificial manipulation of currencies that masks serious problems.

Yes, mild inflation has been going on in Costa Rica for decades, generally slightly higher than the inflation rate in the United States. But since the colón adjusts for this inflation as prices and wages rise, there's no appreciable change for those who own dollars. For example, prices and wages in Costa Rica today are twice as high as they were eight years ago, yet we North Americans receive twice as many colones for our dollars as we did eight years ago. For those of us with dollar incomes, it's a wash. There's no foreseeable reason to expect that exchange rates will vary in any significant way in the future, other than a steady adjustment to world currencies, totally in line with reality.

**DEALING IN DOLLARS** You often hear people say, "You can use dollars just about anywhere in Costa Rica." This is not necessarily so. Yes, businesses that deal with expat residents and visitors commonly accept U.S. dollars. Cab drivers, restaurants, supermarkets, and other businesses that routinely do banking several times a week, or daily, usually have no problem with dollars. They simply deposit them into their accounts. But for smaller restaurants, and businesses with low turnover, accepting dollars would mean having to make a trip to the bank, standing in line and waiting for a turn at the teller's cage just to cash your $5 dollar bill. It just isn't worth it.

Credit cards are usually accepted in larger restaurants and businesses with high-volume trade. But smaller establishments often refuse to take credit cards. Two reasons for this: One, a bank service charge is deducted from each transaction, so the restaurant loses money when accepting a credit card. Another reason: Until recently in some regions of the country, credit cards couldn't be used because there were no telephone connections. Businesses got along just fine by accepting cash, so today they are reluctant to change just because telephone connections make credit cards possible.

When bringing foreign currency into the country, be sure to inspect each bill carefully for rips or tears. Banks refuse to accept any foreign currency if it's torn ever so slightly. Never mind that a 1,000-colón bill you get from the bank teller might look like a dog's breakfast; if that $50 U.S. bill you have isn't pristine, you'll end up taking it back to the States with you. One scam is for a waiter or shopkeeper to take your good $50 bill, then return with a torn bill and ask you for something smaller, hoping you won't notice the tear. The bill is okay, but you'll have to take it home to spend it.

A continual problem is the importation of counterfeit $100 bills from Colombia—so many that shopkeepers sometimes refuse to accept big bills. One place where you might get stuck (so I've been told) is at a gambling casino because in the unlikely event that you win big, the house tries to get rid of the phony bills they previously got stuck with by slipping them to happy gringo winners.

## COSTA RICA **BANKING**

In many ways Costa Rica is a modern country, but for some inexplicable reason a visit to the bank can be an *Alice in Wonderland* experience. It can take forever to do a simple transaction such as exchanging dollars or traveler's checks into colones. Opening a bank account can be a real adventure. Many amusing stories circulate regarding opening an account. Since many banks have no English-speaking tellers, nonfluent applicants are wise to bring along a *tico* who can help out. There do not seem to be common requirements, even among branches of the same bank.

When I accompanied a friend to help her open a savings account, her letters of recommendation were rejected because the clerk insisted on letters from people who had lent my friend money. So she had her friends rewrite the letters to indicate that she had borrowed money. We went to another branch of the same bank and tried again. This time the clerk didn't even ask for letters, just the check for deposit and her passport! I understand that some banks insist on notarized copies of your residency permit, your passport, and documentation of your corporation (if any), as well as a letter from your attorney. Again, an *Alice in Wonderland* experience.

Although each bank handles things a little differently, doing ordinary transactions sometimes involves standing in one line where the clerk checks your passport, examines the bills or checks, fills out forms in triplicate, and pounds everything in sight with a rubber stamp. Then you move to another line and wait until a second clerk fills out more forms in quadruplicate and does more rubber-stamping. One thing to remember: Lines are going to be much longer on days following holidays, when banks have been closed for a day or so, and on the days when pensioners receive their Social Security checks. Some banks provide separate lines for pensioners, which helps considerably.

To be fair, the banks do seem to be gaining efficiency, and the lines are becoming shorter. This is especially so with the appearance of several reliable U.S.-based banks, such as Scotia and Cuscatlán. However, a disturbing development in early 2008 is the reluctance of some banks to accept U.S.-dollar checks over the amount of $1,000; at least one national bank was charging customers $60 for this.

Bank accounts can be in either colones or dollars. An unpleasant and basically unfair bank practice is holding U.S.-dollar checks from foreign banks for up to a month or more before crediting them to your account. For a variety of reasons, most expats also maintain their home bank accounts when they move to Costa Rica. For one thing, the U.S. government will not direct-deposit Social Security or pension checks to a Costa Rican bank, and you certainly don't want those checks floating around Costa Rican post offices. Furthermore, your checks will be tied up for a couple of weeks or more before you can withdraw the cash. With your money deposited in a U.S. or Canadian bank, you can use your ATM card almost anywhere in Costa Rica to withdraw cash as you need it. Some expatriates don't even bother with *tico* banks, relying on ATM machines exclusively. Local businesspeople who know you will usually accept your U.S. or Canadian bank checks. They know they're good, and they don't worry about a long wait because there's always a large balance in their bank accounts anyway. Our local grocery store, where we are well known, cashes our U.S. checks up to $100 anytime we need money.

One of the benefits of Costa Rica's Internet revolution is the ability to pay your bills back home through your hometown bank's Web site rather than to attempting the impossible task of sending a check to your creditor. Between the Costa Rica post office and your U.S. bank is a long and uncertain trail. The time for a check to make the journey to your creditor varies from a span of two weeks to never. The late fees and interest charges can add up quickly. Make arrangements to pay your bills back home via the Internet, and have the bank show you exactly how to make the transfers. You'll never be sorry.

Banks are also where you can usually pay traffic tickets and utility bills and sometimes make Social Security payments for your maid and gardener. Since each transaction requires a flurry of forms, rubber stamps, and calculations, you can count on spending a lot of time in Costa Rican banks. Because of the time-consuming process of dealing with banks, insurance payments, and government bureaucracy, some *ticos* earn their living by standing in line for you or by knowing whom to contact and when. They are called *tramitadores* (from the verb *tramitar,* meaning "to transact," "to take legal steps"). Your friends and neighbors can recommend a reliable *tramitador* to make your life easier. Many people become close friends with their *tramitadores,* dining with them and exchanging presents at Christmas.

Criticize the banking system as we do, the fact is that government banks are financially sound. A few years ago BancoAnglo, one of the big three government-owned Costa Rican banks, was forced to close its doors because of mismanagement and reckless speculation. The situation closely paralleled the savings-and-loan debacle at that time in the United States. Costa Rican investors didn't panic; they simply took their passbooks to any one of the other national banks and exchanged them for new passbooks from that bank. Nobody lost a nickel (or a colón). By the way, the Costa Rican bank officials responsible were immediately arrested. Now just consider how many U.S. savings-and-loan wheeler-dealers were even scolded, much less shown the inside of a well-deserved jail cell.

Costa Rica went one step further: The government decided that those who borrowed money and didn't pay it back were equally guilty. The borrowers claimed that they lost the money, but it was surprising how quickly many "bankrupt" businesspeople found millions of dollars to repay their loans rather than go to prison. Is there a lesson here?

Not all banks are government-owned. Several private banks deal with the public, usually in a much more efficient manner, at least as far as the amount of time you spend in line in front of a teller's cage. But there are two problems with private banks. One is that deposits are often backed only by the bank's reserves. In some cases, limited government funds are available in the event of default. The second problem is that some private investment companies that appear to be banks are outrageously fraudulent, their reserves siphoned into private accounts in the Bahamas. Before you invest in a private bank, investigate its past performance and talk to your neighbors about its reliability. If the bank just opened last March and the main branch is a post office box in the Bahamas, you just might be suspicious.

**INTEREST RATES** At the time of this writing, the rate of interest being paid on time deposits of colones has fallen to around 8 percent or less. (Dollar accounts pay about the same as CD rates in New York.) While 8 percent is a better return on your colón deposits than for dollar accounts, you must consider the inevitability of the colón continuing to lose value against the dollar. You are gambling that the colón will devaluate less than expected, in which case you come out somewhat ahead. If the rates fall at the expected rate, you'll do fine. But if for some reason the colón's value falls more quickly, you could lose money.

A special cautionary note: Private investment funds are famous for failures and outright fraud—especially those that advertise extraordinarily high interest rates. For years some investment funds were paying 3 percent per month to investors. That's right: 36 percent per year! Many expats were living on the income from their savings; $100,000 invested brought in $3,000 a month—a tidy income here in Costa Rica! Tragically, the bubble burst when the largest investment company became snarled in a government investigation, and the other companies also folded, skipping out with whatever was left of investors' money. Some hold out hope of recovering at least some of their money. I sincerely hope this happens, but the chances look very slim.

## MISCELLANEOUS **INFORMATION**

**THINK KILOMETERS!** Distances in Costa Rica are measured in meters and kilometers (*kilómetros*), not in yards or miles. It's not difficult at all, so get used to it. It works like this: a meter is approximately the same as a yard, and 100 meters or 100 yards is the approximate length of a city block, same as in the United States or Canada. So when someone says "50 meters," you simply visualize half a block. A kilometer is 1,000 meters, which equals 10 city blocks. Now isn't that a much easier way of visualizing distance than trying to remember that a mile is 5,279 feet, or 17.6 city blocks? Or that an eighth of a mile is 660 yards?

Why is it important to think kilometers rather than miles? Because when traveling in Costa Rica, all road signs are in kilometers, all road maps use kilometers for distances and directions, the speedometer of your rental car is calibrated in kilometers, and when you ask directions, the reply will be in meters or kilometers. *Ticos* and expats alike think and talk in kilometers, never in miles. They will give you a blank stare if you ask, "How many miles is it to the next gas station?"

**GOLF COURSES** When I first started writing about Costa Rica, golf courses were almost nonexistent. This disappointed many tourists who feel that a vacation isn't complete without a few rounds of golf. For golfers looking to spend a long time or to retire in Costa Rica, the near absence of golf was a severe drawback.

Why the scarcity of golf courses? It's partly a matter of economics. During the rainy months, when golf course maintenance is limited to cutting grass, golf-playing tourists are few and far between. In the dry season, when plenty of tourists are here, sufficient irrigation water might not be available. Another factor is that golf is not a *tico* tradition. The main sport here is soccer, a team sport, with strenuous running, kicking, and body

# GOLF COURSES

- **Cacique del Mar.** Playa Hermosa, Guanacaste; eighteen holes, par 72; members and guests only.

- **Cariari Golf Club.** General Cañas Highway, near San José; eighteen-hole championship course; hotel guests, club members.

- **Costa Rica Country Club West.** In the San José suburb of Escazú; opened 1944; nine holes; members and guests only.

- **Four Seasons Hotel** at the Papagayo Peninsula. Eighteen-hole golf course; guests and members only.

- **Golf La Ribera public driving range.** In La Ribera de Belen near the water park Ojo de Agua.

- **La Roca Beach Resort & Country Club.** North of Caldera on the Pacific Coast; eighteen-hole, par 72 championship course; members and public.

- **Los Reyes Country Club.** San Rafael de Alajuela, near San José; nine holes; members, guests of certain hotels.

- **Los Sueños Marriott.** Playa Herradura. Eighteen-hole, par 72 championship course; hotel guests and public.

- **Marriot Hotel Golf Course.** Nine-hole course reserved for hotel guests.

- **Meliá Conchal Golf Club and Resort.** Playa Conchal, Guanacaste; nine holes, with another nine holes scheduled; par 72 championship course; hotel guests and public.

- **Monte del Barco.** Resort north of Liberia, Guanacaste; eighteen holes; members and public.

- **Parque Valle del Sol West.** San José suburb of Santa Ana; nine holes; additional nine holes could be added; public at present.

- **Rancho Las Colinas Golf and Country Club,** near Flamingo, overlooking Playa Grande in mid-Guanacaste, is the newest course in Costa Rica.

- **Rancho Mary La Cruz.** A half hour north of Liberia; nine holes with another nine holes planned for the near future. It will be an eighteen-hole par 72; members and possibly the public.

- **Tango Mar.** On the tip of Nicoya Peninsula; nine-hole, tough executive course, par 31; hotel guests only.

- **Tulin Resort.** South of Jacó Beach; eighteen-hole par 72; members and public.

contact. The excitement is contagious, with everybody cheering wildly for his or her team. *Ticos* have difficulty understanding golf as a sport. What they see is a few lackadaisical people fooling around with clubs. Someone hits a ball, then rides a sluggish cart to where the ball lands, and then whacks it again. Nobody cheers. Nobody gets excited. There aren't any spectators. It doesn't make sense to *ticos*. To them soccer is more like a real sport.

Since only a few *ticos* play golf and there weren't enough tourists and year-round gringos to play golf, investors were hesitant to build new courses. For years the Costa Rica Country Club nine-hole course and the Cariari eighteen-hole layout were about the only golf courses in the country, and both were private. So if you were addicted to golf, you were restricted to living in the Central Valley, and you had to join a club.

Because of the increase in long-term foreign residents and the large increase of tourism, the situation is changing. As of summer 2008, at least fifteen golf courses were in operation. Some are for members and guests only, but eight or more are open for public play. As tourism increases and more and more full-time gringo residents are moving to Costa Rica, more courses will be opening. See the "Golf Courses" sidebar for a partial list of golf courses open or due to open soon in Costa Rica.

**GAMBLING CASINOS** For those who love the sound of a roulette ball bouncing along the wheel or the riffling sound of cards being shuffled, you'll find no lack of action in Costa Rica. Most gambling casinos are in the San José area, with casinos in hotel lobbies. Sometimes it seems like a miniature Las Vegas. Occasionally gambling casinos are found upstairs over nightclubs or restaurants.

While I sometimes like to gamble, I also like to have a chance of winning. I have the distinct feeling that gaming in the average Costa Rican casino is not really gambling, merely donating to the profitability of the establishment. My understanding is that house rules make it highly unlikely that you will break even, much less win. Some games aren't standard ones that can be easily understood, even though they might seem similar to poker or blackjack. Play is similar to Las Vegas or Reno, but the rules and payoffs are different—sometimes confusing—stacking the odds in favor of the house.

Another disquieting thing about gambling in Costa Rica is that there is almost no government regulation. I doubt very much that the house cheats. It doesn't have to cheat since the odds are so much in its favor, but there is little or nothing to prevent cheating from happening.

Having bad-mouthed Costa Rica gambling casinos, I now have to admit that several friends disagree with me. They claim that the odds and your chances of winning are pretty much the same here as in Las Vegas or Atlantic City. I'll suspend further judgment until such time as I win something.

**HOLIDAYS** Sometimes it seems as though every time you go to the bank to conduct business, it's closed for a holiday. Costa Rica celebrates more than a dozen national holidays and uncounted numbers of local fiestas that call for closing the bank. Watch the *Tico Times* for announcements of upcoming holidays, and plan your official business accordingly. The country's biggest celebration starts a couple of days before August 2, when thousands of people walk along the highways in a pilgrimage to Cartago to honor the national saint, the Virgin of Los Angeles. Drive cautiously at this time.

- January 1: New Year's Day
- March 19: St. Joséph's Day (patron saint of San José)
- Easter Week: Thursday through Sunday
- April 11: Juan Santamaría's Day (national hero)
- May 1: Labor Day
- June 29: St. Peter and St. Paul's Day
- July 25: Anniversary of Annexation of Province of Guanacaste
- August 2: Virgin of Los Angeles Day (patron saint of Costa Rica)

- August 15: Mother's Day
- September 15: Independence Day
- October 12: Columbus Day
- December 8: Feast of the Immaculate Conception
- December 24 and 25: Christmas Eve and Christmas

**RELIGION** Costa Rica is predominantly Catholic but also has a sizable Protestant population. In the village near our home, I would estimate that 30 percent of the residents are Protestant, yet everyone seems extraordinarily tolerant and accepting of other religions. Yes, there can be rivalry between Protestants and Catholics in local politics, with the Catholic priest trying to get as many of his parishioners appointed to town councils and committees as possible and the Protestant preachers doing quite the same. However, I feel it's more of a prestige thing, because the pressure is low-key and everyone works together—at least on the community projects in which I've been involved. Priests often wield political influence in a community, which can dismay some Americans—until they recall that fundamental Christian leaders back home refuse to accept a church-state separation and are continually hip-deep in local and national politics.

All in all, *ticos* are quite casual and tolerant when it comes to religion. Nobody seems to care what religion you may have or may not have. Church attendance also seems to be casual. It's interesting to note that while abortion is illegal, birth control doesn't seem to be an issue here. Apparently abortion is common and rarely prosecuted. Posters in government health clinics urge the use of contraceptives, and my understanding is that morning-after pills are readily available at most drugstores without prescription.

Common-law marriages are frequent in Costa Rica, especially in rural areas, and are regarded as perfectly normal. Couples often live together their entire lives, raising children and grandchildren without any thought of formalizing their relationship. This practice was probably due to the absence of priests in the countryside to perform marriages. Unlike in some Latino cultures, lavish wedding ceremonies aren't important traditions.

# CRIME AND **PERSONAL SAFETY**

I'm always amused when friends visit us in Costa Rica and express dismay when they see wrought-iron bars on our windows. "Is crime so bad here," they ask, "that people must live behind bars?" This question surprises me because bars on Costa Rican windows seem as logical and natural as window screens in Atlanta or storm windows in Cleveland.

Maybe that's because my family moved to Mexico City when I was a youth, a place where homes traditionally have bars on their windows, so I suppose I grew up with the custom. The fact is, in every Latin American country—from the Río Grande to Tierra del Fuego—homes aren't considered complete without a set of wrought-iron bars. To me a Costa Rican home looks naked without them, like a Cape Cod home without shutters or a Southern mansion without a portico and columns. When the first Spanish colonists came here five centuries ago, they brought iron bars with them. Roman settlers brought window bars to Spain 2,000 years ago; for all I know, the Romans picked up the custom from the Greeks, or maybe the Egyptians.

My wife and I recently made a point of checking European homes for iron bars, having spent a few weeks traveling in Spain and Italy, and participating in a lengthy home exchange in southern France. We made a point of observing the various residential neighborhoods we encountered. Without exception, every home we saw had either bars, heavy shutters, and sometimes both. After all these centuries, security is still fashionable in Europe.

Do window bars deter professional burglars? Not really. Not any more than locked doors prevent burglaries back home. Bars and locks simply keep out honest people. However, they do discourage amateur burglars and remove temptation from neighborhood kids. Frankly, I feel quite snug and secure with bars on our windows. (By the way, burglaries while a house is occupied are very unusual. It's much easier to wait until the homeowners are out having dinner or visiting San José.)

I personally refuse to sleep with our metal front door locked. Why? Because after having lived for years in California, another place where earthquakes are commonplace, I don't want to have the metal door jammed should the house twist. I have a fear of being trapped in a house, unable to get out for days, unable to buy cold beer. Seriously, this is also an important issue for wooden houses that could catch fire. You don't want to be rummaging around looking for your keys while the smoke and flames are getting closer! An ordinary door lock on the wooden door is easy to flip open in an emergency.

**NOT CRIME-FREE!** Like every country in the world, Costa Rica has crime. That shouldn't surprise anyone coming from the United States, where crime and personal safety have become a high-priority concern. Take a look at some low-income U.S. neighborhoods: The bars you see on windows and doors clearly aren't meant to be traditional. They are grim attempts to protect occupants from violent crime. The alternative to bigger and stronger bars is moving to a safer place with lower crime rates, perhaps rural Kansas or small-town Costa Rica (that's our solution).

I personally see crime as another one of those annoyances we have to put up with if we want to live here—a nuisance, like potholes. To avoid destroying my car, I have to drive carefully to miss potholes. That's an annoyance. To avoid crime, I have to be careful where I park my car and where I keep my wallet. That's an annoyance. So far I've rarely been affected by crime, but potholes have eaten several of my tires.

Of course there's crime in Costa Rica, but it's of a different nature than crime in the United States. It doesn't seem fair to compare the two places in the same paragraph. While Costa Rica suffers from frequent nonviolent petty crimes, the United States must deal with frequent brutal and violent crimes, which are uncommon in Costa Rica. Criminals don't just rob up north; they savage and maim as well, just for laughs.

Although the overall rate of burglaries in Costa Rica is much lower than in the United States, this statistic is somewhat misleading. Obviously, a higher percentage of break-ins are performed on foreign-owned homes. Burglars know that the average expat home has a nice DVD player, a TV, a microwave, and maybe a stereo. Here again, a little precaution is in order. Besides a protective set of bars, it's worthwhile to contribute to the neighborhood *guardia*, the watchman who patrols your neighborhood on foot or by motorcycle. In some city neighborhoods, every block has one. Because of these watchmen, most middle-class neighborhoods are often as safe as similar places in the United States, where a police car cruises by maybe once a day. In rural areas you seldom find *guardias*, but there are fewer burglaries, so it evens out.

Another big difference is the lack of rampant drug addiction among Costa Ricans. You won't find an army of desperate addicts forced to steal several hundred dollars each day to support a habit. Costa Rican law discourages drugs by handing out a jail sentence of eight to twenty years for anyone involved in drug dealing. Drug use is considered extremely serious, and mere possession of drugs can be interpreted as evidence of drug dealing. By the way, these laws apply equally to native Costa Ricans and gringos. That doesn't mean Costa Rica is drug-free, either. A real problem is when young gringo surfers partying on the beach share crack cocaine with the local kids. So far it hasn't gotten out of hand, but it is unsettling, to say the least. Marijuana is, of course, readily available, just as it is in the United States and Canada. However, this is a common plant that grows like a weed in the tropics, it is not particularly addictive, and it doesn't require stealing to support a habit; just picking.

From time to time the downtown section of San José is bothered by the appearance of gangs of street urchins, called *chapulines,* who rob pedestrians by grabbing wallets and jewelry. *Chapulines* literally means "grasshoppers," describing the way the kids jump on a victim and keep him or her off balance while one of them goes for the wallet. I believe that incidents of this nature have been somewhat overstated. (I personally know only one friend who has been victimized.) The fact that such episodes make headlines in San José newspapers suggests that such incidents can't be all that common. However, the problem was reduced drastically when stricter laws were passed, with stiff sentences for juvenile offenders who previously avoided punishment because of loopholes in the law. Not long ago a San José judge handed out sentences of up to twenty-five years in prison to a band of *chapulines.*

It's best to take basic precautions when wandering about the center of San José—or any other big city in the world, for that matter. To be fair, having a wallet lifted or a gold chain stolen are crimes that plague tourists not only in Costa Rica but anywhere tourists go. Furthermore, this kind of crime can usually be avoided by taking reasonable precautions. Residents and long-term visitors infrequently haunt bad areas of downtown San José after dark, and they know how to avoid pickpockets and the like. In my thirty-plus years of traveling in Costa Rica, I have never had my pocket picked.

## THE **POST OFFICE**

Costa Rican mail service is clearly not up to the standards we expect at home. Let's face it: In a country where streets rarely have names and houses lack street numbers, home mail delivery can't be expected to be "reliable." When a package or letter actually arrives, it's best described as a "miracle." We waited six months in vain for our first checking-account statements. Then one day, out of the blue, they all appeared at once. Instead of complaining, I was astonished that the mail carrier actually found our house. The address on the envelopes read, "300 meters north from Amistad Park, 100 meters to the east, and 25 meters to the south." (But which house?) The poor guy probably carried these bank statements with him every day for months, just in case he deciphered those directions and figured out which house we lived in. Unfortunately, the statements arrived just after we'd sold the house and closed our checking account, having decided that having a checking account wasn't all that convenient.

That's why most folks rely on post office boxes, known as *apartados*. This means a trip to the post office every couple of days, but at least there's a chance your mail might be waiting for you. My post office box in the village near our Guanacaste home costs about $10 a year. I understand the cost is considerably higher at other post offices, and boxes can be in very short supply. In this case your mail can wait in general delivery for you to collect it. To receive general delivery mail, ask friends to address it this way:

> John Doe
> Lista de Correos
> Oficina de Correo Central
> San José, Costa Rica

(Of course, if your name doesn't happen to be John Doe, and if your town doesn't happen to be San José, you need to make the proper address adjustments.)

Not too long ago, the postal system was privatized, but as far I can tell, it hasn't made a lot of difference. The same employees are working in the same offices, and things look normal. I still would highly recommend using one of the courier services or certified mail if anything important or urgent needed to be sent.

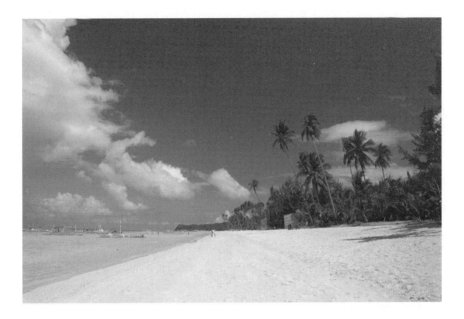

Mail for international communication is a waste of time. Airmail between Costa Rica and the United States or Canada involves ten days each way. That means at best a twenty-day turnaround between the time you send a letter and the time you receive the reply. Now that Internet access is available just about anywhere in the country (there are Internet cafes popping up everywhere), the most practical communication method is e-mail.

**COURIER MAIL SERVICE** When you absolutely need to communicate by regular mail or express mail, the way to beat the system is to use one of several Miami–San José postal services that offer same-day delivery by air courier to and from Costa Rica. Mail going either way gets there almost as fast as if it were mailed in the States. This is the only practical way to subscribe to magazines or newspapers at domestic rates and hope to receive them the same season they were published. If you live in the boonies, your mail service company can usually forward your mail by bus for pickup at the local bus terminal.

Listed below are some popular international and local courier services:

**Aerocasillas.** P.O. Box 4567-1000, San José; Tel. 2-255-4567; Fax 2-257-1187.

**DHL.** Pavas, San José; Tel. 2-290-3020; Fax 2-290-3000.

**E.M.S. Courier.** Zapote, San José; Tel. 2-233-2762.

**Federal Express.** Cetro Comercial Yohan, San José; Tel. 2-255-4567; Fax 2-257-1187.

**Jetex Worldwide Express.** San José; Tel. 2-293-0505; Fax 2-293-0808.

**Mail Boxes Etc.** 150 meters west of the American Embassy, Pavas; Tel. 2-291-0282; Fax 2-290-0806.

**Sky Net Worldwide Express.** Rohrmoser, San José; Tel. 2-232-5678; Fax 232-2797.

**Star Box.** 5177 NW 74th Avenue, Miami, FL 33166; Tel. (305) 257-3443; Fax (305) 233-5624.

# TELEPHONE **SERVICE**

You'll often hear people grumbling about the Costa Rica telephone company (ICE), saying that they can't wait until the system is placed in private hands. But I suspect most complaints come from people who haven't experienced the substandard and expensive telephone service available in most third-world countries. The fact is, Costa Rica has the one of the best and most efficient telephone systems in all of Latin America, with more than a million phones for a population of only four million. (The best part is that you can dial anyplace in the world from your home and connect just as though you were calling across the street. Try that in most third-world countries!) This says nothing about cell phones. There might be a million of them in service, with long waiting lists for more connections. The cellular fad is an astonishing change in communications. Many *tico* families have a cell phone for each family member.

Privatization enthusiasts believe that once the government is taken out of the telephone equation, rates will drop. Well, check this out: Basic telephone service is around $6 a month, with 150 free minutes (no long distance charges anywhere in the country). Additional minutes are 8 cents (U.S.) a minute. Cellular telephone service is also a bargain compared with most other countries. Basic service starts around $7 a month, which includes 60 minutes of free use. Does anyone really believe that a privatized Spanish or German telephone company can cut rates below these levels?

Infrastructure improvement is apparent every year, with more and more isolated communities receiving not only telephone service for the first time, but—would you believe—fiber-optic lines designed for high-speed Internet connections! Ten-plus years ago, to make a phone call from the Guanacaste beach area where we live required driving to the center of the village and seeing which of the three public phones had the shortest waiting line. If we saw teenagers were huddled around one of the telephones, we'd go on to the next. Occasionally, we'd find all three phones hijacked by giggling teenagers, and then we knew we'd have a long, long wait!

A few years later, our lives began to change. ICE telephone trucks arrived, and workers began laying wires (underground, to keep falling trees from messing things up). Suddenly, *everybody* had telephones! Teenagers had cell phones in their pockets. Instead of driving from house to house to find out where Juan Fulano the gardener might be working so you could hire him to work tomorrow, you simply dialed his home and left a message with his wife. Better yet, you could call his cell phone.

Paying telephone and electric bills seems to be different in every community. You don't simply mail a check to the phone company; you need to go to a designated place to pay. This could be a grocery store, a stationery shop, a bank, or some other local business. Phone bills are rarely paid at the same place you go to pay your electric bill, your garbage collection, or your house insurance—that would be much too easy. In the city you may receive a bill by mail, but you have to personally go somewhere to pay it. Many supermarkets can accept phone-bill payments.

I have a friend who owns a small village variety store and collects telephone-bill payments for the area. She speaks almost no English but manages to do okay with gringo customers. However, a couple of times I've had wild-eyed gringos come to me crying, "Please help me, John! I just paid my bill, but that woman canceled my account anyway! She said *'Está cancelada!'*" I calm them down by explaining that the word *cancelada* does indeed mean "canceled," but it was the bill that was canceled, not the service!

## CELL PHONES **AND PHONE CARDS**

Until recently, you had to be a citizen or a resident to get cellular phone service in Costa Rica. And even if you were a resident, you'd have to get on a waiting list. It's much easer today, but you may have to prove you bought your phone in Costa Rica to get it activated. But most cell phones bought outside the country won't work here anyway. You need to be able to switch the frequency to GSM 1800, and most foreign cell phones can't do that.

One of the Costa Rica phone company's modernization projects has been to convert pay phones to accept phone cards instead of coins. The problem with that is when you have to make a call on a public phone that doesn't accept coins, you have to find someplace to buy a phone card. Drugstores often sell them. I like to use phone cards called Servicio 197, which can be used on any telephone by dialing 197 and then the special phone number on the card. This works with all phones, public or private. The phone cards are usually available in denominations of 300, 500, or 1,000 colones. For international calls, Servicio 199 cards work the same way and are available in 3,000- and 10,000-colón denominations.

As of March 20, 2008, the Costa Rican Institute of Electricity (ICE) placed into effect a new system of telephone numbers, adding the digit 8 before all cellular phone numbers and a 2 before all land phone numbers.

Note that all cellular numbers start with either a 3 or an 8, so add the number 8 before the regular number and add the number 2 to all other phone numbers. This change does not affect Costa Rican 800, 900, or 905 numbers.

For example, a land phone number such as 682-1234 is now dialed 2-682-1234, and a cellular number that was formerly dialed as 848-1234 is now 8-848-1234.

## DIALING **IN COSTA RICA**

To reach an AT&T international operator, you dial 0-800-0114-114, no coin needed. Verizon is 0-800-012-2222; Sprint is 0-800-013-0123; Canada Bell is 0-800-015-1162; information is 113. Direct dialing from your home is not only easy but also the most inexpensive way to place an international call. You dial the country code, and then dial the number you wish to reach. For example, to dial the United States from Costa Rica, first dial 001, then the area code and local number. To call Costa Rica from the United

States, dial the prefix 011, then the country code 506, then the local number (there are no local area codes in Costa Rican telephone numbers).

Be aware that some international collect calls can be rip-offs. I've heard horror stories of $100 for calls of fifteen minutes. The bills are collected on the U.S. end, not by Costa Rica. I recommend using the Servicio 199 card, as described above.

Emergency calls can be made by dialing 911, just as you do back home. The fire department is 118; highway police, 117; the Guardia Civil, 127; and an ambulance (Cruz Roja), 128. To report a problem with your telephone, dial 119. For electrical problems dial 126.

# THE WORLD OF **THE INTERNET**

The computer age has arrived in Costa Rica. Wisely, the government keeps customs duties low on items such as computers and accessories. You'll find stores everywhere selling the latest hardware and all the software you could possibly want, at prices similar to what you would pay back home. Internet cafes are everywhere; even the smallest villages seem to have them. For those of us who had to exist in Costa Rica without e-mail or online hometown newspapers, this trend is nothing short of miraculous. Previously we had to depend on expensive telephone calls and faxes to keep in touch with the States, or we wrote letters that took a month for a reply. Now with e-mail, we can touch base daily with family and friends, even hourly. We can do business, sell and buy stocks, or read online, all with a few clicks of the mouse. The downside is that your family and friends can forward stupid jokes and chain letters that will cause seven years of bad luck if you don't immediately forward the message to the few remaining friends who still open your e-mails.

Even though Costa Rica has Internet access, the performance and speed do not begin to compare with high-speed DSL connections in the United States or Canada. Yes, there are some so-called high-speed cable connections, but they are expensive and very slow compared with U.S. standards and aren't available in most parts of the country. In many parts of the country, a "high-speed" ISDN connection is available at a reasonable cost of about $20 extra per month. It's nowhere near DSL fast, about double the speed of a dial-up connection, but that extra speed is truly worth having, not to mention the reliability of the service.

When you have no access to ISDN, your alternative is a dial-up connection through the government-owned Radiográfica Costarricense S.A., commonly known as RACSA. Home service for families and noncommercial users starts at $15 a month for an unlimited dial-up connection. This service can only be used from the specified home connection. You pay extra for the phone time, but the cost is minimal. Regular commercial connections start at $30 per month.

Opening a dial-up Internet account is easy; you don't even have to go to a RACSA office. Just about any computer store has the applications and can set you up with an account and a password while you wait. You'll have to post a $15 deposit, and you have to bring a copy of your telephone bill and your passport. Keep in mind that this account can be accessed only from the home phone number listed on the telephone bill.

If you bring a laptop with you, a RACSA Internet card is convenient, allowing you to go online anywhere you can make a phone connection. This is handy when you're only going to be in the country for a few weeks and don't want to sign up for long-term service, or when you're traveling around the country with your laptop computer. The cost of the Internet card is about $10 for a ten-hour card or $20 for a twenty-hour card. You simply dial 134, and when you connect you enter the password on the back of the card. These cards can be purchased from RACSA in downtown San José and in some computer stores around the country.

A handy and little-known way to access the Internet in Costa Rica is through a "900 toll number." All you need is your computer with a modem connected to a phone line and configured to access via the terminal window after the connection is made. (You might need a computer-savvy friend to help you configure the connection before you make the trip to Costa Rica.) The cost of the service is about 90 cents (U.S.) for an hour-long connection, about the same as a RACSA card. How to do it? Just dial (900) 365-4632. Once the connection is made, the computer screen will show a welcome display. Accept the conditions of the service by pressing any key and then the <ENTER> key. Next, press the <F7> key, and soon you will be able to surf the Internet.

# THE MESETA CENTRAL
## AND BEYOND

Which is the best climate in Costa Rica for expat living? Temperate or tropical? North Americans living here either full- or part-time are almost equally divided over this question. About half settle in the temperate central highlands, while the other half prefer the tropical coasts on either side of the country. Each group can't understand why others could possibly want to live elsewhere. Costa Ricans themselves are also divided about which is best. As proof of this division, roughly half of Costa Rica's four million citizens live in the higher reaches of the country. We'll discuss living in the temperate zone first.

The central highlands—with an altitude of 2,000 to 4,000 feet— provides a year-round spring climate where daytime temperatures average around 77 to 79 degrees, then drop down to the mid-60s at night. People typically sleep under a light blanket. Not just in the spring—year-round.

Costa Rica's central highlands are marked by a low mountain range that begins near the Nicaragua border and marches south, where it crosses the border into Panamá. This range is known as the Cordillera, a picturesque complex of ridges, valleys, peaks, and tablelands, per- petually covered with green vegetation and teeming with wildlife. The

# MESETA **CENTRAL**

*Lake Arenal*

**Nuevo Arenal**

**Tilarán**

**San Ramón**

**Poas**

**Rohrmoser**

**La Garita**

**Atenas**

**Alajuela**

**San José**

**Cartago**

**Orotina**

**Colón**

**San Pedro**

**Grecia**

**Heredia**

**Puriscal**

**Escazú**

**Santa Ana**

**San Isidro del Genera!**

mountains vary from rounded promontories to the rugged peaks of the Talamanca Range, dominated by 12,600-foot Cerro Chirripó. Valleys and rolling tablelands are interspersed between steep hills, volcanic formations, and fertile agricultural country.

# SAN **JOSÉ**

San José is located more or less in the center of the country, an expansive complex of small cities and towns that surround the city of San José. This can be best described as urban sprawl. San José is Costa Rica's only real city, nestled in a wide depression about halfway down the Cordillera, at an altitude of 3,800 feet above sea level. The city, with about 300,000 inhabitants, is surrounded by dozens of satellite communities and small cities such as Heredia, Alajuela, Escazú, and Cartago, all perched at various elevations on the uneven plateau. From just about any point in this area, you are treated to views of mountains and extinct volcanoes that form a half-bowl around the Central Valley (or in Spanish, the *Valle Central* or *Meseta Central*).

Twenty years ago, these towns were distinct entities, separated from others by small farms, fields, and pasture. Today the only evidence of one town being distinct from another is a city-limits sign.

Why so many prefer the Central Valley is a question answered in two words: superb climate. This is the land of perpetual spring. Yet even this weather doesn't please everyone; some prefer temperatures in the mid-80s; others feel more comfortable in the low 70s. Fortunately, in the Central Valley it's possible to "fine-tune" your weather simply by moving a few kilometers in one direction or another. A fifteen-minute drive from anywhere in the Central Valley brings you to a slightly different climate, with more or less rainfall, with warmer or cooler temperatures. It seems as if each town or community brags of having the "best climate in the world." Alajuela is proud of being a few degrees warmer than San José, while Escazú is happy about being a few degrees cooler. Poas boasts of being even cooler than Escazú, and La Garita brags about its *National Geographic* rating of one of the three best climates in the world. The wonderful thing is that all these choices, however slight, are freely available to you. (The weather chart in chapter 2 illustrates this diversity of weather.)

**METROPOLITAN SAN JOSÉ** As their airplane approaches the country's international airport, visitors are treated to the sight of a broad green valley flanked by steep, volcanic mountains that seem to be forever topped with fluffy clouds. The city of San José spreads out below, thinning to a scattering of towns and villages that eventually merge into a lush green countryside. From the air one can see homes and tidy farms lining roads and highways, showing patches of cultivated fields intermixed with wild tropical vegetation.

After passing through the easy customs booths in the modern terminal of Juan Santamaría Airport, travelers make their way toward the city of San José along a modern, divided four-lane highway. Those expecting to see the usual Central American panorama of dingy buildings, shacks, and junkyards will be surprised by tastefully landscaped grounds of light manufacturing facilities, fancy hotel complexes, offices of international corporations, and other evidence of business prosperity. A large Intel computer-chip facility is a proud addition to San José's high-tech ambience. I've heard people proclaim in surprise, "Why, it almost looks as if we are in Europe!"

The closer one gets to the center of San José the denser the population becomes, and the less it looks like Europe. Suddenly, the highway becomes a boulevard when it curves toward downtown and past Sábana Park. The city starts appearing more as you might expect of Central America. By the time the average newcomer reaches the heart of downtown San José, entirely too many vehicles creep along narrow streets, past hundred-year-old buildings mixed with a few modern ones. Dense crowds of pedestrians swarm past a confusing agglomeration of small shops, vendors, and street stands with blaring music. Typically, a feeling of disappointment sets in as the newcomer thinks, "Is this the beautiful Costa Rica I've heard so much about?"

However, it's all in the eyes of the beholder. I absolutely love visiting San José. The city becomes more attractive to me with each visit. We live hours away from the city and get excited every time we plan a shopping excursion to San José. We look for reasons to drive or fly to "San Chepe"—as *ticos* humorously refer to San José—to see our lawyer when the business could just have well been done by telephone. (By the way, *Chepe* is a child's way of pronouncing *José*, thus the nickname San Chepe.)

Those who live here soon learn to appreciate San José for its many cool cultural events. No other place in Central America—or even most cities in the United States—offers as many opportunities for opera, plays, museums, art galleries, symphonies, and foreign artists of all kinds. Once you learn where the good restaurants are, you'll look forward to visiting often. Those who only know downtown San José can never appreciate San José's suburbs—places like Escazú, Santa Ana, Rohrmoser, Heredia, San Pedro, and all the delightful neighborhoods nearby.

San José, the capital and business center of Costa Rica, is a comfortable place despite its large population. Although downtown streets throng with shoppers and automobiles, neighborhoods a dozen blocks away can be tranquil residential areas. San José doesn't suffer from the widespread slum zones that plague many U.S. cities. You'll find modest neighborhoods, to be sure, and a few run-down areas, but not the starkly depressing ghettos so apparent in most large Central American cities, or some U.S. cities for that matter.

There is a slight smog problem in San José's downtown streets, mostly caused by belching diesel trucks, buses, and taxis. However, continuous cross-breezes keep the atmosphere fresh, except in the immediate vicinity of a bus or truck. Some residents disagree with my underemphasis of San José's smog situation. But having lived in Los Angeles and visited places such as Athens and Beijing, I truly appreciate San José's usually transparent air and continual blue skies.

For some reason, people from all over the valley feel a compulsion to do their shopping in downtown San José. This is partly from habit but also because shopping is something of a social event. Every day, crowds of shoppers amble along the streets and avenues, checking out window displays, making purchases, and gossiping with friends. Most could shop in their own neighborhoods, but it's more fun this way, and here is where you will find those scarce items you need. So many pedestrians pack the main downtown avenue (Avenida Central) that the city was forced to turn it into a pedestrian mall.

Although a few neighborhoods in San José are suitable for expatriate relocation, most North Americans are predisposed to congregate in the more costly areas on the edge of the city or in neighboring suburbs. This is understandable since we tend to be much more affluent than Costa Ricans and can better afford upscale neighborhoods. The western edge of San José attracts a large number of foreign residents, particularly around the Sábana Park area (Sábana Sur and Sábana Norte), the upscale neighborhood of Rohrmoser, and some areas of Pavas. Better supermarkets, nicer restaurants, and amenities such as tennis clubs and attractive parks make this a very livable part of the city. The *Tico Times* classified section frequently lists homes and condos for sale or rent in Pavas and Rohrmoser. Rents for condos or apartments typically start around $400, and homes can go as high as $2,000 a month for a nice place. Still farther out, toward the airport, is Cariari, a luxury area with a golf course and country club.

Directly across the valley, the towns of Escazú and Bello Horizonte match Rohrmoser for elegance and expensive housing. Just to the east of downtown San José, Barrio Escalante is an affordable neighborhood of stately older homes. This was the "in" place for wealthy *ticos* years ago and is now in the process of adapting to middle-class families. Still farther out on the eastern edge of the city, Los Yoses and San Pedro supply moderate to expensive housing, with some of San José's most exclusive neighborhoods. San Pedro provides a university atmosphere, with many rentals available at student-budget levels. For the height of luxury housing and opulence, some neighborhoods around Curridabat cannot be topped. One area, known as "Embassy Row," has many stunning homes and mansions, some housing foreign embassies.

By shopping around you can usually find housing that will fit your pocketbook and lifestyle. Remember that ads in the *Tico Times* are directed toward North Americans who can afford to pay more. For less-expensive places, check the classified ads in *La Nación;* that's where *ticos* find their rentals. San José has several apartment complexes renting furnished places by the day or week that make excellent "base camps" while one is looking for permanent quarters or trying out Costa Rica as a place to live.

**FINDING YOUR WAY** Searching for an address in and around San José and its suburbs can be an exercise in frustration; few buildings or homes have street numbers. Even worse, many streets have no names, or at least no names posted on the street corners. Very confusing. Suppose you are looking for the García residence, whose address is listed as "From Caballo Blanco 250 meters west, 300 south." To understand where this house is located, you need to know the location of a store called Caballo Blanco, then go 2½ blocks (250 meters) to the west and then 3 blocks (300 meters) south. At that point, you need to ask someone which house belongs to the García family.

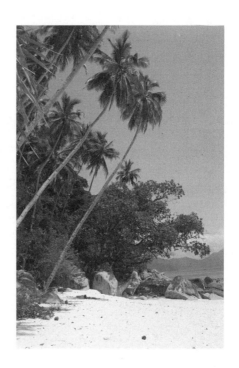

This confusion isn't restricted to residences: Businesses use the same system. On maps, advertisements, and business cards, the word *calle* is often abbreviated as "c," *avenida* as "a," and *central* as "ctl." The distance between two points is usually stated in meters (abbreviated with an *m*). But to make it even more confusing, people occasionally give directions in *varas* instead of meters. A *vara* is an ancient measurement of 33 inches (in English it is called a "pace"), which was in common use before Napoleon's introduction of the metric system in the early 1800s.

Examples of address insanity: The address of the Hotel Presidente would be "c ctl, a 7–9," which translates as "on Calle Central between Avenidas 7 and 9." The address of the bus terminal for Alajuela is "a 2, c 12–14," meaning "facing Avenida 2, between Calles 12 and 14."

Directions and addresses can be vague to the point of impossibility. This is particularly true away from the orderly grid of north-south, east-west streets. An address might be described as, "From the gasoline station, 100 meters north and 75 *varas* to the east." But which gasoline station? My favorite address is on a real estate agent's business card. It says "50 meters south from where the Mas X Menos supermarket used to be."

It doesn't do any good to complain; *ticos* understand the system perfectly and actually become confused when you use logical addresses. Often when I take a cab downtown, asking to go to "Avenida Segunda and Calle Primera," the driver responds with a puzzled frown. When I add

"Teatro Nacional," his face lights up with understanding and away we go, headed for the National Theater, which is on the corner of Avenida Segunda and Calle Primera.

## FROM THE CITY **TO THE MOUNTAINS**

Although many foreigners actually live in the city of San José, the vast majority prefer the smaller communities surrounding the city. These towns range from expensive to moderately priced places to live. For some reason, at least six small towns in the country have the same name—San Isidro—which adds to the confusion of finding your way around. San Antonio is another favorite place-name that is scattered about like leaves in the wind.

As discussed elsewhere, the explanation for identical names is that during colonization, communication was extremely difficult between communities even though the actual distances between them is not far when using modern transportation. People couldn't possibly confuse their San Antonio with another when it took two days' travel by oxcart to get to the other San Antonio.

## ROHRMOSER

Rohrmoser is at the upper end of the housing market in the immediate San José area and is Escazú's main competition for upscale residences. For some folks there is no competition—Rohrmoser wins hands down. Here homes and condos consistently command rents and sale prices higher than elsewhere in the metropolitan area. Unlike Escazú, Rohrmoser looks more like a modern city suburb; it has sidewalks and boulevards instead of narrow roads and streets with dirt shoulders. (For some, an advantage; for others, lacking charm.)

Homes and apartment buildings here are much newer, with some condo development and home construction still under way. Started by a German developer (thus the name), Rohrmoser begins at the end of Sábana Park and runs along both sides of Rohrmoser Boulevard until it reaches the ultramodern shopping center of Plaza Mayor. From that point west, Rohrmoser sits on the northern side of the boulevard, with the town of Pavas on the eastern side. The U.S. embassy, incidentally, is in Pavas, on Pavas Boulevard, a place with dozens of popular restaurants and shopping.

Many North Americans live in Rohrmoser, but the largest percentage of your neighbors will be *tico* professionals who like the convenience of being close to the business center of the city. My wife and I used to own a condo in Rohrmoser and enjoyed the peaceful ambience. We could take a taxi to downtown San José in just ten minutes (traffic permitting). We would stroll from Rohrmoser Boulevard to Pavas (some 4 or 5 blocks) to dine at one of the many great restaurants and return late at night, with absolutely no feelings of insecurity. One reason we felt okay about this was the presence of watchmen on almost every block. We had full confidence in the integrity of our neighbors because most were doctors, professors, attorneys, and the like. Then one day we saw on television that a very nice home a couple of houses away from us had been rented to a gang of professional bank robbers from Venezuela. The bandits had been living there for some time while they committed a string of robberies. They were on the "most wanted" list of the OIJ (*tico* equivalent of the FBI). Despite their occupation, the culprits dressed well, kept their front yard tidy, and paid their rent on time. They couldn't have been all bad.

## ESCAZÚ

Several of the more traditional communities that attract expatriate residents run in a direct line from San José westward, beginning at Escazú— only 8 kilometers (5 miles; around fifteen minutes) from downtown San José—to the town of Puriscal, about one hour from the ocean. Nestled at the base of magnificent ancient volcanic mountains, Escazú has always drawn the affluent and those seeking tranquillity away from the city. Three mountains hover over Escazú. The tallest is Cerro Rabo de Mico, at 7,770 feet; the most spectacular is Pico Blanco, at 7,250 feet, with a dramatic, sheer rock face that has challenged the skill of many a mountain climber. Residential streets on the edge of town ascend the mountainside bravely, presenting an even better view with each gain in altitude.

Escazú used to be somewhat removed from city hustle and bustle. Needless to say, the town no longer has a "village" atmosphere. It is now a city. Originally, Escazú consisted of three separate villages: San Miguel de Escazú, San Rafael de Escazú, and San Antonio de Escazú, each having its own church and patron saint. The red-domed church in San Miguel de Escazú was constructed in 1799 and has survived numerous earthquakes since. Some of the older barrios are famous for quaint old adobe buildings that are painted with a traditional two-color motif. The design is a 3-foot colored stripe painted along the bottom of the home, which was believed to ward off evil spirits and witches. I have to admit that I've encountered very few evil spirits or witches during my visits here.

The villages expanded until they formed one city with a population said to be 40,000. San Rafael is the commercial zone, with an astounding collection of businesses, restaurants, and nightlife. Traffic along San Rafael's main streets is exceptionally heavy, with shoppers and business-people driving automobiles at a snail's pace in traffic.

Trendy restaurants of all descriptions abound, including European, barbecue, Chinese, and even a Cajun restaurant for the yuppie trade. Yet a block away from the main streets, neighborhoods are as calm as they were more than twenty years ago. As San José grew and spread out, artists and those in search of serenity began moving to Escazú. No longer the peaceful retreat of yesterday, the area retains a reputation as an artists' colony as well as a retirement center.

Escazú's higher elevations are ideally suited for those who think that San José's climate is too warm. Many residents consider the weather here to be as close to perfect as you can get, with high temperatures hovering in the upper 70s every afternoon of the year. A large number of North Americans choose Escazú and surrounding towns as their place for relocation. This is where the U.S. ambassador's residence is located. Two famous country clubs provide the area with golf, tennis, and a focal point for the society set. Escazú is the center of much of Costa Rica's expatriate social life.

Escazú and its environs have a sophistication that makes them stand out among San José's suburbs as a prestige address. Although the area admittedly has some of the more expensive places to live, modestly priced homes and apartments are also available throughout the community. Those who choose to live here say they wouldn't think of settling anywhere else. "We have the best of all worlds," explained a couple who owns a small house on the slope of Pico Blanco. "We live in the country with a gorgeous view of the city below, yet we are just five minutes away from stores, restaurants, or whatever we need." They pointed out that although they are close to San José, they rarely go there on other than essential business. Well-stocked supermarkets, shops, doctors, dentists, and a first-class health clinic serve the community's needs quite well.

You'll find no real "foreign colony" in Escazú. Expatriate gringos tend to spread throughout the community, interspersed with *ticos* and other foreigners. Although some prefer to live in "sealed-in" developments—compounds with high walls and twenty-four-hour security—more folks live in ordinary homes or town houses. Those who choose to pay more for the security feel it is worth it, since they can comfortably leave their places unoccupied for months at a time while they return home for visits. Others rely on neighbors and friends to take care of things while they are gone.

## SANTA **ANA**

The first edition of this book described Santa Ana as a "growing village" 6 kilometers (4 miles) from Escazú, separated by fields of sugarcane, rice, beans, and hillsides of coffee. Roadside stands sold braids of garlic and onions, garden-fresh vegetables, and jars of rich local honey. (Despite Africanized bees' nasty reputations, they produce high-quality honey and more of it than ordinary bees.)

Today you'll no longer see farmland between the towns. The most important crops today seem to be condominiums, homes, and gated communities. Santa Ana has become a small city instead of a growing village. For all practical purposes, Santa Ana and Escazú are one today.

The altitude here is slightly lower than either Escazú or San José, making it slightly warmer and drier. A number of small rivers cross the rolling valley, and rounded mountains provide a scenic backdrop. All roads converge upon a central area, giving Santa Ana a true downtown center, casual yet somewhat sophisticated. High above the town, on the mountain Cerro Pacacua, a 20,000-acre forest preserve and bird sanctuary keeps nature ever present in the local ambience.

A few generations ago—before it became an easy thing to drive to the beach for vacations—San José's wealthy families maintained summer homes in Santa Ana. This was the place to spend weekends and school vacations, a place for the upper crust to host parties and entertain lavishly. This old tradition left its traces on today's community, with many nice homes scattered about the area. Many rather attractive developments, complete with swimming pools, gardens, and round-the-clock security, are here.

Santa Ana is well known for polo matches and international equestrian competitions. Seasonal festivals bring an impressive parade of horseback riders, who ride their high-stepping steeds along the streets to the central plaza where the main celebration is under way. (Don't try to drive along the parade route on festival day; horses have the right-of-way.)

Santa Ana has a deserved reputation as a working artists' colony, with a number of writers and artists in residence. The town is famous for ceramics, and production of excellent pieces is a major industry, with almost thirty workshops and more than 150 local people employed in artistic endeavors. Excellent restaurants, first-class supermarkets, and shopping of all descriptions are at hand, eliminating the need to go to the crowded world of downtown San José for odds and ends. Yet when such travel is necessary, it's but an easy drive along one of the country's few stretches of genuine superhighway. What is probably the largest and most elegant shopping mall in the country sits along the divided highway between Santa Ana and Escazú. It's called the Multi-Plaza and is worth a visit.

Every community seems to have an especially popular hangout where expats gather to socialize over a few drinks, lunch, or dinner. The Tex-Mex restaurant in Santa Ana seems to be the place for this. English is spoken here by a ratio of 10 to 1, and the place always seems to be crowded. Another popular place, on the road between Escazú and Santa Ana, is called the Rock and Roll Pollo (*pollo* means "chicken").

# CIUDAD **COLÓN**

Located about fifteen minutes beyond Santa Ana and twenty minutes from Escazú, Ciudad Colón is the next to last of San José's western suburbs. The town is the site of the University of Peace, sponsored by the United Nations, offering graduate courses in peace studies. A growing number of expatriates live here, a close-knit group that welcomes newcomers. The town is very neat and inviting. As far as we can tell, there haven't been any condo developments started in Ciudad Colón, but with population pressure moving from Santa Ana, condos and gated communities seem inevitable.

The word *ciudad* means "city," but that word hardly describes Ciudad Colón. This is a small community where folks stroll to the town center for shopping or to have lunch with friends. One of the restaurants we've enjoyed is a vegetarian establishment called Earthly Delights (even though I'm normally a vegetarian only between meals). There's a sense of peace and personal safety about Ciudad Colón. Although the setting is rural, it is certainly not isolated. The enormous and elegant Multi-Plaza Mall is but a short drive, and Escazú is not much farther. Frequent bus departures from Ciudad Colón take you to the heart of San José for heavy-duty shopping and browsing the interesting downtown areas of a real city.

Of all the Central Valley retirement locations, I suspect that communities from Santa Ana west to the town of Ciudad Colón and on to Puriscal have a great potential for development and property appreciation. The reason for my belief: The government has plans for extending the divided highway from San José through Ciudad Colón that will someday hook up with the Pacific Coast Highway 34. This present highway, by the way, is one of the few made of cement instead of the usual mixture of asphalt, gravel, and oatmeal—or whatever they mix with asphalt to make a dissolvable road surface. The pavement here has endured without damage—not even a tiny pothole—for more than twenty years. Surely the government transportation bosses will someday realize the value of cement highway construction as opposed to disappearing asphalt surfaces.

Anyway, when the highway is extended to the Pacific, this will dramatically cut the driving time to the popular beach communities of Jacó and Quepos. With Pacific beaches just an hour's drive from Cuidad Colón, the convenience will make the area even more attractive as a place to live, and real estate could become an even better investment.

According to news accounts, a contract has been signed to start construction. The highway will be built by a private concession and will collect a toll of about $3. Well worth it to shave two hours off the trip to the beaches. When I mention this news to my *tico* friends, they shrug their shoulders and say, "Don't count on that. We'd be delighted if they'd just fill the potholes on the roads we have!"

## PURISCAL

A few kilometers beyond Ciudad Colón, you'll find a delightful mountain town called Santiago de Puriscal, a self-contained community of about 10,000 inhabitants. Puriscal is in the process of being "discovered" by an ever-increasing number of expats who enjoy the perpetual spring climate here. It's a pleasant alternative to the heat and humidity of Caribbean and Pacific beach communities, and it's set above the smog of San José and the Central Valley. Elevations in this area range from 2,600 to 3,900 feet (792 to 1,189 meters), with homes perched on a series of ridges with spectacular views in all directions.

A massive church anchors the center of town, with a lovely park spread out in front. The church is especially interesting because it is partially in ruins, the result of an earthquake years ago and shifting ground beneath the church. The park in front of the church is a relaxing place to wait for friends and to meet expatriate newcomers. Puriscal offers a surprisingly wide selection of business and commercial services. Probably because it is farther from the urbanized areas closer to San José, central Puriscal has the look of a much larger city. You'll find three supermarkets, several hardware stores, banks, and even several Chinese restaurants.

Puriscal is widely recognized as making the best *chicharrones* (fried pork treats) in the country. During a recent visit we tried them, and I swear they are the best we've ever tasted! You really have to love a town that appreciates good food. Puriscal loves *chicharrones* so much that the people hold a special holiday in honor of the tasty, greasy snack. More than just a holiday, the Festival Nacional del Chicharrón is held over ten days and has dancing, music, sports, and exhibitions. Is that dedication, or what?

If there's something you need and can't find in Puriscal, a good highway links Puriscal to San José, a forty-minute drive or a fifty-minute express bus ride. Actually, many *ticos* commute to San José daily to work, preferring to live in a peaceful community away from traffic and bustle. A bonus of living in the Puriscal area: Now that there's a paved road to Orotina, Puriscal residents are a little more than an hour's drive to the Pacific beaches.

## ALAJUELA

Near the country's major airport, Alajuela is one of the less expensive yet pleasant places for foreigners to live. Situated on the western edge of San José, this small city is convenient to the airport and a twenty-minute bus ride from downtown San José. Clean, modern buses run every few minutes during the day, stopping at the airport on the way to and from San José. (If you have a small amount of luggage, this is an inexpensive way to get downtown from the airport.)

Your first approach to Alajuela can give a misleading impression. The highway comes in on a higher level than the town, providing an unfortunate panorama of tin roofs in every direction—some new, some rusted, some painted red to resemble tile, but actually of corrugated iron, plastic, or aluminum. Of course, in the United States a tin roof usually implies cheap construction, basically used for structures such as storage sheds or temporary buildings. But as explained in chapter 2, this is earthquake country; those picturesque tile roofs can be deadly when they collapse. You may see genuine tile roofs, but you can be fairly sure that underneath all that pretty tile is a heavily reinforced substructure. Since the temperature never gets hot or cold, the insulation value of a heavy tile roof is beside the point.

Alajuela's focal point is a large park in the center of town (called the Parque Central, of course), a pleasant place shaded by tall trees, with chessboards built into some of the cement benches that surround the park. If you would like to meet North American retirees to ask for information about Alajuela, this is the place to come; sometimes it seems that there is as much English spoken here as Spanish. This is the place to find out about housing rentals, who is leaving for the States, who has a car for sale, and who can recommend a gardener or a maid. In the evenings a mixture of classical and pop music can be heard from the park's bandstand, where professional musicians entertain a couple of times a week.

Alajuela was the home of Juan Santamaría, the young hero of the final battle against the American buccaneers under Gen. William Walker. Every year on April 11, the town celebrates Juan Santamaría Day with a jubilant parade through town, a public fiesta, and dancing in and around the Parque Central. On one corner of the square, a museum dedicated to the hero is located in what used to be a jail. About 2 blocks west of the park is the Public Market, the perfect place to find the freshest veggies and choicest cuts of meat.

A good way to become acquainted with the expatriate scene in Alajuela is to visit restaurants and cafes in and around Alajuela center that are frequented by gringos, who drop in for an afternoon snack or a cold drink. If you spend enough time drinking coffee in one of Alajuela's more popular cafes, or sunning yourself on a park bench, you'll likely meet every gringo in Alajuela.

Alajuela is an excellent example of moderate housing costs, for both sales and rentals, in the Central Valley region. Prices are neither as elevated as they can be in upscale areas of Rohrmoser or Escazú, nor are they depressed as in poorer working-class neighborhoods. Neighborhoods here are middle class: Newcomers will feel comfortable, and neighbors can tell you exactly who lives in which house on the street. The expatriate community is scattered throughout the better sections of Alajuela and not very concentrated in any one location. The same is true of Heredia.

# HEREDIA

When we first visited Costa Rica, Heredia was a small provincial capital of about 10,000 persons. Today the population is difficult to estimate. Heredia has expanded to meet Alajuela's growing sprawl until they've essentially joined into one large town, with nothing but a city-limits sign to indicate where one ends and the other begins. Situated northwest of San José on the sloping hills of the Barva and Poás Volcanoes (extinct, of course), Heredia's higher elevation provides a cooler climate and more rainfall, which keeps things looking green and fresh throughout the dry season. Rural areas farther up the sloping hills toward Barva are renowned for quality coffee production. Small- and medium-size coffee farms are scattered here and there, a few owned by foreign residents. Others own homes with orchards of citrus, avocados, and tropical fruit instead of coffee. Most places enjoy breathtaking views of the valley below.

The center of Heredia, like Alajuela, features a large, friendly Parque Central complete with weekly band concerts. This park is shaded by stands of enormous mango trees and has the usual park benches for informal meetings and gossiping. Like the Parque Central in Alajuela,

Heredia's park has a large church at one end—a cathedral, actually—that has watched over the square for more than 200 years.

The center of town is somewhat congested, but that doesn't stop expatriates from meeting at their special restaurant on or near the square, browsing an English-language bookstore, or taking care of banking and other errands near the plaza. One resident points out that "Heredia isn't exactly a 'culinary mecca,' yet you can find some nice restaurants nearby in addition to the McDonald's, Taco Bell, and Kentucky Fried Chicken that cluster around the plaza."

La Universidad Nacional, the country's second-largest university, is located not far from the plaza. A private school, Universidad Interamericana, and several language schools teach Spanish to North Americans here. Many exchange students from the United States and Canada take classes here and become part of the expatriate scene in Heredia.

Heredia's famous market is large, featuring quality meats and exceptionally fresh vegetables, fruits, and greens of all descriptions. Much of the market's exotic produce is grown by local residents in their backyards. Saturday is market day, and selections are bountiful as well as fresh-picked. People from all over the valley come here for their weekend shopping. The market is near the Parque Central and dates back more than one hundred years. Like most other cities on the Central Valley, Heredia homes don't have street numbers. But instead of saying "150 meters north," it's customary to say "150 meters *arriba* [uphill] " because the town slopes uphill toward the north. "Two hundred meters *abajo*" would, of course, mean 200 meters to the south, downhill.

Continuing *arriba* is the town of Barva, location of Costa Rica's largest coffee producer, Café Brit, where many tourists visit for a tour of a coffee plantation. Up the slope toward the extinct Barva Volcano, many lovely homes are tucked away among the tropical vegetation that crowds the side of the narrow highways.

From Heredia's northern edge, hills and mountains rise steadily toward the Poás Volcano. All along these foothills, winding roads travel past beautifully maintained homes, alternating with evergreen forests, small farms, and verdant pastures. This is one of our favorite parts of the Central Valley (we almost bought a coffee farm here a few years ago). As roads climb higher into the mountains, temperatures become progressively cooler, allowing prospective home buyers and renters to make precise adjustments to their environment by buying farther uphill or downhill.

An interesting place to check out is nearby San Isidro, a small village to the east of Heredia. A number of foreigners have made their homes here. They point out that the village is small enough that they can interact with villagers and get to know everyone in town. They enjoy the rustic, rural ambience—a place where oxcarts are often used for everyday farm chores.

Incidentally, those foreigners who own rural parcels and who spend half the year in Costa Rica and the rest of their time in their home country are sometimes willing to rent their property in their absence to ensure that someone will keep an eye on their place and protect it from vandalism. Some attractive rental deals can be worked out in these instances.

## OTHER TOWNS **AND VILLAGES**

To the south of Heredia and Alajuela, several smaller towns and open countryside sprinkled with small farms and beautiful homes draw *ticos* and foreigners alike who want to escape the city's crush. The road from Heredia to Turrucares is particularly striking, with lovely, high-quality homes interspersed with small, neatly kept farms and residences. Our taxi driver, who was renting his cab and services by the day, drove us there and pointed out some of the prettier homes along the way. "I was born in this area," he said proudly. And then, with a hint of sadness in his voice, he added, "Of course, it is too expensive for me to live here now."

**GRECIA** The picturesque town of Grecia is often described as one of the cleanest places in Costa Rica. Positioned northwest of San José, Grecia is situated along the edge the Central Valley with beautiful mountain landscapes in the background. It is in the continual process of being "discovered" by a growing number of expatriates. Conveniently located about thirty minutes from the airport, Grecia's turnoff from the Inter-American Highway is marked by a monument that tries to resemble the ruins of an ancient Greek temple. The town center is reached via a picturesque road that traverses sugarcane fields, high-quality coffee plantations, and small farms. The views are spectacular, overlooking deep valleys and lofty mountains in the distance. Grecia is noted for wide streets and prosperous-looking middle-class neighborhoods.

The center of Grecia features a lovely square in front of one of the country's most interesting old churches. Called the Cathedral de la Mercedes, the deep-red Gothic-style church was assembled from metal pieces imported from Belgium back in the 1890s. Imagine, if you will: Every piece of wrought iron used to construct the church was hauled over the mountains by oxcart from the Caribbean port of Limón, a tedious two-week journey!

A favorite place to meet local expats is the central square located in front of the church. You'll usually find some of them there most week-day mornings, sitting on benches or having coffee in the cafe across the street. Near the plaza is a large central market that, in addition to the usual collection of veggie and meat vendors, has a wonderful *tico* restaurant serving some of the best *comida tipica* we've ever tasted.

English-speaking residents here vow that this is one of the friendliest and safest places in the country, and I tend to believe it. As I've driven the roads in the area, I've noticed a surprising exception to the rule of bars on windows; many homes, especially those up in the hills overlooking Grecia, do not have bars. There doesn't appear to be any one particular enclave where gringos live; they seem to be dispersed about the landscape, sometimes on small plots of land near town or in Grecia itself. Some prefer one of the nearby villages such as San Rafael, San Roque, Tacares, or any number of similar locations.

**ATENAS AND LA GARITA** More to the west of Grecia and only ten minutes farther from the airport, Atenas and La Garita are charming little towns with rural settings and neat town centers with wide streets. These towns sit along the alternate highway that winds down through Orotina, toward the Pacific beaches not far away. Both towns are clean and prosperous looking, with luxury properties interspersed with modest-priced, livable homes. There are adequate community services, including a health center, ambulances, schools, banks, boutiques, and supermarkets. The expatriate population here is said to be around 300 residents.

Atenas and La Garita are gaining popularity with those who want pleasant weather but want to avoid the Central Valley traffic congestion. Residents here are famous for claiming to have the "best climate in the world." They point to an article in *National Geographic* as evidence. Of course, "best climate" is a matter of personal opinion, but there's no question that it is a bit cooler and fresher here than in the Central Valley. Some properties farther up the hill, where the highway crests for its downward, twisty run to the ocean, offer some spectacular views of the Central Valley. A few locations not only overlook the San José city complex to the east, but to the west they have a view of the Pacific Ocean.

Right now, traffic on the highway heading to and from the beaches can be heavy, especially on weekends, when San José residents make their pilgrimages to the Jacó. But this doesn't affect the quiet streets of the towns. When and if the superhighway past Ciudad Colón to the Pacific is completed, the Atenas–La Garita area will be an exceptionally desirable place to live. With the new freeway, Atenas will be thirty minutes from Jacó, ten minutes from the International Airport, and twenty minutes from San José. Since Atenas–La Garita is somewhat more affordable than some other desirable areas, you can find moderately priced homes on good-size parcels of land with wonderful views.

**SAN RAMÓN** An often overlooked possibility for relocation, San Ramón has just as much going for it as most other Central Valley locations. A pleasant and well-maintained city of about 20,000 inhabitants, San Ramón sits almost halfway between San José and the port city of Puntarenas. The exit is just off the Inter-American Highway that joins San José with the Pacific Coast, 35 kilometers (22 miles) from the airport and 48 kilometers (30 miles) from San José. The altitude here is a bit higher than nearby Grecia and Atenas and therefore slightly cooler. Hot, sweltering days are almost nonexistent.

Local residents like to call San Ramón "the city of presidents and poets" because several of Costa Rica's famous political and literary figures were born or were longtime residents here. These include three former presidents, the most famous being José Figueres Ferrer—a champion of democratic reform who abolished the military—and several celebrated poets and novelists. In keeping with San Ramón's cultural past, there is a campus of the University of Costa Rica here, as well as a regional hospital.

This is a place where you can experience the genuine, low-key Costa Rica that you'll not find in busy, tourist-oriented towns. The pace here is slow. The central market seems to be the heartbeat of the city. There is also a huge weekly market. San Ramón is a place where neighbors stop to gossip on the street or meet in the central park around the old church. There is no hurry. At the present time, there is only a small contingent of expatriates living in the city of San Ramón. Most prefer to buy property in the picturesque rural areas within a few kilometers of the city center.

When I asked one resident about the cultural advantages of living in or near San Ramón, he replied: "Well, let's see . . . San Ramón is an hour closer to the Guanacaste beaches. Also, there's a three-screen movie theater, plus a Longhorn Tavern (Casona del Cerdo) featuring great BBQ ribs, cut-with-a-fork *Lomito,* and real corn on the cob, yellow and sweet!" (All of that, plus two kinds of homemade draft beers—what more could anyone ask?)

The North American population here is not overwhelming, by any means. One resident estimated less than one hundred expats in and around San Ramón. "Not nearly as gringoized as Grecia and Atenas, where they have regular gatherings at the park and such," he added. The opening of a store/office/club in downtown San Ramón has created a gathering place. It's called the *Solo Bueno,* or in English, "Only the Best." It offers an Internet cafe, used English-language books, mailboxes, and a real estate office. The owner says: "Seems like whenever gringos come to town, they drop by to see what's happening, have a cup of coffee, check e-mail, or pick up a paperback."

**CARTAGO** Costa Rica's first capital city, Cartago is famous for its rich history. Colonial buildings and ruins dating back to the sixteenth century are reminiscent of an era when Cartago was the center of the country's breadbasket. Nearby rural villages, with ancient adobe buildings and colorful wooden houses, provide glimpses of the region's vibrant past. Sitting at the base of majestic Irazú Volcano, the town of Cartago has an elevation of almost 5,000 feet (1,524 meters) above sea level. This provides a much cooler environment than the rest of the Central Valley.

Cartago used to be a major stopping place on the now-defunct San José–Limón railroad line. While waiting for the train to resume its slow crawl to the coast, we used to stroll around the nearby market and feast on steaming empanadas while we waited for the train's whistle to announce the continuance of its journey. We liked the town at that time, wondering why it wasn't being "discovered" by gringos looking for an "authentic" Costa Rican relocation haven.

Costa Rica guidebooks seldom mention Cartago except to note the ruins of an ancient cathedral dating back to the sixteenth century and the slightly newer cathedral that houses Costa Rica's religious icon, the Black Virgin. Also of interest is the fact that Cartago was Costa Rica's first capital city. Cartago is one of the obligatory places to take visitors—close enough to San José's suburbs for an afternoon's visit to the historic monuments, a lunch at a *tico* restaurant, and then home before nightfall. But that's where tourist interest in Cartago ends.

I feel that things are starting to change. Bearing out my observation that North Americans feel at home almost anywhere in Costa Rica, the city of Cartago and surrounding communities are attracting a few newcomers. This idea isn't exactly new: Some expat residents have lived here for more than twenty-five years. Only ten or so expatriates live in Cartago itself, while at least fifty live in or around the nearby suburb of Paraiso. There you'll find one of those Mega Supers, as well as a shopping mall.

An expat resident from Ohio who lives with his wife in Taras (at the beginning of the road to Irazú Volcano) said, "I was surprised that so many expats say that they live here mainly because of the climate. I always considered it to be cool, and my *tica* wife says it's cold. Also, the rainy season here is probably a little wetter than in San José."

Cartago doesn't seem to have a "hangout" where gringos go for morning coffee like some other towns do. For the most part you run into them in the various shopping centers or on the downtown streets. They will tell you that they enjoy the quality of life in Cartago and that the people really do accept expats and make you feel good about where you live.

## ALSO IN **THE TEMPERATE ZONE**

The following locations do not exactly lie within the Central Valley, but they do have similar climates. These are places for those who don't care to put up with the heat and insects of the jungle, yet they are close enough to salt water that you can usually drive down to the beach for the day and return to sleep under a blanket that same night. Temperatures here are wide ranging, with places like Arenal being very cool and San Isidro del General being rather balmy.

**SAN ISIDRO DEL GENERAL** At first glance, this town would seem to be a rather unusual place for North Americans to choose as a place for residence or retirement. There is nothing spectacular about San Isidro del General; it is an ordinary, small Costa Rican city. It's neat and orderly, with the ubiquitous mountain views common to most other parts of the country. Few vacationers visit San Isidro, and those who have passed through the town may get it mixed up with one of the half dozen other San Isidros in the mountains. But those North Americans who have dis-covered San Isidro's secrets love living here. The climate is considerably warmer than that of San José, which suits some folks just fine, and the pace far slower.

Located on a wide ridge, not far from the high peak of Cerro Chirripó, the town enjoys a continuous breeze that keeps the air clear and aromatic with flower-blossom perfume. Daytime temperatures are pleasantly warm for my taste (maybe hot for some folks), and evenings are tempered by cool air flowing down from Chirripó Peak. Although San Isidro is not as serene and idyllic as some other Costa Rican towns, once you are away from the main square—and the inevitable cars, motorcycles, and trucks circling in search of a parking space—the pace slackens to a very peaceful stride.

Like most older Costa Rican towns, San Isidro features a main square in its center, the usual well-kept park. Since the park is the social gather-ing place for local residents, it isn't surprising that members of the North American community use it as their social focal point as well. The open-air restaurant of Hotel Chirripó faces the park, and at any given time you can count on at least some of the tables being occupied by English-speaking patrons.

Real estate and rentals are exceptionally inexpensive here. Since it is off the ordinary tourist routes, with no beaches and lacking in discos and other flashy attractions, San Isidro is likely to remain inexpensive. On one visit I talked with an American who had just completed building a small, two-bedroom home and was eager to find a tenant. He was offering to rent it for almost nothing just to have someone to take care of it while he returned home.

Several North Americans have taken advantage of the climate and low-cost real estate, living on small farms on the outskirts of town or along the highway toward the beach at Dominical. The views along this road are abso-lutely spectacular, with neat, prosperous-looking farms and picturesque homes in the mountain valleys below resembling toy buildings from a model train set.

**LAKE ARENAL DISTRICT** The northern portion of the Cordillera mountain chain, until recently ignored by North Americans, has one of the better potentials for expatriate population growth in the northern regions of Costa Rica. Certainly that's my opinion and one shared by other North Americans who are buying property around Lake Arenal as quickly (and quietly) as they can. Those who know about Lake Arenal would love to keep it a secret, but truth will

out! The character of this region is so different from that of other parts of Costa Rica that it's difficult to believe you are in the same country.

The Lake Arenal district is in the upper end of the same mountain chain, but that's as far as the similarity with other highland areas goes. As I understand it, the mountains dip lower at this position in the chain to form a low break or window in the Cordillera. This interruption in the mountain ridges permits a reversal of wind patterns, allowing strong easterly winds to bring moist air off the Caribbean with an abundance of rain. There is no such thing as a dry season in the Arenal area; it's a year-round wonderland of greenness and lush vegetation. When I asked one longtime resident how much it rained, she replied, "On average, about fourteen months out of the year."

Before the government started building the dam that created the wonderfully scenic lake, the region was lightly populated. Still, about 2,500 people had to be relocated to make room for the 72-square-mile lake. The project required several thousand workers and support people and took sixteen years to complete. Roads were cut into the area, opening it up to Costa Rican settlers who started farms and small villages. After the lake was created, many workers elected to stay on in the company housing that was built during the construction stages. The population here seems to be growing daily, including numerous foreigners who have "discovered" the Lake Arenal region.

To get here via paved road, the quickest way is by turning off the Inter-American Highway at Cañas, an extremely hot and dusty place during the dry season. Were it not for the ample irrigation water coming from Lake Arenal, Cañas would be more like a desert than a rich agricultural region. An air-conditioned auto and lightweight clothing are necessities here. Yet just 18 kilometers (11 miles) away by a tortuously winding road, the air conditioner is shut off and car windows rolled down to take advantage of the delightful fresh air.

**TILARÁN** By the time you reach the little town of Tilarán, only 23 kilometers (14 miles) from Cañas, a sweater might feel comfortable when the sky happens to be overcast. The countryside changes from pool-table-flat to steep-sided hills; colors change from dusty dry to emerald green. The road climbs gently now, as vegetation seems to become fresher with every curve, past fat cattle grazing fetlock-deep in richly grassed pastures and, where land hasn't been cleared for cattle or agriculture, some astonishingly heavy stands of tropical forest.

A surprisingly nontropical-looking town—with wide streets, neatly maintained homes, and prosperous businesses—Tilarán has become the home base of a number of expatriates. The climate is temperate and springlike due to a continuous eastern wind that drops moisture on Tilarán even during the dry season. Local residents publish their own newspaper, in English and Spanish, which promotes ecology and recycling projects for the nation.

A few miles east of Tilarán, the view of Lake Arenal bursts upon you, one of the prettiest lakes in the world. The fact that it is artificial fades in importance when the overall effect is considered. Sailboarders claim this is the second-best place in all the world to enjoy their sport. What the first place is I don't know, but it surely can't be any more beautiful than Lake Arenal.

Almost all residents in this area live on or near the drive that skirts Lake Arenal. The paved portion of the road has a scattering of European-type homes, chalets, and an occasional commercial unit such as a *pulpería*, those community store–tavern combinations so common in rural Costa Rica. Many homes were obviously constructed more recently, evidence of a developing region.

Several charming little villages and occasional inns or small hotels are spaced along the highway between Tilarán and Arenal. The road is paved and is usually in pretty good condition. A few miles east of the town of Nuevo Arenal, the road turns into graded clay and occasional stretches of blacktop. The condition of the road is never predictable. At the beginning of the dry season, after bulldozers scrape the road into a smooth surface, fill in the gigantic potholes, and sometimes cover it with a bit of gravel, the route feels like a superhighway to drive.

When the road is okay, the distance from Nuevo Arenal to Arenal Volcano seems like nothing, with a wonderful view of the lake and thick tropical vegetation lining the road. Other times the road is an absolute nightmare. Entire sections of the road can be missing. Water and mud can bury a four-wheel drive up to its windshield, and other horrors. I believe the problem is that the steep mountain slopes along the north side of the route come down from rain forests above, bringing water and mud sluicing down onto the road. What doesn't get washed away gets covered with mud. The lesson here is to make inquiries about taking a shortcut from Fortuna to Tilarán. When the road is good, it is very, very good; when it is bad, it is horrid.

**NUEVO ARENAL** The town on the lake is called Nuevo Arenal or, more often, simply Arenal. This is a surprisingly prosperous-looking place, with

## Library in Tilarán

In 2006, when Edward and Leslie Woods arrived in the town of Tilarán, they were very disappointed by the lack of bookstores or other sources of English-language books. Then they realized that neither were there outlets for books in Spanish.

Ed said, "Everything we had read on Costa Rica lauded the education system and near universal literacy. What we found was quite different. Maybe Costa Rica has the best educational system in Central America, but it still leaves a lot to be desired. Students are faced with severe shortages of books in the schools and no options for obtaining books outside of school.

"We wanted to start a library for the local children but had no idea how to go about the start-up or where to source the books. Many gringos told us we were wasting our time because 'ticos do not read.' We were pretty sure the reason they did not read was because they didn't have books. So we persevered.

"On one of our visa renewal trips to Nicaragua, we met the wonderful Jane Mirandette, who has founded a network of libraries throughout Central America. With Jane's help and a starter kit she calls 'Library in a Box,' we began our adventure. We met with the local officials and told them of our plans. The supervisor for the Ministry of Education donated an unused building. The local womens' organization, called Ladies of the Lake, held a fundraiser that provided the seed money to buy the Library in a Box starter kit. Members of the group and spouses volunteered many hours and funded supplies to rehabilitate, paint, and furnish the donated space. We opened our library in May of 2007."

The facility is now open four days a week with a young Costa Rican lady acting as librarian. They learned early on that volunteers can burn out very quickly, so they hired a permanent librarian. Leslie said, "We felt it important for the community to see that we are connected to them and providing opportunity for ticos. We had a very successful 'name the library contest,' receiving 1,200 entries from the local students. The name selected was El Camino del Saber ('The Road to Knowledge'). We had a big celebration of our opening, covered on local radio and with local government officials attending."

As soon as the library opened in Tilarán, the volunteers began to plan a second branch for the town of Nuevo Arenal. They were given space by Kendall Sanborn, a local businessman. This branch opened on February 11, 2008, with the same four-day-a-week schedule and a paid *tica* librarian.

Their biggest issue, of course is fund-raising. It costs over $400 per month for librarian salaries, and additional funds are needed to expand their collection of books. The library currently has 2,000 books in Tilarán (all in Spanish) and about 400 in Nuevo Arenal (as of one month after opening). They receive requests regularly for additional titles and want to begin procuring copies of all the school texts for students to use.

Most of the fund-raising is done by Sarah Benson, who divides her year between Nuevo Arenal and Key West, Florida. Donations of money or books in Spanish would be greatly appreciated. The library's Web site is www.discoverypress.com/TilaranLibrary.

neat little houses interspersed with expensive-looking ones. The town sits high on the sloping bank of Lake Arenal, and most homes and businesses are situated to take advantage of the lake view. Streets are well paved, though parts of town have an oddly unfinished look, as newly paved streets and vacant lots mix with an occasional house. The center of town has the inevitable soccer field with spectator benches curiously pointed toward the street, away from the field, as if the soccer team is so bad that locals would rather watch the traffic, scarce as it is.

Arenal obviously was a development planned by the government during the dam's construction phase. Many of the current homes here are left over from that era. Unlike the traditional Latin American residential style—built close together and against the sidewalk to allocate space for interior patios—some Arenal homes have real lawns, reminiscent of small-town U.S.A. This adds to Arenal's strange, non–Latin American look.

Because of the area's beauty, the temperate-tropical combination climate, and the low cost of real estate, the Lake Arenal region is undergoing a buying frenzy. Buyers from Canada, the United States, and

Europe are furtively looking at property and investing. Germans, Swiss, and Italians appear to be the biggest sharks, biting off chunks of the land as quickly as they can. They try not to appear eager as they snap up bargains, and they do their best to keep this place a secret, lest hordes of other foreigners descend upon paradise and ruin their plans of being the only ones here.

It's not surprising that prices are going up on property around Arenal. It's a very desirable area. Still, it's hard to conceive that inflation could be anything like that along the Pacific beaches. Another favorable circumstance: Since this is lakefront property, it doesn't fall under the complicated and restrictive laws that regulate ownership and construction on beachfront parcels. Here waterfront property is owned outright instead of being leased from the municipality. However, be aware that the water level in the lake fluctuates from dry season to wet season as water is drawn off for irrigation and hydroelectric power. Your waterfront lot could end up with a broad frontage of dry land in the dry season.

**LA FORTUNA** No trip to Costa Rica can be considered complete until you've visited the Arenal Volcano, 13 kilometers (8 miles) from the town of La Fortuna. Active continuously over several centuries, the volcano's northern slope suddenly exploded almost forty years ago, destroying a village and killing more than sixty people. (A geologist had tried to warn them of an impending eruption, but nobody believed him.) The nearest and best place to observe the activity is in the hot pools of Tabacón, a resort wedged into a steaming-hot river canyon at the volcano's base. You can sit on underwater stools at the bar and sip piña coladas while every twenty minutes or so, a jarring explosion shakes the swimming pool, accompanied by puffs of smoke and red-hot boulders tumbling down the volcano's steep side. (That's time to order another piña colada.)

The volcano has done marvels for tourism hereabouts. The nearby town of Fortuna has become prosperous serving the needs of the hordes of volcano visitors. New hotels, restaurants, and stores are appearing each season. Fortuna is an exceptionally neat and pleasant community, one that could well make a good place for retirement. With a relatively new road going through San Ramón, San José is only a two-and-a-half-hour drive away.

A small town with a friendly atmosphere, spic-and-span streets, and a great climate, Fortuna has my prediction of a place that could someday have a sizable expat community. Sitting at approximately 1,312 feet (400 meters) above sea level, Fortuna is too high to be tropical, yet it's low enough to avoid chilly winds. About 16 kilometers (10 miles) from the entrance to Arenal Volcano National Park, La Fortuna serves as an ideal base for tourists visiting the volcano, popular Tabacón Hot Springs, and Lake Arenal. As it's not far from Caño Negro Reserve and such outdoor sports as sailboarding, fishing, and white-water rafting, it's almost obligatory to stay at or pass through La Fortuna to enjoy these activities. The tourism potential will do nothing but grow over time, and this will bring more North American residents. The town and vicinity have a growing number of hotels, *cabinas,* restaurants, and travel/tour agencies. Departing La Fortuna toward Tabacón and Lake Arenal, several new tourist facilities with terrific views of the volcano are always under construction.

A small group of foreigners are now settling into the Fortuna area. Of course, everybody knows everyone here, but to date they haven't formed any residents' club or formal organization. That will come later, when a critical mass of expatriates forms around La Fortuna. In the meantime, as one resident says, "Most of us come here to enjoy living with our *tico* neighbors and being independent."

**SAN CARLOS** When people talk about "San Carlos," they could be referring to the northern region of Costa Rica, from below Ciudad Quesada on up to the Nicaraguan border at the San Juan River. They could also mean the small city known as San Carlos, located in the more southern portion of the San Carlos region. To add to the confusion, you won't find the city of San Carlos on the map, because officially it is called Ciudad Quesada. However, for some reason unknown to me, *ticos* always refer to Ciudad Quesada as San Carlos.

San Carlos offers another example of Costa Rica's microclimates. With a lower elevation than the Central Valley, the region is warmer than the San José area and receives more rain during the dry season. Yet it doesn't have the heavy rainfall of the nearby Lake Arenal area. Agriculture is a year-round activity, with citrus, macadamia, and other orchard crops as well as numerous *fincas* (ranches) with horses and cattle tended by expatriates.

These lands were once tropical forests, which during the past decades have been transformed into cattle pastures and fruit plantations. The exceptionally rich farmland here has attracted a number of gringo farmers and would-be agriculturists. San Carlos's agricultural zone devotes almost 70 percent of the land to raising cattle. The area produces first-quality milk, beef cattle, and agricultural products. Expatriates have set up on small to moderately large spreads; some experiment with reforestation. Some people have been planting teak, even though some experts claim that teak needs definite dry seasons alternating with wet periods to force the tree to produce oil and densely grained wood. Time will tell, because it takes many years before teak is ready to harvest.

Ciudad Quesada, or San Carlos, or whatever, is the main center of services and commerce for the Northern Zone. This prosperous-looking city-town was settled in 1840 when the Quesada family moved here from San Ramón and founded a village. As is the custom, the center of town holds a central park and the ubiquitous Catholic church. Nearby is the customary central market full of colorful stalls selling fruit, vegetables, herbs, and locally made leather products and crafts.

**ACOSTA** A few years ago, the Ministry of Tourism came up with the idea of promoting "rural tourism" as an economic-development project for communities with limited tourist attractions and no hotels or other tourist facilities. The idea is to attract certain types of tourists, those who aren't looking for golf courses, beaches, discos, and the traditional tourist glitz that draws many foreigners to Costa Rica. This special kind of tourist will be curious about the everyday life of the *ticos*: who they are, what it would be like living in a "typical" Costa Rican village. Since these isolated communities rarely have hotels suitable for tourists, local residents organize to turn their homes into bed-and-breakfasts and welcome visitors. Since the community goes all out to make visitors welcome, it occurs to me that retirees might be received even more warmly as permanent economic benefits to the area. A small handful of expatriates live there. A Web site describing the program is found at www.costaricanruraltourism.org. (I have to say that they are very slow in answering queries, but the region is worth a visit anyway.)

Finding this idea intriguing, I decided to investigate by making a trip to one of the designated rural tourism areas, an area known as Acosta, the general name given to a half dozen villages in the mountains south of San José, about an hour's ride by bus from the center of the city. An excellent road snakes its way upward, winding through small villages and past some very interesting homes. The drive is spectacular, with deep valleys and ravines, lush vegetation, and spectacular views of San José and the Central Valley way down below.

The largest village is San Ignacio de Acosta. It's difficult to know the population, because none of the people I met there could make an estimate that agreed with anybody else's. There's a lovely church and a large, landscaped park. The surprising thing is the high quality of the housing. It was explained to me that at one time the *tico* government was making low-interest loans for quality housing, and many people took advantage of this and upgraded their homes. The setting is overwhelmingly beautiful. San Ignacio de Acosta is perched on the top of a rounded mountain, with an astonishing view of other villages so far below that the houses look like toys. San Luis de Acosta is about five minutes away, looking down the other side of the mountain into other valleys. Coffee farms are interspersed with forested land and small farm homesteads. Except for the main roads and some town streets, all roads are graded gravel, some in excellent condition, others not so great. The climate is superb, one of the best in the country, at least for those who like year-round spring-like weather. The temperatures are seldom over 75 degrees or below 65 degrees. Air-conditioning and heating are unknown here.

I was welcomed enthusiastically as a visitor and was given a room in a private home, where I was treated as one of the family. I joined with the family in the local fiesta celebration and was very impressed. In my opinion, a place such as Acosta is a retirement option for certain types of North Americans: those who speak at least some Spanish or those who are willing to learn. Acosta would be appropriate for those who do not require a large circle of English-speaking friends. The local *ticos* are exceptionally friendly and open. I feel that before long, a retired couple could easily be involved with the *tico* society, with friends and volunteer activities keeping them very busy.

# COSTA RICA'S
# **PACIFIC COAST**

The western side of the country is characterized by wet summers, dry winters, regular surf from the open ocean, and a much larger population of foreigners. Although most come from North America, a considerable number of Europeans are moving into the area. Many come from Germany, Switzerland, and Italy; other nationalities are well represented, too. Some expatriates operate successful hotels, restaurants, and other tourist-oriented ventures that the business-friendly Costa Rican government makes possible.

Costa Rica's Pacific Coast can be divided into three basic geographic sections: the Nicaragua border to the end of the Nicoya Peninsula area, the beaches from Jacó to Uvita in the center, and the Golfo Dulce–Osa Peninsula area to the south. Each area has its boosters who will assure you that there is no place in all of Central America as nice as their favorite location. I've seen them all, and I can say that making a choice among them would be difficult indeed.

A nice feature of most of these tropical beach areas is that they are easily accessible from the Central Valley—within a few hours' drive by bus or automobile, almost no time at all by airplane. Some locations

- Panama
- Playa Hermosa
- Potrero
- Flamingo
- Liberia
- Brasilito
- Conchal
- Playa Grande
- Tamarindo
- Junquillal
- Playas del Coco
San Juanillo
- Ostional
Nicoya
- Nosara
- Playas de Nosara
Carmona
- Puntarenas
- Sámara
- Carrillo
Naranjo
Paquera
- Tambor
# NICOYA **PENINSULA**
Montezuma
Malpaís Cabo Blanco

Lake Arenal

require longer driving times than others, but as pavement replaces gravel roads, travel times will decrease.

Eastward from the ocean's surf, rolling hills of forest and farmland spread inland and up the mountain slopes, becoming steeper and more picturesque with each kilometer. Much of this land is wilderness, traversed by occasional dirt roads that become quagmires in the rainy season. Despite isolation and transportation difficulties, foreigners find these rustic sections exceptionally desirable places to live. As the government gradually paves the roads along the coast and into the interior, more and more settlers are swelling the ranks of North Americans and Europeans who live here and operate businesses. With easy access, property values ought to increase dramatically.

## GUANACASTE **REGION**

A number of important beach locations on the north coast attract Costa Ricans and foreigners alike for vacation, retirement, or business opportunities. These beaches are easily reached from San José in three to five hours by car. The main highway is paved and in generally good condition but can be agonizingly slow when you are stacked up behind a string of slow trucks on their way to or from the Pacific docks. Slow as this 16-kilometer (10-mile) stretch may be, you will be glad you have to go slow, because there are some shoulder drop-offs that could be dangerous if you drive carelessly. The secret to driving this section of the highway is not to be in a hurry. Relax and go with the flow. Enjoy the spectacular and ever-changing scenery of the Inter-American Highway.

Rainfall amounts are lower here than anywhere else in the country. Unlike most of Costa Rica, here the dry season is truly dry, with almost no rain falling from January to May. This is similar to much of California, but in reverse. That is, in California it almost never rains between May and October. In Guanacaste's dry season grass turns parched and yellow and many trees lose their leaves, often replaced with a gorgeous display of colorful blossoms. Around homes or along inhabited beaches, however, you'll see more evergreen trees and broadleaf plants because they've been deliberately planted and cared for.

# PLAYAS DEL COCO **AREA**

A quickly developing complex of *playas* (beaches) begins at Playa Hermosa and Playa Panamá, stretching south through Playas del Coco and ending at Playa Ocotal. A nice beach in this complex and one with development potential is Playa Hermosa. *Hermosa* means "beautiful" in Spanish, and Playa Hermosa lives up to its name. This is a lovely place, with a curving shoreline of clean sand and a peninsula that shields it from the open ocean and dangerous riptides.

Playas del Coco, however, is the most commercially developed of all these beach communities. Since the pavement ends in the center of El Coco, tourists tend to stay here rather than braving annoying stretches of washboard gravel roads to get to nearby beaches. Coco's scenery consists of the horseshoe-shaped Coco Bay, with islands in the distance and steep hills and cliffs on either side.

This is probably not the place in which you'd want settle down, not if you are looking for a "typical sleepy fishing village" (as I've seen it described in a recent tourist publication). Actually, I don't believe Coco ever sleeps—it offers some of the wildest nightlife in the country. The town boasts over two dozen bars, discos, and nightclubs that rock all night, every night. There are also two casinos.

There can be no question about Coco's potential for business, retirement, or long-term living. Several very successful American-owned enterprises operate here, and more are probably on the way. But if I don't sound particularly enthusiastic about the place, it's probably because this is where I locked my keys in my rental car and struggled for two hours in the hot sun before figuring out a way to get inside without breaking a window. A good car thief could have done it in less than twenty seconds.

A few kilometers to the south, Playa Ocotal manages to maintain a village atmosphere despite also hosting a deluxe tourist resort. The accommodations are tasteful, blending in with the natural surroundings. The village is on the shore of Bahía Pez Vela (Sailfish Bay), and the fishing is said to live up to the name. Each time we visit, we see a noticeable increase in housing, making this another viable retirement option.

## FLAMINGO **BEACH**

The next beach complex to the north is just a few kilometers away and is probably the most popular residential complex on this part of the Pacific Coast. New paved roads have opened the area to increased settlement. This array of beaches starts with Playa Pan de Azucar and continues south to Playa Tamarindo, including the beaches of La Penca, Potrero, Flamingo, Brasilito, Conchal, Playa Grande, Tamarindo, and Langosta.

By far the prettiest beach is Playa Flamingo. A wide, curving stretch of white sand with startling blue waves that turn to white-capped rollers before crashing loudly against the shore creates one of the loveliest scenes imaginable. Hotels here cater to affluent tourists who can afford to fly in from San José and spend $150 a night for rooms. Tourists on ordinary budgets will find few (if any) reasonably priced rooms. Ongoing building activity may change all this.

As you might imagine, foreigners have taken over this beach and have built some very spiffy places. At one time, I considered Flamingo the "Cadillac" of Costa Rican beach communities, but several other locations along the coast have surpassed Flamingo, at least in price. The hillsides display sumptuous homes, set in tropical landscaping and overlooking a gorgeous beach view. The scene is reminiscent of Acapulco many years ago when it was the playground of the Hollywood and European jet set. Needless to say, Flamingo is not the place to look for inexpensive ocean-view lots.

The beach adjacent to Flamingo is Brasilito. Instead of having a tourist-resort atmosphere, the village of Brasilito is more like a typical Costa Rican pueblo, complete with a soccer field, small bars, and restaurants. This is a bedroom community for workers employed by affluent residents and businesses in Flamingo. It's also an inexpensive place for *ticos* and foreign residents on a budget to find an inexpensive *cabina* or room and enjoy the beach. The beach isn't bad at all; I'm surprised there isn't more commercial development and foreign settlers. For a beach community, property here is reasonably priced.

The next village is at Playa Conchal. The Spanish word *conchal* refers to the shells on the beach. In fact, the entire beach is composed of tiny, water-worn shells instead of sand. This area has attracted numerous expatriates in the past several years. This is another place with a large resort, spread over 2,400 acres of lush land, including a golf course and 350 rooms. Several really nice housing developments are also found here, including gated communities, all near the beach.

Just 2 kilometers north of Flamingo, the tiny fishing village of Potrero has a handful of foreign residents. They're building along the beach toward Flamingo, eventually to become an integral part of one community. The village itself is much more laid-back and relaxed than Flamingo, with some residents' homes built on the hillside overlooking Potrero's exceptionally gentle beach. This is a place where you can hire a local fisherman to take you out in his *panga* to fish for dorado or parga.

# REGIONAL **DEVELOPMENT**

The entire west coast of the Nicoya Peninsula is slated for eventual tourism development by the government's tourism ministry (ICT). Of particular interest, with short-term plans in the works, the stretch from Sámara north to Tamarindo is drawing a great deal of attention. Two circumstances account for this recent flurry of building activity. The first is the newer bridge over the Tempisque River, which cuts at least an hour's driving time from the trip from San José. The second is the possible paving of the road from Sámara north to Tamarindo. Construction is rumored to start in early 2009. (We're not holding our breath.) This plan sets out certain areas as high-density tourism centers, suitable for large hotels, intensive usage of beachfront, and full-service tourist facilities. Sámara and Garza are so designated. Other places are planned for residential and low-intensity tourism.

Nosara was supposed to fall into the latter category, much to the delight of local foreign residents. This is precisely what they wanted: protection of the beach and forest, yet development of low-impact tourism to boost prosperity for the natives. Unfortunately, the desire of local residents has little effect on the determination of tourists to enjoy the Nosara beaches. Not to mention the determination of developers to accommodate tourists and new residents. The region is booming, with more facilities and homes being built every year.

## TURTLE **BEACHES**

An excellent example of how tourism and conservation can work hand in hand is found from Playa Grande south along the peninsula beach communities. One noteworthy turtle conservation project is at Playa Grande, just north of Tamarindo, a broad, sandy beach area famous as nesting grounds for endangered leatherback turtles. It used to be that local residents awaited the arrival of these huge, prehistoric survivors, collected the eggs in buckets as they were being deposited, and sold the harvest to bars and restaurants all over the country.

Alarmed by the possibility of the turtles' extinction, the Costa Rican government instituted a model conservation program. Local people are enlisted to help protect the nesting grounds; guarding the beaches and guiding tourists through the nesting grounds put local people to work. Hotels and restaurants have opened to accommodate the ever-increasing number of tourists; jobs are created for even more local residents. This boom has only begun, and future ecotourism development seems inevitable.

Conservationists have expressed mixed feelings about this program. While they praise the protection of the nesting grounds, they point out that the extra tourist foot traffic causes damage when visitors inadvertently step on the hatchlings. On the other hand, the number of baby turtles killed in this manner is nothing when compared with the unborn ones that used to end up as tasty *bocas* in San José bars.

**PLAYA GRANDE** Turtles need a wide, sandy beach with ample portions not touched by normal high tides, and Playa Grande fills these requirements admirably. It used to be relatively unpopulated, with few human footprints to disturb the solitude. Until a few years ago, only a handful of homes and one or two tiny motels were to be found near the beach's access roads. Today development is under way. However, as part of the Tamarindo Refuge, the beach area will always be somewhat restricted in tourist development, even though the region's natural beauty and wildness are bound to attract even more people in the future.

One place I looked at was a large, tastefully constructed home with a neatly manicured lawn ending at a beach wall marking the 50-meter boundary. The owner half-apologized for the home's isolation and lack of anything to do, adding, "The hope of this little community is that things won't change. What we offer here is location, nothing else." He indicated the broad expanse of beach visible through a stand of coconut palms and said, "The whole idea here is to fit into the ecology without disturbing things, particularly not the nesting turtles and their life cycle." The house's window frames were made of wood instead of the more practical aluminum "because metal frames reflect moonlight and confuse the hatchling leatherbacks. We don't allow any lights from our homes to escape at night. For bright lights and nightlife, you have to go to Tamarindo." Since my writing of these lines, a number of bars and restaurants have opened near Playa Grande, and several housing developments are under way.

Local turtle-watchers report some good news: The number of turtles visiting the beaches to lay eggs grows each year, with new turtles joining the flock (or should it be covey? Band? Could it be a herd of turtles?). The numbers still remain below what they were in the 1980s, but locals are hoping this will become a trend.

**PLAYA TAMARINDO** Playa Tamarindo begins where Playa Grande ends; a picturesque estuary separates the two. Tamarindo is where leatherback-turtle-watchers find hotels. Launches begin ferrying passengers across the estuary around midnight. Visitors tiptoe quietly along the beach and pause to observe the huge turtles as they awkwardly pull themselves up on the beach to bury their eggs 6 feet deep in the sand. This is an unforgettable sight; some of these turtles are said to grow to more than 12 feet across and weigh up to 1,500 pounds! The one I watched laying eggs may have been a pygmy; she was barely 6 feet wide. Our guide claimed that during the peak of the season, as many as 350 turtles can be on the beach in a single night. What an amazing sight!

Because of excellent surfing beaches and nearby Playa Grande turtle beaches, Tamarindo has always been a magnet for tourists of all ages. The coastal region here is easily accessible by pavement rather than gravel and dirt roads. This ensures a steady stream of visitors as well as new residents who often become part of the business community. The new international airport in nearby Liberia has also accelerated development. Arriving passengers no longer have to stay overnight in San José, with a long drive to the coast the next day. An hour or so in a rental car or taxi, and you're on the beach the same day.

Tamarindo's popularity with tourists and expatriate residents has transformed the sleepy village of a few years ago into a busy, highly commercial entity. The town is a textbook example of foreign development of a Costa Rican beach community: totally developed, and with a cosmopolitan mix of nationalities. Almost all businesses—restaurants, hotels, shops, bars, and so forth—are owned by foreigners: North Americans, Italians, Germans, and French, with several other European nations also represented.

Some residents and longtime visitors lament these changes, while others appreciate the presence of upscale restaurants and quality retail and food shopping options, including a supermarket and conveniences that a mere village would lack. While some yearn for the "good old days," Rob Gibson, a Tamarindo homeowner, says: "The surroundings are still spectacular, and the relative success in protecting Playa Grande and the estuary behind it from unbridled development has been key to maintaining its attractions."

A few years ago, a Tamarindo *tico* complained to me: "We keep selling our land and moving farther back into the hills. Now we are working for foreigners on land we once owned. Before long we won't be able to afford to live in our own village!" That prediction has come true; the price of real estate makes property ownership impossible for local families, and hotels are priced out of range for vacationing *tico* families. However, Rob

Gibson—who speaks Spanish with local working people—observes no general sense of resentment. "Most *ticos* say that tourists and part-time residents are good because they bring money and create jobs in the area. I love the practicality and lack of xenophobia among *Costarriquenses*, and if we gringos behave decently, perhaps we can keep it that way." Rob also points out that there are definite advantages to living in an expatriates' enclave. "I don't know how much my gringo neighbors would help me in a crisis, but it is nice to have so many of them around."

For those with school-age children, this is the only region outside the Central Valley with an international K–12 college-prep school. Country Day School Guanacaste is a private facility located between Tamarindo and Flamingo. It isn't inexpensive, but as one parent said, "The school is small enough for the teachers to have a one-on-one relationship with their students." There's also a bilingual elementary school, Niños del Mundo, with classes for students from pre-kindergarten to fourth grade.

**PLAYA JUNQUILLAL** South of Tamarindo the coast is lightly populated by foreigners or *ticos*. This is partially due to the seasonal condition of the dirt roads along the coast. Most residents believe that a paved road will be built not too far in the future and that beaches along this coast might have potential for development. A series of beaches front the Pacific along this coast, some with tiny villages, others almost unpopulated. Among the beach villages are: Playa Avellana, Playa Negra, Playa Junquillal, and Playa Lagarto. These beaches are graced by large waves rolling in from the open Pacific and are very picturesque. Since I'm not an expert swimmer and know little about ocean currents, undertow, and riptides, I can't vouch for the safety of these beaches. You'll need to consult local authorities on the subject. This is a sensible practice anywhere in the country.

A place that's attracted our attention is Junquillal, a growing village positioned on one of the longest beaches on the Nicoya Peninsula. The region is known for exceptional surfing waves in the Playa Negra and Junquillal areas. Endangered leatherback and green turtles come ashore to lay their eggs in the sand. Most businesses in the area are owned by Americans, Canadians, Italians, and Germans who are trying to develop more tourism in the area. Meanwhile, residents are hoping that Junquillal doesn't develop to the same extent as the more popular beach towns.

One Canadian expatriate said, "We like progress, but we'd prefer to keep the area as a serene place to come for relaxation and the natural beauty."

One small hotel, right on the beach, is owned by several California couples who take turns managing the establishment as their excuse for a working vacation (presumably tax-deductible). One partner said, "It's a very small operation. We consider a month successful when we don't have to dig into our pockets to make the payroll." A few kilometers from the village center, an elaborate residential development is being purchased exclusively by Canadians and Americans. Construction quality is tops, with all amenities. Since Junquillal has a small population, major shopping and other services are available about forty-five minutes away. There is, however, a mini-supermarket that provides most basic supplies.

## BEACHES OF **NOSARA**

We "discovered" Beaches of Nosara (Playas de Nosara) more than twenty years ago, while researching Guanacaste beach communities on the Nicoya Peninsula. Driving north from Sámara over a dirt road that parallels the ocean beaches, we stumbled on an almost isolated beach community inhabited exclusively by North Americans and a few Europeans. Because the road was not paved, and several rivers need to be forded, few tourists bothered to investigate the heavily forested and lightly populated community. Over these years, we've been privileged to see many profound changes to Beaches of Nosara.

Starting at the Nosara River, three lovely beaches and a wildlife reserve extend south along Playa Nosara and Playa Pelada to Playa Guiones (*playa*, of course, means "beach"). Nosara started as an experiment in a different concept of foreign development. The emphasis was on private homes and pristine beaches rather than tourism and commercial enterprise. Along more than 8 kilometers (5 miles) of beaches, to this day only two small restaurants are located on the beach. As you stroll the ocean's sandy shores, you'll see no discos, fast-food restaurants, miniature golf courses, or other evidence of higher culture. Just beach and jungle. At least for the first 200 meters—after that, all bets are off. There's a possibility that in the future the government could relent and allow building closer to the beach, but residents are hopeful this will never happen.

Don't misunderstand; you can find plenty of services like the above (well, maybe not miniature golf), just not on the beach. Two hundred meters is as close to the water as they can legally be located. So when you are strolling the beach, swimming, or sunning, there's nothing to remind you that you are not in pure paradise. The major exception to this rule is a small *tico* bar and restaurant, Olga's Bar, which has occupied a patch of beachfront for the past thirty-plus years and is therefore grandfathered (or grandmothered) into acceptance. Thirsty residents concede that they need at least one bar on the beach!

A major problem has always been that newcomers aren't as ecologically aware as the original owners. Residents and old-timers continually try to educate newcomers about the importance of not cutting down the trees or destroying the animals' habitat. Howler monkeys need regular "trails" through the treetops that they use daily to go from one feeding area to another. Since the project is set in the forest, a great deal of the Nosara project was zoned as greenbelt, forever to be public parklands, never to be developed or built upon. Until recently parklands have been sacrosanct, with development verboten. Longtime residents are determined that their parklands remain protected from development. This is their insurance that their unique forest won't be replaced by lawns, T-shirt shops, and condos.

When this book first described Nosara, development was still in its infancy. Services were limited and property prices were very modest, probably one-half to one-third of more accessible beach locations such as Tamarindo or Flamingo. Then, at the turn of the new century, change began accelerating. New residents began arriving in a steadily increasing stream, looking for homes to buy or construction lots. An astounding amount of commercial construction seems to be going on everywhere. Many original residents shake their heads in disbelief at these radical changes. Others are happy, convinced that this growth will force the government to pave the road. At the present time, it takes an hour to drive a dirt road to the nearest pavement. That doesn't stop newcomers.

Despite changes in character and lifestyles, I'm firmly convinced that Nosara will maintain its charm and forest ambience. There is room for all.

## SÁMARA AND **CARRILLO**

A welcome development for those traveling to the Pacific Coast from San José and points inland is the "Friendship Bridge" constructed by the Taiwanese government. This bridge replaced the cumbersome ferry across the Tempisque River. In the time it would take the ferry to cross the wide stretch of water, carrying a limited number of vehicles, a thousand cars and trucks can zip across the bridge. Travel time to the peninsula has been shortened by about an hour. This access is having a profound impact on the development of the entire coast, with Sámara and Carrillo being affected the most.

Much of this area is already developed, particularly in and around Sámara. New hotels and condos are going in, and more expats are building homes south of town, extending toward Carrillo. However, this is only the beginning. As we noted earlier, the Tourism Institute has targeted the Sámara-Carrillo area for high-intensity tourist use. We expect to see some large hotels and probably a resort going in before long. Smaller hotels, restaurants, and shops will naturally follow. If Sámara develops as did Tamarindo, we can expect a large percentage of new businesses to be owned by North Americans. It seems to be working out that way.

Sámara and Carrillo share opposite ends of the same bay, one of the most beautiful imaginable in a country of beautiful beaches. Several long stretches of beach are flanked by a wide road fringed with coconut palms, making the beaches freely accessible to all. At the northern portion of the bay, Sámara attracts more *tico* tourism from the Central Valley area at the moment (on weekends and holidays they arrive by the busloads). Toward Carrillo, more hotels cater to foreigners and are higher priced. This is where the airstrip is, which makes it handy for visitors.

All along this part of the coast, some low mountains sit back about a kilometer from the shore, and here is where many expats make their homes. The views of the bay are magnificent up here, whereas homes built at sea level have views of nothing but trees or the nearby hotel.

An item of interest about Carrillo: A short distance south of the airstrip there is a bridge over a small river where two large crocodiles lurk. Local residents regularly feed them by throwing frozen chicken carcasses tied with nylon line into the river. They then troll the tasty morsels toward the bridge to lure the monsters from their hiding places. Although the river isn't posted against swimming or wading, I would strongly recommend that you refrain from this activity. Naturally, the crocodiles strongly disagree with this advice.

# LOWER **NICOYA PENINSULA**

On the southern tip of the Nicoya Peninsula, a string of beaches with tremendous potential are undergoing development. The beaches run from Naranjo on the Gulf of Nicoya side to Cabo Blanco at the very tip of the peninsula, and then up along the coast via impassable roads, toward Carrillo. Most investors agree that the economic growth between Cabo Velas and Cabo Blanco could be among the best in the country. It all depends upon when (and if) the roads will be made passable.

Getting to this area from the northern part of the peninsula has always been a problem. The paved highway ends abruptly at the little town of Carmona, presenting about a 30-kilometer (19-mile) stretch of dirt road to the coast. The road paralleling the Pacific Coast dwindles to a trail from time to time, and you have to ford several good-size streams. Even rugged four-wheel drives avoid the coastal route. An easier way is to take a ferry from Puntarenas to Playa Naranjo or Paquera, which shortens the drive considerably. It's possible that the road is currently in much better condition. Make inquiries first.

**PLAYA TAMBOR** The setting of Tambor is an extraordinarily calm horseshoe bay called Bahía Ballena (Whale Bay). Two long projections of forested and rocky coastline protect beaches from ocean swells. A major tourist attraction used to be the migration of whales into the bay's protected waters during the summer season to give birth. Nowadays, probably because of the increased boating and fishing activity, whales stay further offshore. Bahía Ballena's beaches of dark volcanic sand and shallow water offer perfect swimming for even the most timid of bathers. It's not good for surfing, but it's great for snorkeling and diving. The nearby Curu Wildlife Reserve is known as a place for viewing wildlife and lush vegetation.

This is also the location of a controversial hotel-resort by the Barceló chain. I say controversial because a few years ago the construction caused a maelstrom of controversy, with ecologists accusing the hotel chain of doing damage to the environment in the construction of the hotel. Oddly enough, the huge Playa Tambor resort doesn't seem to affect the atmosphere of the village of Tambor. It's the same laid-back, friendly place as before—ever popular with retired foreigners, who appreciate the conveniences that Tambor offers. You'll find golf, tennis, and a small airport with daily twenty-five-minute flights to San José.

The reason tourism at the expensive resort hasn't affected the town could be the fact that the hotel and grounds are self-contained and guests seldom venture elsewhere. Interesting to note: The hotel enjoys a nice white-sand beach (ecologists complain the sand was imported from elsewhere). The little surf that Tambor beach gets is rather gentle, always peppered with little *tico* children splashing and laughing.

Several gated communities set back on the hillsides are in place, and others presumably are on the drawing boards. A little farther west, the gated community of Tango Mar provides an elegant contrast to funky Playa Tambor. Tango Mar is basically a private (and expensive) resort with deluxe accommodations; it is also a retirement community featuring a small golf course, tennis courts, and a lovely beach.

**MONTEZUMA** Located about 30 kilometers (19 miles) down the road from Playa Tambor, the village of Montezuma is the entry point to a beautiful string of beaches. A description of "laid-back" or "tranquil" would hardly describe this picturesque little village. It is widely known for its bohemian flair and reputation as a party town. Although many tourists you meet are younger, many residents are older, reliving the continuous party scene of the 1970s. Along Montezuma's main street, you'll see a continuous parade of characters, such as aging hippies, tattooed surfers, and Rastafarians, plus some occasional visitors who seem overwhelmed by it all.

Just a few steps from the hustle and bustle of the town center, you find yourself on Playa Grande, a great place for a walk to secluded coves, tide pools, and sunbathing. The village itself is sheltered by vertical cliffs overgrown with vines and green tropical foliage. Several streams flow down from the hills, creating scenic waterfalls and natural swimming pools. Monkeys, parrots, and other wildlife are frequent visitors.

Montezuma is not only a mecca for backpackers and surfers but also a special retirement place for more mature counterculture people. (Maybe I fall into the latter category, because I've always felt right at home in Montezuma with kindred spirits my age blending into the scene.) It's not for the early-to-bed set, needless to say. Gringos who love the Montezuma scene enjoy a lively and active social life; those who covet peace and quiet will probably want to look elsewhere. Residents and businesspeople are very ecology-minded and maintain a continual campaign for clean beaches. The last few miles of road to Montezuma are usually bad during the rainy season.

**MALPAÍS** Malpaís is Spanish for "badlands." The region certainly lives up to its name, with rugged, twisted, and bizarre rock formations breaking the surf as ocean waves crash into spray and foam. Malpaís is said to be one of the better surf destinations in Costa Rica—actually it's at nearby Santa Teresa. The settlements here are located about as far as you can drive around the tip of the peninsula. The road up the other side of the peninsula is just about nonexistent. I've heard people claim they've driven four-wheel drives up the western edge, all the way up the coast to Sámara, but that seems reckless to me.

Along with most of the Nicoya Peninsula's tourist areas, the Malpaís area is continually growing and attracting more retirees and businesses. I can see a promising future for the region if the road is ever paved. The government is eager to develop places such as this and will surely devote whatever resources are available for roads and infrastructure.

Unlike Montezuma, the village of Malpaís can truly be described as tranquil. The area is sparsely settled, with not much in the way of a village commercial center. Rather it's a long collection of houses, restaurants, and small hotels scattered along about 3 kilometers (2 miles) of gravel road parallel to the ocean. Cabo Blanco Nature Preserve is to the south. Despite the small population, a surprising number of expats live here. They live in houses dotting the beaches, some more cliffs than beach. The area seems to be peaceful and quiet, probably as quiet as Montezuma is noisy. The last time we visited, there were a number of development sites being laid out in anticipation of new expatriate settlers.

## MID-PACIFIC **COAST**

If there is any place in Costa Rica that's bound to bloom with foreign investors and retirees, it would have to be that stretch of beachfront from Jacó to Dominical and, with the recently paved road, south toward Palmar Norte.

Although pretty beaches line the entire Pacific Coast, the Mid-Pacific beaches are the most readily accessible for residents of the populous Central Valley. A short drive or bus ride makes this coast practical for overnight sojourns. A weekend home here is convenient and usable by family and friends, whereas one that requires a five-hour drive over horrible roads might sit vacant most of the year. When the coastal highway has been totally paved and time-saving shortcuts completed, a drive from Escazú or other suburbs will take as little as an hour to Jacó or two hours to Dominical. Today, add an extra hour to allow for the dirt road south of Quepos to Dominical.

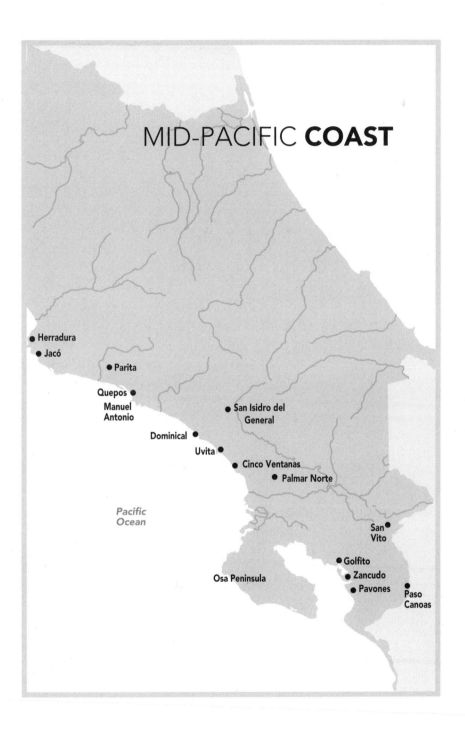

# MID-PACIFIC **COAST**

Herradura

Jacó

Parita

Quepos

Manuel
Antonio

San Isidro del
General

Dominical

Uvita

Cinco Ventanas

Palmar Norte

*Pacific
Ocean*

San
Vito

Golfito

Zancudo

Osa Peninsula

Pavones

Paso
Canoas

**PLAYA JACÓ** Very popular with residents of the San José region, Playa Jacó and other nearby beaches offer the most convenient opportunity to enjoy Pacific Ocean beaches. From the residential resort at Punta Leona to communities south of Jacó, a string of beaches attract thousands of weekenders for surfing, swimming, and partying. Since Jacó is about a two-hour drive from San José, it's entirely possible to drive here in the morning, enjoy the surf, and be home in time for supper. No surprise that many Central Valley residents have weekend homes here. Several hundred North Americans and many Europeans make their permanent homes here, either seasonally or year-round.

Jacó is the largest and most developed town along this portion of the coast, with about 6,000 year-round inhabitants, with at least double this number during the peak tourist months. The town has everything you need, from good medical care to discos and casinos. The main street is sprinkled with open-air restaurants where members of the foreign community can be seen socializing, day or evening. Discos, nightclubs, casinos, and salsa bars make Jacó come alive every night. This is especially attractive to the younger crowd, although it may turn off some of the more sedate residents.

Since Jacó is one place where beach property can be owned rather than leased, it's possible to find a home right on the ocean, with beach and surf for your front yard. Jacó's 3 kilometers (2 miles) of beach are fairly pedestrian and uninspiring when compared with beaches such as Manuel Antonio. Instead of white sand, as you might expect in the tropics, the beach here is dark gray, probably of volcanic origin. However, the surf is more than adequate for those more interested in waves than scenery. There have been a few complaints of pollution from a river that empties into the ocean here, but at last report, the municipality is working on a solution.

Many if not most tourist businesses here are owned by gringos and Europeans. Some do quite well because the area's many tourist attractions bring streams of visitors in search of adventure. Every surf and nature sport, from surfing to crocodile safaris, ensures plenty of tourist business. Two eighteen-hole golf courses are open to public play here, one at Marriott's Los Sueños resort, 5 kilometers (3 miles) north of Jacó, and another 15 kilometers (9 miles) south at Quebrada, Amarilla, the Tulin Resort.

**PLAYA HERRADURA** Playa Herradura is smaller than Jacó, enjoys gentler surf, and has more shade trees. At the moment Herradura offers economical tourist hotels and weekend homes for highland residents, both *ticos* and gringos. But the town extends a promise of better things to come. For a beachfront community, Playa Herradura boasts property that is reasonable—at least compared with prices at Jacó or Manuel Antonio. Many building lots can be found within walking distance of the beach, and construction is booming. An upscale development known as Los Sueños overlooks Playa Herradura. With its large-scale marina, luxury homes, and condos, Los Sueños raises the general tone of Herradura and brings in more development. An eighteen-hole championship golf course is located in the Los Sueños complex.

About 10 kilometers (6 miles) north of Herradura (30 kilometers, or 19 miles, north of Jacó), Punta Leona has an attractive private club (with day admission for nonmembers) with a complex of condos and cottages owned by retirees and weekenders from the Central Valley. Like Los Sueños in Herradura, there is a very safe feeling about these gated communities, but prices reflect the additional costs of privacy and luxury.

**MANUEL ANTONIO** It was the middle of February, and we were sitting with a group of friends in a restaurant overlooking the Pacific. A long, palm-fringed beach stretched out into the distance as far as we could see. Behind us loomed mountains covered with rain forest, sweeping down to accent the beach, with its azure blue water and sparkling surf. The sun was at its zenith, beating directly down with dazzling strength. Two members of our group were complaining about the heat. We consulted a thermometer and found that the temperature was 85 degrees. Suddenly they broke into laughter as they realized that Baltimore, their hometown, was dealing with 4 inches of sleet and snow. Two weeks of Costa Rica's idyllic weather had turned them into indignant complainers over an ordinary 85-degree day at the beach! We all ordered cold beer served over ice cubes (a Costa Rica tradition) and looked out over the panorama with renewed appreciation for where we were: Costa Rica's famous Playa Manuel Antonio.

Manuel Antonio? What kind of name is that for a beach? According to legend, a husband, worried about his pregnant wife, placed her in a dugout canoe and headed north toward Puntarenas, hoping to find a doctor to deliver the baby. But before they could go very far, the wife went into labor, and they paddled ashore to camp in the shelter of a gentle beach cove. His wife gave birth to a healthy child, whom they named Manuel Antonio; the beach has been called that ever since. Travelers who have visited beaches all over the world swear that Manuel Antonio is the most beautiful of all.

The coastline north of Manuel Antonio is a long shore of golden sand that catches the full force of the Pacific's waves as they roll in from China. Then, at Manuel Antonio Park, a narrow peninsula juts out into the ocean, curving to form two protected coves on either side of the land. Here the waves suddenly become gentle, a place where you can float on your back for an hour without worrying about getting surf in your face. You'll often find a sailboat or two anchored here, gently swaying, resting on the way to the Panama Canal or the big voyage north to Acapulco.

Originally United Fruit Company banana property, the area was made into a national park in 1972 with almost 1,730 acres (700 hectares) of land, partially expropriated, partially donated. The park contains three beaches, each with its own character. The first is Playa Espadilla Norte, which sees occasional riptides, although many people swim here anyway. Next

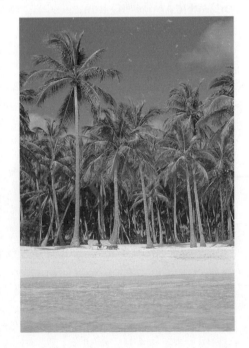

is Playa Espadilla Sur, and then Playa Manuel Antonio, both quite safe for swimming and snorkeling. From the beginning the emphasis has been on preserving the natural beauty and protecting wildlife. Whiteface capuchin monkeys frolic in the trees, competing with arboreal iguanas for food. A tropical storm in 1993 ripped up some of the trees, causing the sloth population to go elsewhere, but other than that the damage was minimal.

Since Manuel Antonio's fame makes it an almost obligatory part of a tourist's itinerary, a bed-and-breakfast or room rentals can be a viable business. Rooms are likely to be rented solidly through the Costa Rica "summer" (December, January, and February) and to have low vacancy rates during the rest of the year. On a past trip we rented an apartment from a woman who came from Florida several years ago to build a small house for herself. She added a couple of rooms for extra income during the tourist season. As the volume of tourism during the off-season increased, she added more rooms until she had a pleasant ten-room hotel, plus two apartments across the road, all with a splendid view of the ocean. "I hadn't considered becoming a hotel owner when I came here," she explained. "It just happened to work out that way."

Over the thirty-plus years that I've been visiting Manuel Antonio, I've seen the most profound changes of anywhere in the country. It has changed from a very rustic, low-density tourist destination to a full-tilt, full-service community. The road from Quepos to Manuel Antonio Park is jam-packed with hotels, restaurants, and other tourist accommodations. Scarcely a square meter of land remains undeveloped. Oddly enough, this doesn't seem to detract one iota from the region's beauty and charm.

**DOMINICAL** South of Quepos and Manuel Antonio, along the 45-kilometer (28-mile) stretch of gravel road to Dominical, you'll find country that is for the most part either palm-oil plantations or flat farming land. This part of the Pacific Coast Highway is a surprise because of the terrible condition it is in. Until recently it took a full two hours of 20-kilometer-per-hour (12-mile-per-hour) driving and bouncing to navigate it. However, the road crews have been doing some impressive work, smoothing roadbed and replacing old, one-way bridges, preparing the road for eventual pavement. Now the driving time to Dominical is closer to one hour.

Before long the Pacific Coast Highway will be paved all the way to Panamá, joining the Inter-American Highway at Palmar Norte. This route will take considerable pressure off the present Inter-American Highway as well as open the region to tourism and development.

As paved roads replace the almost impassable stretches of rock-and-mud obstacle courses, ever-increasing traffic streams along the coast—tourists looking for rooms and retirees buying property. Dominical and its surrounding communities can't help but flourish. As you might guess, many foreign residents prefer things the way they are; they dread the thought of developments and tourists destroying the peace and tranquillity that have been theirs for so long. As one man said, "It is funny to think that in a few years we'll be looking back fondly to the time when there were no traffic lights in Dominical."

If you want to drive on pavement, instead of gravel and rock, all the way to Dominical, travel south on the Inter-American Highway and turn toward the Pacific at San Isidro del General, then just follow the signs through town. Because of San Isidro's system of one-way streets, you may have to ask directions by pointing in whichever direction you are going and asking "Dominical?" Someone will steer you in the right direction.

In its own way, this road is one of the more scenic in all of Costa Rica. The narrow pavement traverses rich farming country, up somewhat steep grades, running along ridges with breathtaking views on both sides of the road, looking into deep valleys where the farmhouses are so distant that they seem like toys. Even during the dry season, the countryside is lushly green, plants heavy with foliage and banana trees shading the roadside. Although the drive is less than 25 miles, it takes about forty-five minutes. That's the way it should be, because the scenery is so spectacular that you might miss something if you could whiz along at 60 miles per hour. Also, the pavement has a way of disappearing from time to time, turning into stretches of gravel road where construction crews are still at work. The problem is not serious; just slow down and relax.

The paved highway ends at the recently paved coastal road at the Barú River, a picturesque mountain stream that empties into a lagoon at this point. A turn to the left, over the river's cement bridge, and you find Dominical. Take the first right turn past the bridge. This is another place I've watched develop over the years, from a sleepy village to an awakening, cosmopolitan community. It is my impression that this region is one of the fastest growing along the coast—at least as far as residential development is concerned. Excellent restaurants and other retail businesses seem to be popping up in response to the growing number of expatriates in the Dominical area.

Dominical's main street follows the river past several rental cabins, motels, restaurants, and businesses. It ends at the beach, where another road follows the shore down to Punta Banda, also known as Roque Azul. Camping beneath a grove of shade trees is free on the edge of the broad, sandy beach of Playa Dominical. Restrooms and showers are strategically

spaced along the beach. For the most part, campers
backpackers, but all are welcome. As with anywhere
careful of leaving valuables in a tent while you are sur
restaurant.

Open ocean surf here is spectacular, booming ac
occasionally making swimming hazardous when riptides h
used to handling them. "You usually don't realize what i.
said a longtime resident here. "It seems as though you are .
the water, yet the beach is moving away from you. We lose
tourists every year to these tides, and it isn't necessary. Instead
swim against the current, the best thing to do is relax and leis
parallel to the beach, until the shore stops moving away. The
only a few feet wide. Then work your way back to shore, pausing
on your back and rest. The water is so warm and salty that you c
all day long and never get tired. There is no reason for anyone to
in a riptide."

The road from Dominical south to Palmar Norte (where it joins
highway going to the Panamanian border) is brand new and a ma
compared with the old rock-and-mud nightmare trail of a few years a
South along this coast, numerous beaches face the open ocean, som
with houses or tiny farms, places that will someday become villages. On
of the prettiest on this part of the coast is called Punta Dominical. A high
point juts out into the ocean, with cliffs and surf reminiscent of California's
Big Sur or Spain's Costa Brava. Below a small hotel, cliffs and rocks catch
the full force of the ocean's strength as waves crash and send cascades of
white foam flying high in the air.

**UVITA AND OJOCHAL** Playa Uvita, according to tourist publications, is
one of the top six most beautiful beaches in Costa Rica. Long described
as a sleepy little village, the town of Uvita has been awakened by the new
paved road from Dominical to the Inter-American Highway at Palmar Sur.
Rapid development is under way as much prime land is now available for
development. According to one report, Uvita now boasts two banks, a
new supermarket that offers a wide range of formerly hard-to-get products, a large new furniture store, and a new appliance store. Residents of
Uvita and nearby Ojochal no longer have to drive to Palmar Sur for shopping. Newcomers seem to be buying property almost weekly.

A longtime resident named Lillian said, "We looked all over Costa [Ric]a before settling on Uvita. We found a ten-hectare [twenty-five-acre] [lo]t up on the mountainside. Not only do we have a gorgeous view, but [th]ere are also six beautiful waterfalls on the property. For me it's like hav[in]g my own national park." She added, "We are holding it in trust for our [tw]o granddaughters, as a future for them."

Nearby Ojochal, 13 kilometers (8 miles) south of Uvita, is about halfway between Dominical and Palmar Norte. The first time I made the drive from Dominical to Ojochal, in 1993, the trip took two hours of hard driving. Today, with the smoothly paved highway it's just a matter of twenty minutes or so. The road zips on down the coast past areas that before were seen only by four-wheel-drive daredevils. This growing little paradise village consists of a variety of hotels, restaurants, bars, and various businesses. Ojochal offers many amenities, including a doctor's and a dentist's office, hardware store, supermarket, beauty salon–barbershop, and more. According to locals, the village is growing and attracting newcomers from the United States and Canada. A new hospital is located in Ojo de Agua, just 13 kilometers (8 miles) to the south of Ojochal. This is in addition to the hospital in Palmar Norte.

One very interesting place we encountered on a trip to the Osa Peninsula is called Cinco Ventanas, a little north of the village of Ojochal. Even though development here is rather new, there are already 1,400 properties owned by foreigners (only a few live here full-time). A fourteen-unit shopping center, including a small supermarket, gasoline station, and restaurant, serves the area. The majority of the foreign property owners are French-Canadian, but other North Americans are discovering the area and will be moving in as well.

The developer explained why there are so many French-speaking residents: When she and her husband started their project here, they advertised heavily in the Quebec area as an experiment. They sold building lots by mail, with the buyers being assured that if they didn't like the property when they arrived, they could either have their money back or choose another lot. Before long, most of the lots they had were gone, bought by French-speakers. "They just love it here," she said, "and since French is similar to Spanish, they have no problems with language."

Just east of Ojochal and Cinco Ventanas, the mountains quickly rise to more than 3,000 feet, probably providing the same kind of "air-conditioning" as in Dominical, with cool breezes coming inland during the hot part of the day and flowing down the mountains at night. By the way, the name Cinco Ventanas (Five Windows) refers to some natural caverns in the cliffs by the water's edge. Residents in this area have exclusive rights to cross the private land between the highway to Playa Ventanas, a small bay with a wide beach and bordered on both sides by rocky cliffs ranging in height from 60 to 200 feet, making this one of the few "private" beaches in the country.

## SOUTHERN **COSTA RICA**

For years I had heard people speak of Golfito and the Osa Peninsula. The area sounded like a place of adventure—panning for gold in forest streams, fishing for trophy sailfish, or hiking rain-forest trails. In order to complete research for this book, I resolved to spend some time around Golfito to collect information. But when I asked folks around San José who either owned property or regularly visited here, I found their answers short and vague, always skirting the subject as if trying to draw my attention elsewhere. When I spoke with a man who owned property on Zancudo Beach, his face burned angrily as he said, "Zancudo is my special place, and I don't want any damned travel writers drawing attention to it! It would destroy things for all of us!"

Obviously, our interview was over, but now I knew I had to go! I jumped in a car and was soon on my way to Golfito, the jumping-off place for the Pavones–Zancudo Beach area. The drive south on the Inter-American Highway is gorgeous. One unbelievable view after another invites a pause wherever the car can be parked safely off the pavement. Ordinarily the trip takes six hours, but by the time I stopped several times to sample pork *chicharrones,* marvel over the views, and take a nap in the shade of a banana tree, the trip stretched into an eight-hour day.

**GOLFITO** Golfito is the jumping-off place for nearby and regional expatriate communities. This is an often neglected part of Costa Rica, with scanty information provided by most tourist guides. The town of Golfito began its existence as a banana port for United Fruit Company but was abandoned when a disease damaged the banana crops and the company decided that the operation had become unprofitable. When it was a banana port, there was no incentive to develop it as a tourist attraction, although today the area is trying hard to do so.

The town itself can hardly be described as anything but picturesque. It looks like a cliché movie set of a banana-shipping port. Just a few blocks wide, the town follows the water's edge, with some houses actually standing over the water on stilts and others clinging to the cliffs and hanging out into empty space. A couple of excellent hotels accommodate the growing number of curious tourists, but many lodgings are rather ordinary to downright rustic. They are often full with Costa Rican shoppers who take advantage of the port's duty-free warehouse. From the slope of a low mountainside overlooking the town, a rain forest serves as a wildlife preserve and watershed, ensuring Golfito a pure water supply.

Golfito's main commercial street, looking delightfully ramshackle and picturesque, climbs a hill that parallels the highway and waterfront. Foreign residents patronize a couple of open-air restaurants here, as well as hardware stores, shops selling tackle and boating supplies, and several red-light bars. A surprising number of North Americans live in or around Golfito. A few actually live in town, but most have places scattered along the shores of Golfo Dulce and commute via motorboat. Ferries commute between Puerto Jiménez and to Zancudo. You'll often see expats hanging out in the restaurants in the commercial area or along the waterfront. Ask around to find out which are the favorite haunts of the day.

The government is working hard to bolster the economy in this region, trying to attract new businesses to fill the void left when United Fruit abandoned ship. One popular program that brings hoards of residents into Golfito: duty-free warehouses. Anybody, resident or tourist with a passport, can obtain a permit to enter these warehouses and purchase a wide variety of goods duty-free. To make sure that Golfito tourist facilities gain from this, buyers must register the day before—thus ensuring that they will spend money on meals and accommodations. You are allowed $500 per person tax-free every six months.

Another project that helps local commerce is a Free Trade Zone, a special place for manufacturing and exporting by Costa Rican and foreign businesses. Those operating within the zone's coverage are exempt from some taxes and customs on importation of raw materials, components, and parts. This should attract investors who would like to take advantage of the tax breaks and the availability of good local workers.

**ZANCUDO BEACH** Although Golfito is the central focus of the area, many North Americans prefer to live nearby rather than in the town. Their homes and business interests are in nearby villages or on isolated bays around the Golfo Dulce. Playa Zancudo is one of the secluded communities that attracts expatriates. It's a relatively small village stretching along one sandy street with a handful of restaurants, cabin rentals, and a small hotel or two. The black-sand beach is backed by homes not far from the water's edge but concealed from the view of swimmers and surfers by the usual coconut and strangler fig trees. Zancudo is a popular place for local *ticos* to come to swim on weekends. Unlike Pavones, the famous surfing beach to the south, Zancudo's beach is very swimmable, with gentle surf.

Several bars and restaurants serve as social centers, with occasional weekend dances. A stop at any of the local open-air restaurants will usually find a table or two of North Americans or Europeans discussing local news and making plans for the development of their properties. Paving the road is a common topic. Those who own homes along the beach shudder in horror at the image of the throngs of tourists, property buyers, and developers a paved highway will surely bring. They feel that since they have discovered this part of Costa Rica, it is rightly theirs, and it would be downright rude for others to crowd in. (I'm exaggerating, of course. Residents of Zancudo are as gracious as you will find anywhere.) Actually, those who have businesses, who depend on tourists and new residents to make their enterprises grow, eagerly look forward to the road and the increased prosperity popularity brings. Property owners are delighted to see values of their holdings increasing.

We spoke with several folks who routinely come here for three months or longer every year. A house or a cabin with a small kitchen, right on the beach, can usually be found at reasonable rents during the off-season. By all means, stay for a couple of months before deciding to invest or build, get to know the other expatriates, and know whether you will find enough compatible friends. This will also give you the opportunity to talk with local residents and get the latest on land values and who has properties for sale.

A local resident remarked, "Everyone wants to come here in the winter months [referring to winter and summer in the North American sense]. People seem to think that summer is a total monsoon. But the weather is wonderful then. It's actually a little cooler during June, July, and August. Every morning is sunny, and at least part of the afternoon is usually rain-free. Often it doesn't rain at all." The hottest month of the year is March, according to local residents, just before the rainy season gets started.

Buses and stake-bed trucks bring families from nearby towns on weekends, loaded with children eager to enjoy the beach. The waves are gentle, the water's warm, and the kids are in danger of nothing worse than sunburn. An easier way to get here is by water taxi from Golfito. Schedules vary with the tides.

The shortest way to the beach is a two-hour drive over a gravel and sometimes rocky trail. This same road splits off and goes to Zancudo's sister beach to the south, Pavones. During the rainy season this route requires a four-wheel-drive vehicle, and it's not all that great in the summer. Maps don't help much in finding either Zancudo or Pavones. I have three different maps; for all practical purposes they might as well have been of three different countries, because each has a different version of the road system, none approaching reality. It's best to stop often and make inquiries.

**SAN VITO** Shortly after World War II, Luigi Sansonetti and his three sons, from Italy, decided to investigate Costa Rica as a place for a new beginning, away from the chaos of postwar Europe. They fell in love with a beautiful valley surrounded by mountains and rain forests. Their discovery was in the canton of Coto Brus, just north of the Panamanian border, in one of the coastal mountain ranges of the southern region. At 3,200 feet (975 meters) above sea level, with cool mountain breezes and ample rainfall, this seemed to be the perfect place to grow coffee and begin life anew.

They notified friends and relatives back in Italy of their discovery and invited them to relocate here. Before long, Italian immigrants were settling the town of San Vito de Coto Brus and planting coffee on the hillsides. It wasn't easy. The pioneers suffered hardships as they established their colony: hand-sawing huge trees for lumber and cutting them into boards to build houses; no electricity; little food; having to wait for three years for coffee to be ready for harvesting. Partly by courage but mostly by stubborn determination, they survived.

Fortunately, in the early 1950s the world market for quality Costa Rican coffee was at an all-time high. Coffee plantations could not help but prosper. Their economic success is reflected in San Vito's infrastructure today and in the quality of homes and farms surrounding the town. You'll find banks, supermarkets, Internet centers, great restaurants and bakeries, and taxi service, as well as a hospital and nearby airport. A charming plaza in the town center makes a pleasant place for young people to congregate and residents to relax.

San Vito's population today is around 10,000, and the town still displays prosperity, even though the coffee market tanked several years ago. Many of the original families have moved on, but they've left their mark on today's population. Around the square and in outdoor cafes, you'll see beautiful young people with faintly olive-colored skin and strikingly beautiful gray-blue eyes characteristic of regions in Italy. You'll often hear Italian spoken. You might hear *ciao* instead of *adios* when someone says goodbye.

San Vito's best restaurants are Italian, as you might expect. One is the dining room of the popular Hotel Ceibo, where lasagna, scaloppine, and other traditional dishes are served. The owner, Antonio Papili, was one of the original settlers; he was five years old when his family immigrated from

Italy. He is proud of his heritage, and it doesn't take much encouragement for Antonio and his wife, Carmen, to talk about the old days.

I have to admit that I had reservations about including San Vito in this book. Why? Because I made friends with some of the North Americans who've relocated here, and because some worried that publicity might cause a land rush, bringing hordes of new residents, along with some undesirables. I gained their grudging support when I pointed out two things: First, adding a few new residents would only increase their support group of English-speaking neighbors, and second, the undesirables they have in mind are the types who prefer the action of beachfront discos and all-night reggae or rap music. All of which are extremely rare in San Vito.

I am convinced that it will be some time before we'll see surfboards and party animals elbowing aside the two dozen or so expatriates in residence in San Vito. The most exciting things to do here are gazing at breathtaking vistas of the mountainous Amistad International Park and the volcano across the Panamá border; visiting the nearby, world-famous Wilson Botanical Gardens; and having cocktails at homes of other San Vito expatriates.

# THE
# CARIBBEAN COAST

The same mountain chain that creates the delightful temperate weather in Costa Rica's highlands separates the country into eastern and western tropical zones. Because of this separation, the Caribbean and the Pacific zones have dissimilar personalities. Not only will you find differences in weather patterns and varieties of animal, plant, and marine life, but distinctive cultural differences as well. The Caribbean is Jamaican/African; the Pacific is Latin/European.

The word *tropics* implies long stretches of deserted beaches with thick jungle hovering at the edge of the sand. It means monkeys jostling branches in the strangler fig trees while parrots, macaws, and a thousand other birds screech, twitter, and sing lyrically in the sunset. Costa Rica's Caribbean Coast has all of the above and much more.

Often referred to as the Talamanca Coast, it consists of two distinct regions. The northern half is almost uninhabited, visited mostly by fishing fanatics, tourists, and ecology students. (Incidentally, Costa Ricans usually refer to this entire coast as the "Atlantic" rather than the "Caribbean.") The southern coast is populated with a mixture of Jamaican culture and black, white, and Indian races, creating a distinct type of *tico* personality.

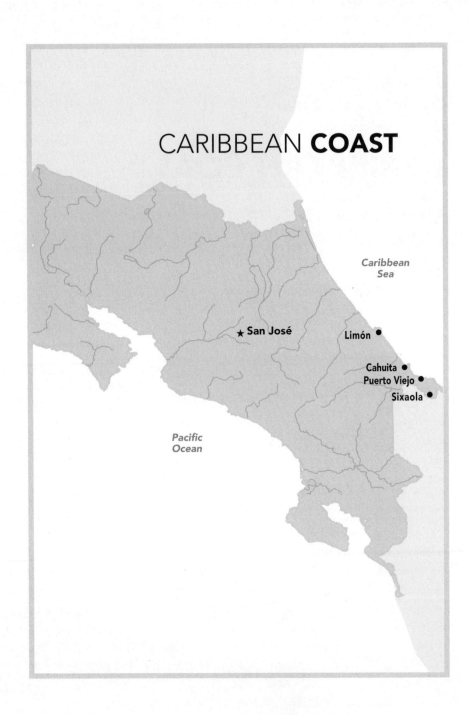

CARIBBEAN **COAST**

Caribbean
Sea

★ San José

Limón ●

Cahuita ●
Puerto Viejo ●
Sixaola ●

Pacific
Ocean

The northern inland lagoons and waterways are famous for world-class fishing of all kinds. Record-size tarpon and snook are routinely hooked in these scenic jungle rivers and inlets. The best snook angling is usually from the shore, around river mouths, with twenty- to thirty-pounders not uncommon. Fishermen also bring in jacks, mackerel, barracuda, snapper, and other species when fishing the Caribbean Coast. While waiting for exciting action, you are treated to the sight of monkeys frolicking in the trees, an occasional parrot or toucan darting among the branches, and sometimes a crocodile lurking along the shoreline. The Tortuguero area is known as an important nesting place of the endangered green sea turtle.

No passable roads enter this northern region; the only way to get here is by airplane or motor launch. My belief is that the area is far too isolated and the climate too humid for development other than ecotourism projects.

## SOUTHERN **CARIBBEAN**

The southern Caribbean Coast attracts surfers, snorkelers, and reggae enthusiasts, as well as ordinary tourists and ecology buffs who want to savor the unique tropical environment. Weather patterns here are unpredictable, with no sharp distinction between winter and summer. Rain can fall at any time and usually does. Winds often blow down from the north, sometimes causing the Caribbean Coast to replicate Miami's weather. The plus side of the Caribbean weather is that things stay green and lush year-round, unlike the Pacific Coast, where it seldom rains between December and May. The downside is that this weather is always more humid, and insects tend to grow healthy and robust on this edge of the continent.

There is a tendency among North American expatriates to view this region with suspicion due to crime and drug use. There have been a couple news stories of crimes that did severe damage to the tourist image. However, those who live here paint an entirely different picture. They point out that these incidents can happen anywhere, and just by chance they occurred in their region.

Our experience with this area is limited to short stays and visits with friends, never staying more than a few weeks at a time. Therefore I felt it would be best to get opinions from folks who actually live here before making recommendations for relocation. We've interviewed several expatriates who live on the Caribbean Coast for their views and recommendations. One person—who prefers to be called "Expat Hatch"—lives near Puerto Viejo and had the following to say about the eastern coast of Costa Rica:

"The Talamanca Coast (not Limón city, but from Hone Creek to Puerto Viejo, then down to Manzanillo) to me represents what *pura vida* is all about: the jungle, the beach, the environment, and the people. A unique mix that you either love or you hate. I happen to love it.

"Yes, there is the Caribbean drug corridor, but the serious things that go down remain largely invisible—just don't get involved. And yes, you may find yourself feeling even more laid-back after breathing the ganja-laden collective cloud coming from backpacker and surfer hangouts and wafting over the area from Playa Negro to Playa Cocles. But if crime were truly serious here, you wouldn't see the elderly gringo ladies who live here riding their bikes up and down the road with smiles on their faces.

"I personally believe that most of the negative hype about the Caribbean side boils down to culture shock. Things are definitely not clean and tidy there. Limón is a third-world city populated by Caribbean descendants of Jamaica, Panamá, and Nicaragua. If that's not what you want to experience, then don't go there, because it's not been prettied up for tourism at this point.

"But as you go from Limón down the Talamanca coast, you will meet a broad mix of people: *ticos*, indigenous Indians, Jamaicans, Panamanians, Nicaraguans, and Europeans such as German, French, Polish, and Italian. It truly becomes a rainbow soup of humanity, which I personally think makes it that much more interesting.

"But *pura vida* does have a price here—forget making a list of twenty things to do in the day. Because you'll only get two of them done if you're lucky. Things are more primitive here. I just smile, say *¡Pura vida!* to myself and chalk it up to the universe forcing me to slow down after working seventy-hour weeks in the U.S.A. rat race for so many years. The bottom line for me is that I can sit in a hammock writing on my laptop, with the beach in front of me, the jungle behind me, and howler monkeys making awesome sounds while they meander through the trees in my backyard. That's why I moved to Costa Rica—not for conveniences."

**LIMÓN** The city of Limón, a two-and-a-half-hour drive from San José, is probably where Columbus sighted the American mainland for the first time back in 1502. Since nothing of value was found, the explorers moved on, leaving this coast to the native Indians. Later, scattered villages cropped up where bananas were grown for export. Until a railroad was constructed from San José to Limón, the area was mostly ignored by those living in the highlands. Many of the settlers were English-speaking Jamaicans of African descent. Many came to work on the banana plantations and later to build the railroad.

At best, the city of Limón has always been a ramshackle affair—a tropical banana port, too large to have the charm of a small town, yet too small to offer the amenities of a real city. The population is predominately black, and the major business here is related to shipping. Not many expatriates will care to relocate here, in my opinion.

Having exposed my bias toward Limón, I must point out that there are those who disagree with me. A number of North Americans who reside in the community testify to the charm and friendliness of their African/Jamaican neighbors. Racial tensions, resentment, and animosity that are so common in some U.S. cities are virtually unknown here. The social atmosphere here is relaxed, friendly, and neighborly. In fact, Costa Rican race relations and attitudes toward citizens of color are very different from those in many other parts of the world. Because many people in Limón speak perfect Spanish as well as English (with a British-Jamaican accent), those with education are much in demand in the business world. They often find positions as supervisors or managers. They can communicate with London, New York, or Geneva (English being the lingua franca of business today), and they can deal with North Americans and Europeans who speak very little Spanish.

The number of foreigners living in Limón is difficult to ascertain. I asked a friend who lives in Limón to make an estimate, and he replied, "I can't put a solid number on the expats here, but we just celebrated Thanksgiving with about twenty-five of them. We had a great dinner with turkey and all the trimmings—a full-blown Turkey Day, including watching football. I've met teachers in the Caribbean School [English-Spanish], Peace Corps people, semiretirees, evangelical missionaries, and ship's chandlers [people who are commissioned to buy or supply provisions for all the freighters that come into port]. We have also run into a few retired people who have been here for many years and still haven't learned any Spanish."

**CAHUITA** More than 150 years ago, the beaches of Cahuita and Puerto Viejo were uninhabited except for seasonal campsites of Miskito Indians who followed the migration of green and hawksbill turtles. ("Miskitos" are a mixture of native Indians and escaped African slaves who fled Jamaica and Cuba to settle the coasts of Nicaragua and Panamá.) The newcomers named their camp *Cahuita*, which means "Point of blood trees" in Miskito dialect, because of the large number of blood trees growing on the promontory now known as Cahuita Point.

The region remained uninhabited until the late 1800s, when William Smith, an English-speaking Afro-Caribbean who came from Panamá every year to fish and hunt turtles, decided to build a permanent home on Cahuita's beach. He was joined by a group of Jamaicans who originally came as construction workers on the railway from Limón to San José. In addition to working on the United Fruit Company's banana plantations, the settlers worked at subsistence farming, hunting, fishing, and small-scale cultivation of cocoa. Settlers here were pretty much self-sufficient, having had little contact with the rest of Costa Rica. (In fact, for many years the central government prevented people from the coast from traveling to the highlands for fear of spreading yellow fever and malaria.) The first road to Cahuita didn't connect with the outside world until 1976. This isolation enabled people here to preserve their African-Jamaican-Caribbean heritage and bring it intact into the twenty-first century.

Because English is the area's first language (usually spoken with a delightful Jamaican patois), this area is favored by tourists and visitors who don't want to bother learning another language during their stay. The genuine lack of racial tension here is refreshing for those of us who have been used to the self-imposed social barriers and chasms of hostility that separate black from white in some areas of the United States. I personally feel welcome here and enjoy basking in the warmth of genuine hospitality.

The village of Cahuita is a three-and-a-half-hour scenic drive from San José. It's about four hours by bus. The village's Afro-Caribbean setting has a picture-book quality. Many houses stand on stilts to discourage insects, as is the custom in African and Caribbean villages. These buildings tend to be painted with bright, contrasting pigments similar to the flamboyant styles of Jamaica. Slender, colorfully dressed women and girls carry bundles on their heads with grace and enviable posture. It's easy to imagine you are in an African seashore village.

The main road follows the shore, past black-sand beaches and coral reefs to the north and past more coral and beaches of yellow sand to the south. Along the yellow-sand beach is Cahuita National Park, a 13-kilometer (8-mile) stretch of jungle complete with howler monkeys (which the Costa Ricans call *congos*), feisty parrots, and wildlife of all descriptions. A foot trail parallels the beach through a

thick tangle of tropical trees, vines, and orchids. Butterflies, orange and purple land crabs, and iguanas keep you company on the hike.

Many North Americans and Europeans live here year-round, some operating successful businesses. Others regularly arrive in November and head home by May. I had the good fortune to meet a young Californian couple who invited me to visit their winter quarters in Cahuita. They lived in a picturesque, thatch-roofed cabin perched next to a coral reef and shaded by graceful coconut trees. Their house was very rustic, with minimal furniture, but they enjoyed their winter home immensely. Surf washed over rocks in front of the home, spilling into a small depression of smooth black coral where their children played in their own private saltwater swimming pool.

**PUERTO VIEJO** The village of Puerto Viejo is 16 kilometers (10 miles) south of Cahuita by road and somewhat less by the beach trail. To make matters a bit confusing, there are two Costa Rican places called Puerto Viejo. The one here is formally called Puerto Viejo de Limón, and the other is a small river town in the northeast, near La Selva Reserve: Puerto Viejo de Sarapiquí.

This Puerto Viejo, on the southern Caribbean Coast, used to be much more sleepy than its sister village of Cahuita. Things have changed, with surfers, Rastafarians, and tourists of all descriptions now thronging through the town. Puerto Viejo has the reputation of being one of the hippest spots in Costa Rica. When discos are going full tilt, especially on weekends, you might find it impossible to find a room. Young visitors and adventure seekers, mostly from North America and Europe, crowd the streets in the evening, visiting bars and restaurants throbbing with reggae music.

Yet, intermingled with the under-twenty-five crowd, an older generation of expatriates has its own parallel scene. Dozens of retirees, residents, business owners, and seasonal visitors age fifty and way above live here, many of their homes just steps from the main street action. They blend in with the younger generation as smoothly as cream and coffee liquor.

There's no question that the beaches here are much nicer than Cahuita, as is the case down the coast, toward the Panamanian border. Not only that, the businesses, bars, restaurants, and so forth are just steps from the beach, often visible through palm trees from the bar stool where you are sitting. An additional attraction is that homes can be built within 328 feet (100 meters) of the surf, a happy condition of which many expatriates take full advantage.

## WHY THE **CARIBBEAN COAST?**

People who love Cahuita and Puerto Viejo will tell you that the rest of Costa Rica is too tame for them. They prefer this movie-set tropical ambience: romantic, picturesque, and inexpensive. One bar in the very center of Cahuita features on its front porch extraordinarily powerful loudspeakers blaring Jamaican rock music day and night. The volume was such that it rattled windows a block away and peeled the paint off passing automobiles. I love to visit here, but for long-term living in the tropics, my personal preference would be the Pacific Coast. It's my age, I suppose.

Others have a completely different take of lifestyles on the Caribbean. To get yet another viewpoint and perspective, I took advantage of my friendship with a couple who make their home in Puerto Viejo by asking how they made their decision.

Doug and Rosin Warren, who moved here from Arizona a few years ago, said that numerous other people had e-mailed similar questions about living on Costa Rica's east coast. They wanted to know the "whys" of choosing the Caribbean side rather than other, more popular, sections of the country. Here's what Doug had to say about living here:

"We made our decision from the position of someone who wants to live on or very near a beautiful, tropical beach," Doug says. "We realize we're in the minority, since many more people prefer the Pacific beaches. Our viewpoint is sort of a Caribbean versus Pacific comparison, so here it is:

"We honestly believe that the southern Caribbean Coast is the best-kept secret in this entire country. The 20 miles [32 kilometers] or so from Cahuita down through Puerto Viejo and Manzanillo and to the Panamanian border have some of the most beautiful beaches I've ever seen, with white sand and palm trees, where the jungle comes right down to the shoreline. For the most part, the beaches are almost deserted. You can have a whole cove all to yourself if you want.

"On the last 5 miles [8 kilometers] of this section, from Manzanillo to the border, there's not even a road! You walk along an easy trail, right on the beach, and you see nobody. Beaches here are spectacular, clean, unspoiled—if you feel like skinny-dipping in crystal-clear, warm water, knock yourself out!

"Weather is another important factor: 70 degrees early in the morning and then about 85 degrees in the afternoon—that's all twelve months of the year! We don't keep blankets on the bed, just a couple of sheets. The downside is that there is no defined dry season. It can rain anytime, but the showers are usually short, and the rain is always warm.

"Another reason for choosing this area is the price of land. It's much cheaper than just about any place the Pacific side. Our house is 100 meters [328 feet] from the beach, sitting back in the jungle. When we relax on our veranda, we can hear the ocean, but we can't see it. On all four sides of the house, trees grow 30 to 60 feet [9 to 18 meters] high; it's lush with vegetation—all you can see is green. In the front yard we frequently see three-toed sloths, iguanas, parrots, gorgeous blue morphus butterflies, and more. I'm the first to admit that this is not paradise, but it is damn close to it.

"We had the house built a few years ago: two bedrooms, one bath, a little more than 1,300 square feet, with a huge veranda out front, a covered carport, and gorgeous hardwood floors (we sort of splurged on that).

Total cost of land and building was about $45,000. Try doing that over in Tamarindo, with just a minute's walk to the beach!

"Another reason we love it here: Small villages are cool places where everyone knows everyone else. When we go into the grocery store, the hardware store, or the bank, they call us by name. That's a touch you just don't find anymore. Yes, I've read about how crime is so bad on this side of the country, but I really have no idea where all that comes from! Sure, petty theft is 'alive and well' over here (as it is everywhere); we've had hiking boots and other items taken from our porch when we were foolish enough to leave them out at night. But neither our house nor our car has ever been broken into. (By the way, we do not have bars on any of our doors or windows. I refuse to live in a prison.) We feel perfectly safe strolling through the village at night or walking along the beach at any hour. We do it all the time; we just use common sense.

"Maybe the main reasons we chose this coast are the attitude of the people and the laid-back lifestyle. There's a very strong Jamaican 'yeah, Mon' sort of thing here; it's unlike anywhere else in Costa Rica. You almost get the feeling that time stood still on this coast. They say it looks pretty much the way it did forty years ago. On the other hand, you'll find places on the Pacific side where, if you didn't know better, you'd think you were in San Diego or Hawaii. Thank God, the big resorts and commercial developers haven't discovered this place yet.

"I will be the first to agree that this coast is not for everyone: no shopping centers, no movie theaters, no golf courses. But that is exactly why we live here! If we had wanted all of that other stuff, we would have stayed in the States! To sum it up in terms of my '60s generation: 'If you were a yuppie, you belong on the Pacific side. If you were a hippie, come on over here!'"

# A HEALTHY **COUNTRY**

Costa Rica is a healthy place to live. The United Nations noted that Costa Rica is in first place in Latin America for the development of preventive and curative medicine, ranking with the United States and Canada among the twenty best in the world. Infant mortality is lower in Costa Rica than in the United States, and the average life expectancy is longer than in the United States. This is not happenstance: The Costa Rican government spends a great deal of money on health care.

For example, in many third-world countries, you play a game of Russian roulette every time you choose a restaurant. A dining room can look wonderful, with white tablecloths, gleaming silverware, and tuxedo-attired waiters, but the kitchen can be a virtual cesspool. Not so in Costa Rica. If a restaurant looks good, then its kitchen will probably be just as nice. I've found very few places where I would hesitate to eat, and I've never been served spoiled food. This is due in some measure to the high quality of the underground water supply but also to the *ticos'* natural inclination toward neatness and order. The level of cleanliness of Costa Rican restaurants is remarkable. This is reinforced by frequent visits by health inspectors to make sure that the normal *tico* cleanliness is maintained.

Another factor in restaurant safety is the relative scarcity of houseflies in most parts of Costa Rica. Since this is the tropics, you might expect to see more insects than you would in the temperate zones of North America, and you do, but in balance. For some reason you'll see remarkably few houseflies, true villains in spreading intestinal disease. In San José and other towns on the Central Plateau, you can eat outside at a sidewalk cafe without sharing your lunch with flies. This seems strange to visitors from North America's Midwest, where the fly population blooms in the

summer to a plague. Yes, an occasional fly might drift past, curious as to what you are having for lunch and hoping to join you, but nothing like you expect back home in the summer.

The same thing goes for mosquitoes: In the dry season they are as scarce as houseflies. In many areas of Costa Rica, people don't use window screens. (I wouldn't advise this, because you never know what kind of critter might be attracted to house lights in the evening.) However, when in an area where dengue fever is known, mosquito repellent is essential. Mosquitoes can carry this flulike illness, which has also appeared in the southeastern United States. So far it's affected only a few parts of Costa Rica, around Puntarenas and Cañas. A continuing campaign to wipe out the particular mosquito that carries the virus is under way.

One health condition that never fails to impress visitors: You can drink the water. Unlike most Mexican and Central American cities, safe drinking water is the rule rather than the exception. Most smaller towns have excellent-quality water, as do most hotels, where drinking water comes from safe wells. As part of its commitment to serving the public, the Costa Rican government spends large sums of money on water and sewage treatment. All water systems, even private ones used by only a handful of people, are strictly monitored. Every two months, at a minimum, tests are made for purity and submitted to the government agency overseeing water control.

## COSTA RICA **MEDICAL CARE**

The U.S. health-care system, with its exclusion of more than forty million citizens from the ranks of the medically insured, is a major reason some folks think favorably about living in a country where health care is not only available but affordable. In a typical U.S. hospital, for example, patients with Medicare coverage usually pay more for the deductible share of an operation than the total surgical and hospital bill might cost in Costa Rica.

Should you visit an emergency room in the United States, you have to provide proof of a hospitalization plan or a personal credit card. If you have neither, you could be told to get lost. If you have Medicare, you will find a growing number of doctors who won't accept you as a patient. When someone goes to an emergency room in any government hospital in Costa Rica, there is no mandatory charge for resident, visitor, or even someone in the country illegally. If you can pay, they appreciate it, but you will never be turned away. This affordable medical system is another of the benefits Costa Rica enjoys because there is no military or defense industry to absorb resources. Statistics show that the general level of care is equal or superior to that in the United States—and it's available to all citizens, not just those who can afford premiums.

Obviously, the level of health care and facilities cannot be the same in rural and isolated communities as in the metropolitan area of San José. Yet the government tries. To ensure that most villages have medical backup, a system of mandatory medical service sends newly graduated doctors to remote or rural settings for a one-year period. These new doctors have to work for minimum wages for this time as a way of repaying the country for the education received in state universities.

Why is quality health care inexpensive in Costa Rica? A prominent physician (in private practice in San José) explained it this way: "Here, our government considers medical care a public service and obligation, just as it considers education and highways a public responsibility. The government builds hospitals and trains medical specialists to serve the people, not as a business. But in the United States, medical care is a profit-making industry, a big business where profits are maximized to the highest point people can pay. Here, a doctor working for a government clinic earns between $2,000 and $4,000 a month. In the U.S.A., where doctors work for profit, $20,000 a month is more common."

The doctor went on to say, "Where there is no competition, medical specialists can charge what they like. But here in Costa Rica, we have competition between our free public hospitals and private clinics staffed with private doctors such as mine. We private doctors must keep our fees in line or we lose our patients to free clinics."

## MEDICAL **BILLS**

In San José a routine visit to a private physician's office costs between $25 and $50. Specialists tend to charge toward the upper end of the scale. A day in a first-class private hospital can cost less than $200. Hospital food is excellent, by the way, not the skimpy, tasteless food we're used to in U.S. hospitals, but delicious food and usually more than you can eat. That $200 rate is at one of the country's better hospitals—for a private room, a private bath, and a color television, plus an extra bed and meals for an *acompañate* (a companion). It's customary for a family member or friend to spend the night in your room after an operation or when you are in serious condition, at no extra charge.

If you are willing to put up with sharing a bath with the room next door and can do without your own private phone, the daily room cost can drop to almost half. Think about it: A day in a first-class hospital in Costa Rica costs the same as an ordinary hotel room in New York City! Compare these prices with those in your community. In the United States, if you can get out of a hospital for less than $2,000 a day just for the room, consider yourself lucky.

## MEDICAL **INSURANCE**

An appreciable number of folks decide on Costa Rica residency because of the country's excellent and affordable health-care system. This applies particularly to those quitting their jobs and retiring before the magic age of sixty-five, when Medicare kicks in. With no health care benefits coming from the workplace, early retirees join the forty-million-plus U.S. citizens who face total disaster should a life-threatening illness or an accident strike.

There are two systems of medical insurance available in Costa Rica for residents. The government's INS insurance monopoly coverage, and the government's Social Security system. Some people choose to belong to both plans, for reasons that will be explained later. Understand, Medicare is not valid outside of the United States.

The government insurance plan costs around $50 a month for men under age fifty-nine, and around $85 a month for men between the ages of sixty and seventy-five. The plan covers 70 percent of examinations, doctor visits, prescription drugs, hospitalization, and 100 percent of surgeons' and anesthetists' fees, up to a limit of $17,500. You can choose your own doctor, which is important. Over age seventy-five, you cannot apply for coverage. Dependants under nineteen years old pay about $22 per month; women between ages nineteen and fifty-nine pay about $75 a month, and women sixty to seventy-four pay about $110 monthly. Therefore, a couple in their early sixties would be paying under $200 a month for excellent coverage, impossible to match in the United States.

Several clubs and organizations offer insurance with a group discount (usually 10 percent). Among these are the Association of Residents of Costa Rica (ARCR), the American Legion, and the Canadian Club; sometimes a property owners' association can obtain the discount. Most plans allow you access to any doctor, hospital, clinic, lab, pharmacy, or provider of medical goods and services of your choice. Under other policy plans, you are given a list of affiliated providers.

Foreign residents can also "buy into" the Social Security system (*Caja*, as it's called in Costa Rica) by paying $37 per month for a family where the principal insured person is over fifty-five years of age, and $58 per month where the principal insured is under the age of fifty-five. It may sound odd that younger policy holders pay more than older ones, but this is because if you're younger than fifty-five, your premium includes a compulsory pension fund payment. Presumably, at some time you will receive this back.

However, since Costa Rica's Social Security medical care is almost free, it isn't surprising to find the public system well used and crowded. When people don't feel quite up to snuff, they traipse off to the hospital to see a doctor. This means long waits. For emergency treatment there is no problem—you are seen immediately—but for an ordinary office visit with a government doctor, you could find yourself standing in line or sitting in the waiting room for a long while. And you don't have a choice of doctors. For elective surgery, you can expect a wait of several months for your turn.

However, there is a better way. By joining both systems, you can use your personal family doctor who is in both public and private practice. That way you can see your private doctor by making an appointment whenever you have a minor problem and paying for an office visit. But if something expensive comes up, such as a major operation, your doctor will check you into the government hospital for free treatment—and you are treated by your personal doctor.

Even if you don't choose to have medical insurance, costs are ridiculously low compared with those in the United States. For example, in San José the typical bill for a gallbladder operation is $2,500, and for an appendectomy, $1,200 to $1,800. Again, for those with Medicare, be aware that you're not covered outside the United States. If something really serious comes up, you can always fly back to the States and use your Medicare benefits.

All expatriates we interviewed swear by the quality of Costa Rican medical care. A friend told me: "I've had good and bad experiences with the *Caja*. I had an emergency appendectomy, got great treatment, speedy, all good, that would have been a whopping $300 out of pocket if I had not had the *Caja* (at Hospital Mexico)."

Another says, "My son has had excellent care since birth for his hyperthyroid condition, and an operation he had for frozen head plates came out fine. Hospital de Niños is first-rate. But my cancer situation was different. I had a couple of small operations, then went out of the system for a third, because I felt I was not getting the kind of care I needed. My out-of-pocket for massive surgery (radical neck dissection), six hours in the O.R. at Clinica Biblica, whole thing, O.R., surgeon (U.S. residency at U Michigan and U Miami, head and neck ontological surgery specialty), anesthesiologist, two nights at the hospital, excellent service, food, care, etc., was $6,000, and subsequent radiation at a state-of-the-art outpatient center was $3,000."

# DUAL **SYSTEM**

After graduating from medical school, many Costa Rican doctors go to universities in the United States for further study and to do residencies. This is particularly true for specialists; since Costa Rica is such a small country, there aren't enough patients with the same problem to give a doctor the opportunity to see the wide variety of patients needed to get experience in his or her specialty.

I asked a physician from the United States who had retired to Costa Rica some years ago, "Why would a Costa Rican doctor who does a residency in the United States or Canada return here to work for Costa Rican medical earnings?"

"You have to understand," he replied, "that most doctors only work half-time for the government. The rest of the time, they work for themselves. Take the case of a cardiologist who charges $50 an office visit. If this doctor sees five patients a day, that's $250 a day, or about $50,000 a year, plus his salary from the government. Many doctors in the United States have to pay two or three times that amount just for malpractice insurance. When you consider that income taxes and the cost of living are far less here, and that high malpractice premiums aren't necessary, a large percentage of the doctor's earnings are available for savings or investment. Even though Costa Rican doctors earn a fraction of what U.S. doctors do, they live here just as well or better. And the best part is, they get to live in Escazú instead of Kalamazoo!"

## SAN JOSÉ **HOSPITALS**

Three large Social Security–system hospitals provide San José with round-the-clock emergency care, with regular hours for laboratories, X-rays, pharmacies, and doctors' appointments. These are the Calderón Guardia, San Juan de Díos, and Mexico. Some private hospitals are the Clinica Santa Rita, the Clinica Biblica, and the Clinica Católica, all excellent hospitals.

Next to the Clinica Biblica is the Clinica Americana, an office complex with a group of English-speaking doctors, most of whom did residency in prestigious U.S. university hospitals. The KOP Medical Clinic in Escazú specializes in treating foreigners, with a staff that speaks English, French, Spanish, and Japanese. They offer a wide range of services, including obstetrics, gynecology, pediatrics, and dermatology.

Some emergency rooms specialize; for example, Hospital Mexico specializes in heart problems, and San Juan de Díos has a burn center. All towns of any size will have a hospital, and those that are too tiny often still have a doctor or paramedic and emergency equipment.

The latest and most impressive addition to Costa Rica's medical care system is Hospital CIMA San José, which is located in Escazú. This is one of the largest, most modern facilities in Central America, offering complete clinical laboratory services, radiology (including the only open MRI in Central America), and a full range of medical and surgical specialties. The hospital is affiliated with Baylor University in Dallas, Texas.

## MEDICINES AND **LIFE EXPECTANCY**

Most prescription drugs cost slightly less in Costa Rica than in the United States, but for Costa Ricans, prescriptions are horribly expensive. Note that Americans commonly spend more for hypertension and cholesterol-lowering medications and other drugs every month than the average *tico earns* in a month! Costa Rican physicians are reluctant to prescribe drugs unless the patient absolutely needs them, such as antibiotics to halt an infection.

I find it interesting that, according to recent statistics, the male life expectancy in the United States is 76.9 years. In Costa Rica the life expectancy is 76.3 years. That would indicate that despite spending three or four thousand dollars a year for the latest pharmaceuticals, and despite the availability of the most ultimate in high-tech medical treatment, the average American lives only six months longer than the average *tico*, who cannot afford prescription drugs. Go figure.

## ASSISTED **LIVING**

Retirement in Costa Rica has always been popular, but it began in earnest in the mid-1980s. In those days, folks didn't retire at an early age, as they often do today. They typically held on to their jobs to age sixty-five, or retired at sixty-two at the youngest. Not like today, when retiring at the earliest possible moment is in vogue. If my math is correct, those who retired in the late 1980s are now in their eighties or nineties. As much as we hate to admit it, the time comes when all of us must evaluate our options in advanced-age living accommodations. Many decide to give up Costa Rica and return to their hometowns, where they have family and friends to rely on for help in case of need. When everyday living becomes difficult, they can always move into a modern assisted-living facility where their children and grandchildren can visit frequently.

However, suppose you hate your hometown and have no friends there? Suppose your children and grandchildren are scattered to the four winds? Furthermore, can you afford the $5,000- or even $6,000-a-month fee to live in a modern assisted-living facility? What about a cut-rate old-folks home where conditions are basic, but the monthly cost is only $3,000 a month? Suppose your Social Security check is only $1,500 a month; will you have enough assets for a long stay? What are your alternatives should you choose to tough it out in Costa Rica?

A few years ago, there were few alternatives. I only knew of a couple of assisted-living facilities in the country. Actually, this is a rather new concept, because *tico* families traditionally take care of their elders at home. However, as I write these words, at least a half-dozen assisted-living centers are under way, some by American expats, others by *tico* health specialists. At least one of these facilities offers specialized care for Alzheimer's patients: Golden Valley Hacienda in Alajuela. Another place I've heard of is also in Alajuela: the Villa Comfort Geriatric Hotel, which specializes in folks who are not bedridden but who need care in everyday living. A facility in Los Yoses, the Hogar Retiro San Pedro, was given high praise by an American woman for the care there.

Understand, this is by no means a complete list, and I haven't investigated any of the facilities mentioned here, so I cannot make recommendations. If you are not fluent in Spanish, my recommendation is to personally check out the facility and speak to the employees to see if indeed they can communicate. Management can exaggerate the facility's English-speaking ability in order to gain new patients. Not being able to communicate your needs can be very frustrating. I have a friend who was in a recovery facility that he had been assured was bilingual. Once he had a terrible pain in his back and called for some medication. Instead, the confused aides couldn't understand what he wanted. They brought him a washcloth, then a glass of water, and finally some cigarettes (he didn't smoke).

At the time of this writing, several retirement facilities owned and managed by North Americans or Europeans were either open or under development. Estimated costs range from about $1,500 to $2,500 a month. For those who are fluent in Spanish, there are places that are much less expensive, reputedly around $1,000 a month. Again, I cannot make recommendations without having personally investigated these facilities.

However, the aforementioned facilities are called "assisted living," which implies that the patient gets around okay but needs "assistance": getting bathed and dressed, taking medications, having meals cooked, and so forth. But what about someone who requires round-the-clock care? Someone with Alzheimer's, or too weak to even feed himself? According to the Alzheimer's Association, the average lifetime cost of Alzheimer's care for an individual is $170,000. Even in Costa Rica, care will be expensive.

Let me give an example of how friends of ours handled this problem. Our friend's father—in his late eighties—wasn't totally incapacitated, and he was more or less lucid, but nevertheless required supervision twenty-four hours a day. They investigated a dozen facilities in their home state of New Jersey and found none of them acceptable, much less affordable. The father's only income was $1,500 a month in Social Security. Although he had savings and investments, paying the $6,000-plus a month required by a so-so New Jersey nursing home would have soon bankrupted the entire family.

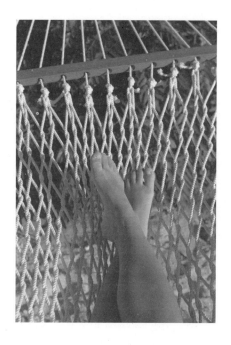

Retiring in Costa Rica was what my friends had planned on for years. They had built a beautiful home with a view of the Pacific Ocean, but they couldn't just leave the father alone in New Jersey. After much thought, the group solution was to take Dad with them! They bought him a small two-bedroom house in the center of the village, near a twenty-four-hour doctor's office. Three village women were hired to be with the father around the clock, and a *tico* with paramedic experience was hired to oversee everything. The total cost came to $1,800 a month, which included salaries for the caregivers, food, and miscellaneous expenses. They were able to visit their Dad at least once every day since his home was only a fifteen-minute drive from theirs. At least a couple of times a week, the couple would take him to dinner at a local restaurant, and he would absolutely beam with smiles. We felt this to be a heartwarming story; the father spent the last three years of his life happy in Costa Rica rather than lonely in New Jersey.

## COSTA RICA **DENTISTS**

The University of Costa Rica trains medical specialists of all kinds, including highly skilled dentists, periodontists, and orthodontic surgeons. Like medical expenses, dental expenses in Costa Rica are affordable. I go to an English-speaking dentist in Pavas who has a very modern clinic. After he received his degree in Costa Rica, my dentist did postgraduate work in the United States.

When asked about Costa Rican dental prices compared with those in the United States, the dentist replied, "Depending upon where you live in the United States, dental care there can be three to six times as expensive. For example, in Costa Rica the standard price for a porcelain cap is $135. In Los Angeles the same work costs from $600 to $700. A bridge typically costs $375 here, but a similar job in Los Angeles would cost at least $1,800. I've had patients who fly here, pay for their hotel, food, and airfare, and still save money."

What about quality? "Dental work in Costa Rica is equal to that done in the U.S.A.," he replied. "There is absolutely no difference in the competency of the dentists. However, the quality of dental laboratory work is usually better here in Costa Rica. Don't misunderstand, the U.S.A. also has excellent dental labs, but because they can get the work done cheaper in the Philippines, many dentists routinely send bridgework and dental caps overseas to low-cost laboratories. The quality just isn't up to the standards of Costa Rican or American labs. If I were to have caps or bridgework done in the U.S.A., I'd certainly insist that my dentist use an American dental laboratory."

Charges for dental work vary widely, depending on the part of the country in which you live and on the financial status of the dentist's clientele. You'll pay more in the more affluent suburbs of San José and less in small cities in the provinces. Many smaller towns and few villages have no dental services other than visiting dentists who are sent in by the government to take care of schoolchildren's teeth.

Along with cosmetic surgery, cosmetic/restorative dentistry is becoming a big business here, with huge savings over the cost in the United States or Canada. People have reported savings of $6,000 to $18,000 over prices quoted in the United States and Europe. They've reported satisfaction with the treatment and quality of the dentists.

## PLASTIC **SURGERY**

Costa Rica has gained worldwide recognition for another of its medical services: reconstructive surgery, commonly known as plastic surgery. San José is becoming known as "Beverly Hills South" because of the number of people coming here for body renewal. Several excellent surgeons specialize in face-lifts, liposuction, breast reconstruction, and other corrections of nature's imperfections. Not only are Costa Rican plastic surgeons ranked among the best in the world, but their fees are based on Costa Rican medical standards: in a word, inexpensive.

Why would Costa Rica be so popular with those wanting to rid themselves of wrinkles? Besides affordable costs and quality surgery, it turns out that San José is a perfect place to slip away to have an operation because of its climate—never hot, never cold—which makes recuperation faster, safer, and more comfortable. Since the healing process takes three or four weeks, many patients find this a great time to learn Spanish in one of the many "total immersion" schools around the city. These schools provide for homestays with Costa Rican families and have small classes or even individual instruction if you prefer.

Another attractive thing about Costa Rica as a base for cosmetic surgery is that many folks feel embarrassed about having their friends and family know they are going to have it done. Therefore, a growing number of them vacation in Costa Rica, where they are unlikely to run into acquaintances; they have the operation; and they return home a month later, when all traces of the surgeon's handiwork have disappeared.

What does all this cost? Happily, the cost of a face-lift, a breast job, a tummy tuck with liposuction, or a body-lift, including surgery, postoperative care, and hospital stay, is a fraction of what one might pay for a similar procedure in the United States. For example, a complete face-lift costs from $2,000 to $6,000, plus $1,300 for the operating room and two recovery days in the hospital. The same operation in New York or Los Angeles would be $25,000, plus much, much more for the hospital.

San José's leading plastic surgeon is Dr. Arnoldo Fournier, who did his residency in reconstructive surgery at New York's Columbia University and who has the oldest established plastic surgery practice in Costa Rica. Dr. Fournier charges $800 to $1,500 for an eyelid operation when done separately. Nose surgery or liposuction to abdomen and thighs costs about $1,500 to $5,000, compared with U.S. rates of about $15,000 for the same procedures.

How safe is it? Costa Rican hospitals are excellent, with all modern equipment. Personnel are highly trained. Dr. Fournier points out, "Most of my surgery is done under local anesthetic and sedation. The patient is given some pills a couple of hours prior to the operation, and intravenous medication is given by an anesthesiologist during surgery. This is much safer than using a general anesthetic. Some patients just stay one night in the hospital and then check into a bed-and-breakfast for a few days. Others prefer to stay a while, since hospital rooms don't cost much more than a first-class hotel." For information about plastic surgery, go to www .drfournier.com/ing.

# THE **REAL ESTATE GAME**

A common mistake newcomers make is rushing to buy a home. You really should rent for a while to get an idea of where you want to live. Communities and neighborhoods vary greatly in quality of shopping, access to transportation, compatibility of neighbors, and, of course, price. There are some areas where you definitely wouldn't want to live—you can usually detect "bad vibes" quickly—and there are other areas that may look great at first, but later you could be sorry you didn't know about another, more interesting neighborhood. Take your time when looking for a place to live, and ask many questions of fellow expatriates.

To get an idea of what you might have to pay to rent a house or an apartment, check the *Tico Times* classifieds for a wide range of rents. The last time I looked, houses and apartments were offered at rents ranging from $350 to $2,500 a month (and even higher). While the $2,500 place should be spacious and luxurious, chances are the $350-a-month place could be perfectly livable and just as nice as places back home that rent for twice that amount. Don't rent on price alone, however; check out the neighborhood closely.

For many Costa Rican families, the idea of paying even $350 a month is prohibitive. (Remember, $350 is considered a nice monthly salary for many *ticos*.) So if you are looking for the rock bottom in rents, check the classifieds in the Spanish-language newspaper *La Nación*. The ads in that paper are read by local people who do not have the ability to pay higher rents. Better yet, when you find a neighborhood you like, don't hesitate to ask at stores and businesses if they know of rentals, or even ask people walking along the street.

When trying out Costa Rica for livability, most people don't enter into long-term rentals or sign leases until they are certain they want to settle in for a long time. An ideal way to savor living in the country, particularly in the Central Valley, is to rent an apartment by the month or the week. Short-term rentals are particularly useful when determining which neighborhood you'd like to settle in. San José has several *apartotels,* small furnished apartments complete with cable TV, telephone, and cooking utensils—in short, everything you need for a trial of Costa Rican living.

Another excellent way to discover whether you like a neighborhood or a city is to rent a room in a Costa Rican home. Because of pressure on hotels for tourist rooms a few years back, many private families converted spare bedrooms into rentals for the busy seasons. They're delighted to host North Americans on their visits, to take them into their homes and treat them as part of the family. Another possibility is a bed-and-breakfast located in the neighborhood you want to investigate. The owners can provide invaluable information about the area.

The standard recommendation to visitors is to wait at least six months before buying property. However, many catch real estate fever within the first few days of their initial visit and end up buying something anyway. For a while the buying spree in Costa Rica increased in volume, with people from all over the world plunking down money to buy something—anything—before it was all gone. At the present time, the dollar is weakening against foreign currencies, down more than 30 percent under the European euro. This makes Costa Rican properties, which are traditionally priced in dollars, very attractive to Europeans who desire to move to Costa Rica.

Some people are surprised when researching home prices on the Internet or by looking at ads in the *Tico Times*. Prices are sometimes higher than expected. There are plenty of properties to be found at bargain prices, but you must realize that there are several levels of real estate, from the very cheap to the ultraexpensive. If you're looking for something at the lower end of the scale, the Internet and English-language newspapers aren't the best places to look. When property is a real bargain, it won't be on the Internet, and it probably won't be in the *Tico Times* either. The more affordable properties are usually bought and sold by *ticos*, who read *La Nación* or *La Republica*, and who don't have access to the Internet. When the price is much over $60,000, most *ticos* and those gringos with

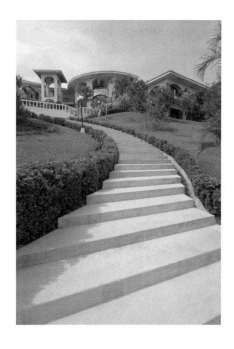

ordinary budgets can't buy. The advertisement for these properties goes into places where well-to-do buyers will see it, like on the Internet. The same goes for rents. A house or apartment that rents for $400 a month doesn't need to be advertised in a newspaper or posted on the Internet; word of mouth takes care of it. But a luxury place that rents for $3,000 or sells for $500,000 needs to be exposed to a different market.

For more than twenty years armchair experts have been saying that Costa Rica real estate is overpriced, that the market has peaked and is sure to tumble. Overpriced compared to where? Clearly, you can buy a home in Nicaragua, El Salvador, or Honduras for a fraction of the price in Costa Rica. If you want to live in Honduras, be my guest. These same experts predicted the collapse of California real estate for forty years. Yet prices kept going up, despite the fact that you could buy cheap property in places like Oklahoma, Nebraska, or Kentucky. The reason Costa Rica real estate is priced higher than Nicaraguan properties is a basic principle called "supply and demand." When a surplus of buyers feel they'd rather live in Costa Rica than Nicaragua, prices will be higher in Costa Rica.

The real estate market in the United States is in a downturn at the time of this writing (mid 2008). Inflated prices, shaky mortgages, and foreclosures have halted the upward surge of prices, forcing asking prices downward by 10 to 20 percent in some parts of the country. It stands to reason that property here in Costa Rica will be affected somewhat by conditions in the United States. However, since most properties in Costa Rica are sold on a cash basis, foreclosures do not enter the picture. Folks with paid-for properties aren't forced to sell for a loss, so if they can't get their price, they tend to hold on until demand for property resumes. This has happened several times in the recent past. My guess is that the real estate boom will stall for a time, then resume when the next sellers' market appears on the horizon.

Having pointed out that bank-financed property in Costa Rica has been the exception rather than the rule, I must say there has been a slight trend toward U.S.-style financing. A few private banks recently started granting mortgages. Previously, this was unheard of. Sales had to be handled by cold cash up front. Of course, the loan will be in dollars, and interest rates are somewhat higher than you'd pay up north. (A friend is paying 8 percent variable on a fifteen-year loan.) If you're not a resident or a resident in progress, you'll probably pay a higher percentage of interest. I hope I'm not making this sound easy, because the few people I know that have received financing had to wade through complicated applications and provide letters from their home bank and/or employer. Obviously, banks are concerned that you can and will pay off the mortgage rather than walk away and leave them with a foreclosure.

## PLAYING THE **REAL ESTATE GAME**

Many, if not most, countries in the world severely restrict the rights of foreigners to buy property. Some absolutely prohibit it. Not so in Costa Rica. This is one country where you needn't be a citizen, or even a legal resident, to own property. If you're financially capable of buying real estate, it's yours. However, too many newcomers fail to understand how the real estate game is played in Costa Rica. In this chapter we'll try to explain the rules of the game. In my opinion, this chapter is one of the most important in the book.

First of all, in North America, the vast majority of property sales are conducted through professional real estate offices. A real estate professional brings the buyer and seller together and helps negotiate the deal.

But this is a North American concept that is foreign to Costa Rica. Almost all real estate offices in Costa Rica belong to foreigners. Costa Rican buyers and sellers simply do not use third-party negotiators. Traditionally, they sit down with family members to negotiate, with trusted lawyers sitting in. This is why you almost never see *tico* properties listed with an American real estate company. Also, you rarely see Costa Rican real estate offices.

**HOW THE GAME IS PLAYED** Newcomers with stars in their eyes do not realize how different these customs and the laws are. They take it for granted that the game rules are the same as back home. Let's look at the differences and see how they could affect your financial future in Costa Rica.

**Back home:** You visit a convenient real estate office and choose a salesperson you like. It really doesn't matter who, because all real estate offices and real estate salespeople are pretty much the same. Brokers and agents have taken the same real estate classes, passed identical tests, and have basic experience in real estate before being granted a license. All sales practices are governed by specific laws.

**In Costa Rica:** There are neither training, tests, licenses, nor any laws regarding real estate sales. To become a broker or a salesperson, you simply announce that you are now available to sell property. Having printed business cards is all you need. (Even business cards aren't necessary.) Anyone, even tourists, can and do sell property and collect commissions without violating real estate laws.

**Back home:** You sit down with the real estate agent and go through the area's Multiple Listing Service (MLS). That is, descriptions of each and every home for sale in the community, in the price range you can afford. There's no need to go to another sales office if you can't find something you like, because all real estate offices have the exact same list of properties.

**In Costa Rica:** There is no such animal as MLS. Sales offices and individual agents keep their listings to themselves and would be fools to share information with competitors. Therefore, you have no way of knowing what properties are for sale without going to each and every real estate sales office in your target area.

**Back home:** The salesperson conducts a tour of all available properties so you can narrow your choices.

**In Costa Rica:** You will never be given a tour of "all available properties." You'll see only those under contract to that particular salesperson or office. You have to go to all real estate offices. Even then, you won't see listings for properties for sale by owners. You'll have to ask around the community for available properties. Local *ticos* and gringos pretty much know what is for sale and how much the seller is actually asking.

**Back home:** You look at the list of comparable selling prices, which is a list of every home sold recently and the transaction price. By law, all selling prices are available to the public. You quickly determine which of your choices are overpriced and which are bargains.

**In Costa Rica:** In Costa Rica there are no comparables. The actual sales price is a carefully guarded secret. Well, everyone knows how much is asked for a property, but not the final price. This is because property taxes and transfer fees are based on the reported selling price, and because of income tax and capital gains issues. To be blunt, many people fib about how much money they received or paid for a property.

**Back home:** You know more or less what the owner will settle for, so you make an offer a little below the asking price, assuming that the price has been boosted in order to have room for haggling. Eventually you reach a happy medium.

**In Costa Rica:** You haven't the vaguest idea of the price the seller wants for his property, because the real estate agent could be keeping this a secret. If so, the agent will refuse to give you a way to contact the seller so you can find out. Why? Too often, the property is being sold on a net listing contract. In most North American states or provinces, this type of contract is illegal.

A net listing works this way: The agent asks, "How much do you want for your property?" Let's suppose the seller wants $100,000. The salesperson writes a contract guaranteeing the seller $100,000 less a 5 percent commission. Then the salesperson lists the property at $150,000, not $100,000! If there's a buyer, the seller receives $95,000 ($100,000 minus $5,000 commission). However, the salesperson's cut is $55,000 (the commission plus the extra $50,000)! If the home doesn't sell, the salesperson hasn't lost anything. Yet, the seller could have lost several potential sales because the asking price was too high, and would never know.

Since there are no laws or regulations in Costa Rica, this is perfectly legal. In the United States or Canada, the agent could go to jail for not properly representing his client. If the salesperson wants your listing, he or she will agree to a commission-only contract. If not, look for another salesperson.

**Back home:** When your offer has been accepted, you can safely assume that the deal is solid. You will soon have a home that will be livable, with no hidden problems. You can be confident that the seller actually owns the property, there are no major leaks in the roof, the title to the house is in order, the boundary lines of the property are exactly as represented, the house hasn't been condemned, there isn't an outstanding mortgage worth more than the house, or other routine problems. The law back home demands that these problems must be disclosed.

**In Costa Rica:** There is no obligation to disclose anything. It's up to your attorney to check out the legal aspects of the deal, and up to you to look carefully at the physical condition of the property. This is why a competent lawyer on your side is worth his or her weight in gold. Your lawyer has seen through every possible trick.

**GAME RULES** Although buying property in Costa Rica should be rather straightforward, it can be hazardous if not handled carefully. The following are some points to keep in mind. (For more legal details, see chapter 18.)

**The first rule:** Under no circumstances should you use the same lawyer who represents the seller. Find a competent, English-speaking attorney to handle the deal for you. This can be a challenge in itself. Too many Costa Rican lawyers are part-timers and aren't truly familiar with the buying and selling of real estate. Inquire around the North American community for recommendations.

Why is this important? For one thing, your lawyer needs to make sure the person who is selling you the property actually owns it. It's up to your lawyer to make absolutely sure that no liens, mortgages, or second deeds are attached to the property. Your lawyer needs to examine the deal with a legal microscope, looking for bugs and hidden risks. The seller's attorney has no obligation to do all of this; it's up to your lawyer. Legally, an attorney can represent both sides of a transaction, but if the lawyer's first client is a crook, look out. The lawyer may well be part of the scam himself. It happens often since they aren't breaking any laws.

**The second rule:** Never count on a verbal contract. A handshake means nothing. You may think you have a deal, but when you return with the cash, someone else owns the place and is moving in furniture. Get everything in writing, in Spanish as well as English.

**The third rule:** Do not trust the seller or real estate agent just because he or she is a fellow North American! There's something about Costa Rica that seems to bring out latent tendencies toward larceny in some of our compatriots. An astounding number of confidence men come out of the closet the moment they arrive in Costa Rica. Most of the real estate agents who are just starting out are rank amateurs, but since they deal with people like you and me—also rank amateurs in business deals—even honest amateurs can cause serious damage.

**The fourth rule:** Do not be so overwhelmed by the beauty and tranquillity of Costa Rica that you pay the first price asked. Gringos and *ticos* alike can display irrational streaks of optimism when valuing their properties. Foreigners, bloodthirsty for profit, can be the worst of all.

**The fifth rule:** If you're buying unimproved land, be absolutely positive you can bring electricity and year-round water to the property. (Some parts of Costa Rica suffer water shortages every dry season.) If there is no water connection possible, make sure that the local municipality will grant a permit to drill a well, and that a well will have water. Have the soil tested to be sure it's suitable for a septic system. If sewage can't be treated properly, it will sit around, back up, and make your new home smell like a cesspool. Some of these conditions could prevent you from getting a building permit, making your property virtually useless except for raising goats.

If you have to bring electric power to your place from the nearest source, it could mean paying a fortune to install power poles and electric lines. The last quote I heard was $15,000 a kilometer! The cost could be many times the price you paid for that lovely parcel in the mountains. Solar-power installations are not cheap, and they limit the appliances you can use. Don't believe assurances that telephone and high-speed Internet lines, or a paved highway, are on the way. They could be years away, or not even on the drawing board.

**The sixth rule:** When selling property, be wary of a listing agreement that doesn't pay you the full sales price less commission. As discussed earlier, these contracts are known as "net listings." I've seen net listing sales where the agent boosted the sales price of property by 100 percent over the price asked by the seller, keeping the balance, plus a commission. The agent can end up with more money than the property-owner client! If the salesperson wants your listing, he or she will agree to a commission-only deal. If not, look for another salesperson.

**The seventh rule:** When buying property, insist on talking with the owner. Ask him what his bottom-dollar price would be, and ask about any problems that the selling agent might not be aware of. If the real estate agent refuses to allow you to speak with the seller, you have every right to be suspicious.

**A final suggestion:** When buying property, the title is often in the name of a Costa Rican corporation, or *sociedad anónima,* which is good. If not, one of the first things you'll probably want to do is form a corporation. This may sound strange, but there are several advantages. (The section on offshore corporations in chapter 18 explains how corporations are set up and how they are used in buying property.) Although offshore corporations are sometimes used for avoiding taxes, hiding assets, and other marginal activities, there is nothing at all questionable or illegal about placing home ownership in a corporation.

# NATIONAL **REGISTRY**

Since Costa Rica is so small, the government can keep all land records in one place, at a central title registry called the Registro de la Propriedad, or Registro Nacional. Most people just say "Registro." All valid liens and attachments against a property must be registered here, and the books are open to the public simply by going to the Registro's Web site. This makes it easy for your attorney to double-check the Registro before making an offer. You can check properties out yourself, although the final check needs to be done by your attorney. At the end of chapter 18 you'll find instructions for using the Registro Nacional's Web site.

If your lawyer finds no liens or mortgages registered against the piece of real estate and has no questions about the legal standing of the owners, you can safely transfer the property to your name or to your corporation. Any outstanding debts or obligations that didn't appear on the Registro records are none of your concern. But don't feel smug until you make sure that your lawyer actually registers your new property and the documents are stashed away in your safe-deposit box.

Incidentally, another valuable use of information provided by the Registro is checking the ownership of motor vehicles. You'll find the complete legal history of the automobile, motorcycle, or pickup you might want to buy. Before putting up the cash, you can see who actually holds the title to the car, whether there is a loan, and who the previous owners were.

# *TICOS* ARE **NOT NAÏVE!**

Newcomers to Costa Rica often have the mistaken notion that there are two prices for real estate: the "gringo price" and the "*tico* price." They sincerely believe that *ticos* are simple country folk who have no idea of the real value of their properties. The theory is that bargain real estate can be purchased simply by paying a Costa Rican to buy it for you.

First of all, it is more than a little arrogant for strangers to come to Costa Rica and assume that they know more about the real estate market than Costa Rican landowners. After all, *ticos* have lived here all their lives and are thoroughly familiar with the current market. To assume they might sell property at less than its value to another Costa Rican is actually naïve on the part of the prospective buyer. When we are talking about desirable properties—those with ocean views or in pleasant neighborhoods with elegant homes—you must realize that virtually all of these properties are already owned either by wealthy *tico* families, North Americans, or Europeans—none of whom are ignorant of the value of their property.

Obviously, isolated land, up in the mountains, accessible by dirt road, will usually be owned by *ticos.* It's entirely possible that they have only a vague idea of the value of their properties. Yet, who does know? Certainly not a newcomer to the region. If that's the kind of land you want, having a *tico* bargain for you makes sense only because the landowners probably can't speak English. But it is a mistake to think that you can pick up land like this at a below-market price because these are "simple people."

# DECIDING **WHERE TO RELOCATE**

Unlike some foreign countries, expatriates in Costa Rica don't feel compelled to isolate themselves in gated or protected enclaves. Most North Americans feel at home in Costa Rica's city and suburban middle-class neighborhoods throughout the Central Valley. They don't feel the need to group together, living in compounds or sealed-off neighborhoods as expatriates do in other foreign countries. Because Costa Ricans and North Americans are similar in personality and worldviews, most expats feel right at home with their neighbors. Since juvenile delinquency isn't out of control in most middle-class residential areas, and because neighborhood kids are generally well behaved, Americans don't feel threatened as we might in some low-income areas back home. Granted, North Americans do tend to congregate in the more expensive areas with nice homes, condominiums, and plush housing developments. But not everyone can afford to live in these upscale neighborhoods, and not everyone wants to live in an English-speaking enclave. Therefore, you'll find foreigners scattered all over the Central Valley and, in fact, all around the country in small towns and villages.

One expatriate who has lived here for twenty years with his family of five said, "We live in a Costa Rican barrio with *ticos* who are typical of most Costa Ricans I know. They love their families, neighborhood, and country, and [we] all work together at watching out for one another. Our home has never been broken into, and we don't live in a fortress. We have no walls, pit bulls, Dobermans, or security systems. Five minutes and a crowbar could gain entry."

Not only are foreigners right at home in city and suburban areas of Costa Rica, but those who speak fairly good Spanish find that they are accepted without any fuss in rural settings and villages away from the Central Valley. This is something you'll definitely not find in the rest of Central America or even in Mexico. In other cultures, a gringo family living in a native community would stand out like pigs wearing miniskirts. Your neighbors would think of you as a little eccentric, and you would feel bewildered and lonely because the culture is so different. Not so in Costa Rica. I know many gringos who enjoy living in rather humble (and inexpensive) lodgings in picturesque villages, and their neighbors are proud that foreigners would like them so well that they'd want to be neighbors.

## BEACHFRONT **PROPERTY**

Ocean real estate is wildly popular with Europeans and North Americans. Prices are somewhat erratic, in some areas having gone wild, while other places still have bargains available. The situation is somewhat murky, because some building lots right on the ocean often have tough building and ownership restrictions that you might not be told about until you are denied a building permit. Foreigners are supposedly limited as to ownership of property near or on the beach, but they manage to sidestep this law by putting the property into a Costa Rican corporation.

Property owners on most beaches are restricted as to how close to the water they can build. The most important point to bear in mind is that you usually cannot own beachfront property outright; it must be leased from the local municipality. Make sure you're comfortable with this concept before deciding on that wonderful stretch of coconut trees and sand.

Chapter 18 discusses beachfront property in great detail, but generally, the law goes like this: The first 200 meters ashore, starting halfway between low-tide and high-tide lines, is the "maritime zone," and it belongs to the municipality. It cannot be sold, but it can be leased. (This lease is called a "concession.") The first 50 meters from the beach is the "public zone," which belongs absolutely to the public and is off-limits to construction of any kind.

Construction between the 50- and 200-meter points must be approved by the municipality. Building permits are sometimes issued only for tourist-related projects. Remember, that $150,000 lot on the beach is not an outright purchase; you actually pay that money for the right to renew a lease every five years. It's yours provided you do everything right: make the lease payments, pay taxes on time, and obey all the rules.

Caution: A seller may claim that an existing building that falls within the first 50-meter mark is legal because it's been "grandfathered." That's possible, but more likely someone in the past ignored the rules and the bureaucracy hasn't gotten around to enforcing the laws. The government could force you to dismantle the buildings and restore the property to its original state, when and if it chooses to do so. Check grandfather clauses with a skeptical eye—and a good attorney.

## SQUATTER **PROBLEMS**

Anyone who has followed the battles between North Americans and squatters in the *Tico Times* is aware of hair-raising stories concerning squatters and legitimate property owners. The popular name for a squatter is *precaista*. If you're thinking of buying a piece of rural property, or any land that could possibly be farmed, you need to be aware of the squatter problem. The problem is with agricultural land, not with residential property.

We've all heard stories of North Americans who purchased lovely tracts of forested land with the intention of building a home someday, and then, when they returned a few years later, they were surprised to find the land cleared and a family living in a rustic home, raising cows. Squatters strike again!

If the property you are interested in has an extra house with a *tico* family living in it, beware. Don't let the seller glibly pass this off as the "caretaker's residence." It could be a squatter's home. "This family takes wonderful care of the place!" the seller might exclaim. "They never leave the property unattended." The seller should add, "They'll never leave, period!" Make sure you see documents proving that this is indeed a care-taker employee, not a squatter. In order to be an employed caretaker, the employee must receive the legal minimum wage rate, including Social Security, and all other legal benefits. The papers proving all this must be up to date. Insist that your lawyer examine the proof. If someone is paid to simply look over the property on a regular basis, make sure there's a written receipt that he is being paid for this service and is not a squatter himself.

To most of us the idea of someone simply moving in on your property is outrageous. It's trespassing! It's theft! Can this really happen in a law-abiding country such as Costa Rica? Aren't property owners protected by the law? Isn't all of this illegal?

Well, it turns out that to a certain extent, it is legal. There are laws to the effect that unowned or abandoned property is open for homestead-ing, just as it was in the early days of the United States and may still be in some western states. These Costa Rican laws were intended to prevent a few wealthy people from hogging land they don't use and don't need.

This is precisely what happened in some other Central American countries, where 2 or 3 percent of the people own 90 percent of the good land but don't use it. One reason Costa Rica is so much better off than its neighbors is that citizens have access to land. The laws are well intentioned and fair. The problem lies in how these laws are interpreted and who is doing the interpreting. Too often the bias is in favor of the squatter. (Remember, this only applies to agricultural land. Residential properties cannot be claimed as abandoned.)

Just when is a piece of land abandoned? One law, which seems clear, states that after property goes unattended for ten years, whoever has been using the land in a "continuous, open, and peaceful manner" for those ten years may apply for a title. The intruder will be successful unless the original owner has a good lawyer and a valid excuse. Another principle of law is that the squatter must show that he had reason to believe the land was abandoned. This means that someone who was being paid to watch your land can be removed if he attempts to take it over for himself. (Remember, you need receipts and canceled paychecks.)

Typically, the scenario goes like this: A choice piece of unattended property becomes a tempting target for a *precaista*. He'll construct a cabin and plant a crop in the hope that he won't be discovered for a year. If the occupancy is less than a year, it's considered trespassing and is handled by the Ministry of Interior and the courts. If the trespass is less than ninety days, you call the local police, and they are obligated to evict the squatters and "present you" with a paper that confirms that you are the true owner of the property. (If the police fail to act, your lawyer can do something about that.)

But let the problem go a full year and the situation becomes a bit more serious. The owner usually has the option of paying the squatter for his expenses and "improvements" or else going to court. ("Improvements" could include cutting down all your beautiful trees to make a pasture.) When the bill is too high—you can be sure it will be padded—sometimes it's cheaper to walk away. Understand, these problems seldom occur anywhere but on agricultural land. Land zoned or used as residential property doesn't fall under the category of this law.

The solution to this problem is a matter of prevention. While you are out of the country, have a friend or a management agent drop by the property at least once every three months. At this point, a simple complaint to the police is usually enough to boot someone off your land. Be sure to keep records of expenses and improvements to the property as proof that you haven't abandoned your land. Paying someone to clear brush once in a while is good enough. Be sure to keep a record of how many hours he worked and receipts for how much you paid him. Any place where there are a lot of foreign property owners, you'll find someone who watches property as a paid service. However, be absolutely sure you know who is taking care of your property, and keep records that he is being paid. My attorney advises, "Hire someone to check on the property, and then hire someone else to check on the person checking on your property." The last thing you want to do is hire a squatter to watch over your property!

Occasionally a problem arises when a foreign resident decides to return to the United States for an extended stay and has to lay off the maid, gardener, or other employees. If the property owner isn't familiar with the laws and neglects to pay workers' benefits such as severance pay, accrued vacation, and year-end bonuses, the employees could feel justified in taking over the land as compensation. Chapter 12 covers this in detail.

However repugnant the idea of squatting may be to you, it is important to operate within the law. After all, *precaistas* have rights, like it or not. One woman who had just purchased some property told me that she had been informed that "the only way to deal with squatters is to burn down their houses," and that's what she intended to do if she ever found any on her property. I was horrified to think of someone on a tourist visa, a guest in the country, taking the law into her own hands! This is the way the problems start, and problems of this nature have been known to escalate into gunfire. Sometimes squatters are well organized and have their own ways of striking back; the best advice is to leave this problem to the law. The law may work slowly, sometimes not at all, but this is better than killing or being killed for a piece of farmland. I have friends who had no problem kicking the rascals off their land and watched while the police burned the squatters' shacks.

If you are an absentee owner of undeveloped land and have reason to believe that your property is a target of squatters or property-theft scams, you should do the following: Make sure you are the legally registered owner; if you live out of the country, ask your attorney to conduct a title search from time to time to make sure you are still on the title, or at least check the Registro Nacional Web site yourself. (See instructions for checking the Registro in chapter 18.) Let the neighbors know who you are and that you own the property. Fence the property if possible, and post signs. Have a friend walk the property boundary lines every two or three months and file a complaint against any squatters encountered. If you hire a caretaker or agent to watch the property, make sure you have signed receipts showing that you've paid the caretaker for this purpose. Understand, these precautions are only for undeveloped property that is left untended by absentee owners for long periods.

# BUILDING **YOUR OWN HOME**

Okay, you've made the big decision? You've done your on-location research? You've traveled Costa Rica to check out climates and expat communities? You know exactly where you and your spouse want to settle in?

Congratulations! Your next decision is: Do you rent, do you buy, or do you build?

Unless you have the capital to invest, the obvious decision is to rent. The downside is that you'll have to accept whatever lifestyle and home designs are available instead of what you'd really like. Another problem is that many homes are used as vacation homes for the owners, so you'll be limited as to when you can stay in the house. Being forced to move from one place to another is a frequent consequence of renting. Even with a long-term rental, there's no guarantee the house won't be sold out from under you.

Buying is the best and simplest solution for most people. You choose from among the best-designed homes on the market and simply move in. More often than not, the house will come completely furnished, including refrigerator, washer, and dryer. Often these are turnkey setups, including kitchen utensils, bedding, and garden tools, especially when the owners are returning to their homes back in the United States or Canada. It wouldn't make sense to drag furniture back home.

Building your home is the third option, the one my wife and I adopted, twice, but only after looking over the homes-for-sale market. We found features we loved in each of the homes we considered buying. Yet every home had at least one flaw we didn't care to live with. We decided to build instead of buy—that way we could incorporate all the nice features we'd seen and eliminate the problems.

First we needed a building site. We narrowed this down to two choices. The first choice: a lovely lot, high on the mountainside, with a gorgeous view of the beach. But the location was a ten-minute drive to the beach. We wanted walking distance. When friends and family visit, we didn't want to operate a taxi service back and forth to the beach. The second option was a lot where we could hear but not see the surf, priced at a quarter of the cost of an ocean-view lot.

Next came the wonderful and exhilarating process of designing our dream home. We converted our dining-room table into a work space, and we each began to make sketches of how we envisioned the layout should look: which features would be included; how bedrooms should be positioned; where stairs to the upstairs living quarters would go. At first, none of the drawings had any similarities. We debated and argued for our designs, making changes over and over. Finally, we arrived at a consensus. The design retained all of the good features and eliminated the bad. Or so we thought.

Our next step was consulting with our contractor. We handed him our final drawings and eagerly awaited his enthusiastic approval. Enthusiastic was not exactly his reaction. He pointed out several flaws in the design. One important flaw was that the stairway to the upstairs deck would end up in space, 4 feet beyond the house, rather than on the deck. Another error: We forgot to allow for a door into the downstairs bathroom. Back to the drawing board. The process continued with our altering designs and the contractor correcting them.

Finally we all agreed on the design. Next steps: finding an architect to approve the plans and getting building permits from the municipality and a construction engineer's report on the suitability of the building site and septic tank capability. Costa Rican architects have a strong lobby in the National Assembly; the law says you must use blueprints from a licensed architect, and the fee shall be a hefty percentage of construction cost. Actually, an architect here does much more than design: He/she is sup- posed to supervise all phases of the construction. Since the architect is paid a percentage of construction costs, he/she has no incentive to keep costs low.

However, it turns out that there are many more architects in the country than building projects to keep them busy. Architects who work part-time at their profession are often willing to negotiate the fee, especially when the contractor is a friend or relative. This architect will look over the plans and recycle a similar blueprint for a negotiated price, resulting in significant savings for the client. Not all architects will do this, and those who have plenty of work will not do it this way. Again, it helps if your contractor and architect are friends or relatives. If you are building anything more than a basic, plain vanilla house, you probably don't want to take shortcuts. Hire a skilled, reputable architect, and have your lawyer help negotiate, to be absolutely sure you are aware of the contract agreements.

When estimating how long it would take to build our house, our contractor wisely said, "I might finish in three months. *No hay problema.* But since this is Costa Rica, I will promise *five* months. That way you will be delighted if I finish in only *four* months." Actually, he finished in four months to the exact day. He asked one of the workers to stop us that day, before we could get to the building site. The man took us to lunch and stalled for an hour while the crew installed the last of the windows. The contractor met us with a proud smile and took us through our new house.

When the day came to begin construction, the work crew set about cutting just enough trees to lay out the house. I watched over them to make sure they didn't cut too many. They thought this amusing. (Little did I know that trees here grow so fast they have to be continually trimmed and finally removed before they damage the roof and windows.)

I made friends with the workers by providing cold beer at lunchtime. They started calling me *"don John"* (a term of friendship and respect accorded to those older than you and who are well liked in the community). They still call me *don John*—twenty years after our first house was completed. As I drive to or from the village, someone is always waving at me and saying, *"¡Hola, don John!"* I've gotten into the habit of waving at everyone for fear I might hurt someone's feelings by not being recognized as *don John.*

Watching over the crew is a good idea, by the way—not because they will loaf, but because when you go away for a few weeks, contractors have a tendency to take their men and go work elsewhere. You can't blame them, because there is a labor shortage from time to time. They figure they can always get back to your house before you return. It does not always work that way.

During the early construction phase, I stayed at a nearby bed-and-breakfast and arose at dawn to hang around the building site and observe the wildlife that is so bountiful at daybreak. Monkeys, coatimundis, parrots, and other animals put on an early-morning show. Hanging around my building site at dawn brought surprises other than wildlife. I discovered something about the *ticos* who worked on my project: Not only did they arrive on time for work, they were there early—quite unlike the case in other Latin countries I can think of. Starting time was 6:00 a.m.,

and at exactly 6:00 work commenced in earnest. They worked hard, with regularly scheduled breaks, until 3:30 p.m. (a nine-hour day). The famous *mañana* mentality wasn't apparent on this job. I'm not saying all *tico* workers are like this; I'm only relating my personal experience.

Don't misunderstand: Our building experience was not all peaches and cream—all expected problems raised their ugly heads, and a few creative problems joined in the fun. We quickly learned a Spanish lesson: the difference between *Hay un problemcito* ("There's a little problem") and *No hay problema* ("There's no problem"). Essentially, it's as follows: *Hay un problemcito* translates as "We have a problem here, amigo, and it's probably going to cost money." On the other hand, *No hay problema* usually translates as "We may or may not have a problem, but it's not my problem."

The above experiences describe the first home we built, about twenty years ago. However, we finished our second home in 2006, and the conditions haven't changed. We have a Web site with pictures and construction progress of our last house at www.discoverypress.com/new_house.

# BUSINESS **OPPORTUNITIES**

Just a few years ago, the vast majority of those coming to Costa Rica for long-term stays were traditional retirees. By "traditional" I mean affluent couples about sixty-five years old, retired after forty years of loyalty to a benevolent company. They enjoyed a nice pension and looked forward to enjoying their "golden years" and a lifestyle of leisure. Retiring any earlier than  sixty-two would have been unusual. Their ideal was a Costa Rican beach house overlooking the surf at Flamingo, or perhaps a stately home perched above Escazú with a gorgeous view of the valley and volcanoes in the distance—ideally with a lifestyle that allowed ample time for bridge, cocktail parties, and golf with other expatriates, plus an occasional charter fishing trip.

A few years can make a lot of difference. For one thing, the retirement age has dropped—quitting work at fifty is not unusual. For many, retirement isn't voluntarily: Fifty is the age at which many employers like to trim the payroll, before pension benefits accumulate. Today there is no such thing as company loyalty or loyalty to employees. People are hired for whatever skills are needed at the moment—and are dropped the minute they're not needed. Many of today's retirees are casualties of the "dot-com" meltdown; since that time, most good jobs have moved to India or China. Other people are simply tired of working for someone else and recall thirty years ago when "dropping out" was idealized. In the new millennium, "dropping out" becomes a goal as much as an option.

This creates a restless population of not-yet-ready-for-retirement people who are itching to do something interesting with the rest of their lives. In fact, the word *retirement* isn't in their vocabulary. These are the youth-oriented activists who in the 1960s and 1970s used to say, "Don't trust anyone over thirty!" Determined not to get "old" in the way they perceived their parents to be, these youngsters are eager to get on with life. They have energy, talent, and workplace skills that they don't care to waste by playing bridge or swinging in a hammock. If they can't find a good-paying job in Costa Rica, the next option that comes to mind is going into business. And many of them do. Some popular tourist locales have more businesses owned by foreigners than by native *ticos*.

## A FRIENDLY **BUSINESS CLIMATE**

Many countries severely restrict foreign business investment as a way of protecting their national businesses and industry. Special tax breaks are given to local commerce, and roadblocks are thrown in the way of foreign investors. There's some justification for this, because many foreign businesses only want to take advantage of cheap wages, then ship the products—and the profits—out of the country. But Costa Rica takes a positive attitude toward foreign investment. Outside money is encouraged as a way to spur development, yet labor laws and wage minimums are enforced, giving the average *tico* worker enough income so that local stores, shops, and businesses flourish.

The end result is that Costa Rica is probably the most business-friendly country in Latin America. Foreign investment and foreign entrepreneurs are welcome. One obvious result has been the relocation of several high-tech corporations to take advantage of Costa Rica's educated and computer-literate workforce. This business-friendly climate has earned Costa Rica the reputation as Central America's "Silicon Valley." Companies such as Acer Computers, Microsoft, Abbot Laboratories, and General Electric have established sizable production facilities here. Intel Corporation's three production facilities here produce one-third of Intel's computer processor chips, creating thousands of good jobs for *ticos*.

Any investment that promotes tourism, creates jobs, and doesn't harm the environment is considered welcome here. Another plus: Many foreign investors in Costa Rica actually live in Costa Rica. For them, the whole point of going into business is to be able to enjoy living in Costa Rica. They spend and reinvest profits in the country, further bolstering the economy.

To attract desirable businesses, Costa Rica offers generous incentives and tax breaks. Depending on the enterprise, there can be a twelve-year

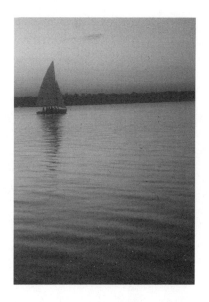

exemption from income taxes as well as waivers on import duties. When ecology is concerned—particularly projects involving reforestation—tax exemptions can be forever. Be aware, however, that continuing changes in tax laws may affect some of the tax breaks for tourist-oriented businesses.

Investments of $50,000 or more in specially approved projects can qualify the investor for immediate residency. With $150,000, the investment can be in any enterprise. Of course, to qualify for any of these special investment provisions, you need to proceed with government approval. Your lawyer can help you with this.

Remember that reforestation projects aren't just a matter of deciding to start sticking trees in the ground. You need to present detailed plans prepared by an approved forestry technical expert. If your reforestation project is a good one, you can also be eligible for government subsidies. (A friend is receiving about $5,000 a year under one of these programs.) Once planted, the property can be resold, as long as the purchaser agrees to continue with the reforestation project.

## GOING INTO **BUSINESS**

Before we delve into the subject of doing business in Costa Rica, you should ask yourself some important questions. Do you really want to move to a beautiful country and spend your time working at a business? Ask yourself whether you'd be better off bird-watching, swimming, or tanning on the beach instead of doing bookkeeping, tending bar, or changing linens in your bed-and-breakfast. Do you feel up to the challenge of dealing with a quixotic, entangled bureaucracy, in a language you don't entirely understand? And finally, if it's so easy to start the business you have in mind—and make large sums of money from your idea—why hasn't somebody else already filled that niche?

Too often, dreamers feel confident that all that's necessary to become a successful businessperson in Costa Rica is to show up and dazzle the country with entrepreneurship. Well yes, this can happen, but mostly to those who know what they are doing, who employ skills and special knowledge gained from business experience in their home countries.

Most North Americans who go into business in Costa Rica don't bother qualifying under the $50,000 or $150,000 investment laws, since tax advantages accrue to most qualifying businesses anyway. Also, because a Costa Rican passport isn't an enticement to those already holding U.S. or Canadian passports, few people bother with the special arrangement.

Since most businesses are registered in the name of a corporation or *sociadad anónima*, even a foreigner on a tourist visa can effectively control and manage the enterprise. While it is against the law for noncitizens to work at an ordinary job without permission, it's perfectly okay to oversee your own business. Discretion is required here, since part of the scheme is to create jobs, and if a business owner is doing work that could be performed by a Costa Rican, complaints could arise. This seldom happens, but it can happen.

Some North Americans have done exceptionally well in Costa Rican business ventures. They bring enthusiasm, expertise, and imagination, often re-creating successful enterprises they operated in their home country. One businessman from Illinois, who started a successful beach resort in Manuel Antonio about twenty years ago, said, "It's interesting to see who makes money here and who goes belly-up. Those who succeed are those who come here because of the attractive Costa Rican lifestyle and who go into business as a means of staying in Costa Rica. They usually make money despite themselves. Those who face one problem after another, and finally disaster, are those whose main interest is making a pile of money."

Foreigners often feel confident that they can be successful in tourist-oriented businesses because they understand the wants and needs of other foreigners who visit Costa Rica. That's often the case. Some restaurants and bars are popular with tourists because the owners know what tourists like. However, as in any business endeavor, you should know what you are doing, particularly in the restaurant or bar business, where the failure rate is unusually high.

Real estate development projects have created fabulous success stories as well as woeful tales of spectacular flops. Too many optimistic types start creating developments and resorts that look great on paper but never get past the fantasy stage. Be cautious about floating your investments on blue-sky dreams.

You needn't start your own business; numerous in-place enterprises are always available through ads in local newspapers. Of course, just as is the case back home, you need to investigate why the business is for sale. Maybe the reason is too much work, not enough profit, illness, or perhaps the owner feels it's time to cash in the equity and stash the profit. Don't consider buying a business unless you're competent to handle it and understand exactly why the enterprise is up for sale. What makes you think you can make money at this if someone else failed?

Among the many businesses advertised in the *Tico Times* are bed-and-breakfasts, car-rental agencies, pharmacies, travel agencies, and tons of bar-restaurants and discos. Also, apartment buildings, hotels, and beach resorts are usually on the market.

A business consultant I once interviewed said: "Remember, it's just as easy to lose money in Costa Rica as it is back home. For a stranger in a foreign land, it's even easier. You must know what you are doing. My best advice is to come here for six months and look around. Study the existing businesses and find out why some are successful and why others fail. Above all, don't jump into a business just for the sake of being in business—particularly a business that you don't know much about."

# BEWARE OF **SCAMS**

Because of Costa Rica's liberal attitude toward foreign business ventures and sometimes lax enforcement of regulations, a surprising number of foreigners feel as though they have complete freedom to operate as they wish and that ordinary laws and ethics don't apply to them. This is probably why Costa Rica draws more than its share of swindlers, crooks, and con artists.

The Costa Rican government does what it can to keep on top of offenders, but it's impossible to do much more than prosecute crooks after the damage has been done. And prosecution rarely happens, because the swindler simply skips the country before the trial date. For this reason, look very carefully at any business deal presented to you. Make sure you have a good, English-speaking lawyer check with all the proper government agencies and verify the integrity of your deal before risking your hard-earned money.

Popular scams include phony mutual funds, nonexistent banks, so-called tax-shelter investments, gold mines, hotels and resorts that never leave the drawing board, and real estate that is sold to several people or that didn't belong to the seller in the first place. You'll be offered phantom teak, macadamia, and jojoba plantations—all the get-rich-quick schemes you can imagine.

After pointing out all the pitfalls of going into business, I have to admit that many people are having fun doing so. You can feel a dynamic sense of progress and excitement in Costa Rica. This is the country of the entrepreneur, of wide-open opportunity, inexpensive land, dependable labor, and a relatively honest government. Modern-day Costa Rica is reminiscent of the old frontier days of the United States and Canada, full of success stories about North Americans who've opted to "start all over again."

When interviewing entrepreneurs, I always ask: What is the best part of doing business in Costa Rica, and what is the worst part of doing business here? The replies are often: "The best part is that I can afford to live in Costa Rica. The worst part is I don't make enough money to live in the style I'd like."

Just be aware that there are as many tales of failure as there are of success.

## EXAMPLES OF **BUSINESS VENTURES**

I had a discussion with an expat businessman about the high rate of business failure by Costa Rica newbies. He said, "If you take restaurants out of the equation, business success rates are probably not much different than in the United States. The problem with restaurants is that most start-ups are opened by people who have absolutely no experience. Yet a restaurant is usually their first choice."

What happens is that people fall in love with Costa Rica and decide to chuck everything back home and move to paradise. Too young to retire, they want either a job or a business. They've always loved to cook, and friends always praise their culinary skills. "Everybody always said I should open a restaurant when I retire." Good luck. One expat said to me, "It amazes me to see a new restaurant open up in our village, where there are already eight other restaurants. When one of these restaurants started to serve pizza, each of the other restaurants immediately bought pizza ovens and put pizza on their menus. Unless you have something extra-special to offer, how can you possibly succeed?"

Sometimes this works. A very successful Italian restaurant in our community was started by an Italian insurance executive from Naples and his wife, who was an accountant for a chain of hardware stores. They knew nothing of the restaurant business, but their location was wonderful, and there were no other Italian restaurants in the region at that time. To succeed, food didn't have to be more than just okay. Surprisingly, they eventually became gourmet cooks!

But all too often, novice restaurateurs have no clue as to what to do after making up a menu. Imaginative menus and good cooking are only part of the restaurant business. Without knowledge of buying, food spoilage, theft, and dealing with Spanish-speaking employees and suppliers, the new entrepreneurs are lost at sea.

**GOURMET RESTAURANT** The following business profile is an exception to a rule. Instead of accidentally going into a business she knew nothing about, Debbie Crawford had studied and prepared. She opened the Vista de Paraíso restaurant in Nosara forewarned and forearmed.

Debbie says, "All my life I dreamed of becoming a chef. I was premed in college and got my degree in chemistry. I worked in restaurants while going to college and loved the life. I am a very social person and love to talk. Chemistry, though, fit the financial backing." After receiving her chemistry degree, she worked in environmental chemistry and plant processing for fifteen years before making a career change.

She explained, "I was earning a six-figure salary, but I wasn't satisfied. Then, I found an opportunity to go to chef school full time. I quit my job and went to the prestigious Alain & Marie LeNotre Culinary Institute for an intensive, full-time program. Most classes were taught in French, and we needed a translator. A couple of the chefs spoke English, but all were master chefs, either in pastry or cuisine. After my time in culinary school, I applied and was accepted to the prestigious Accellis Culinary Arts Challenge. There were over 5,000 applicants across the United States and Canada, but only twenty were to be accepted. I came in third but felt like a winner before I ever got there!"

When Debbie returned to the States, she decided to move to the tropics to open her own restaurant. Since she already knew Nosara and liked the people and the climate, her decision was easy. She found a gorgeous ocean-view property in an unbelievable tropical setting.

She says, "I named it Vista del Paraíso, or 'View of Paradise.' I built the house, the restaurant, and a new life here in the tropics. I have nothing physical left in the States except some of my best friends. My children are now both bilingual, and we are able to spend 100 percent of our time together in our home-restaurant. They play in the swimming pool while

I prepare the evening's menu. I also have a wonderful Costa Rican boyfriend without whom I could not have gotten this far as fast as I did."

The restaurant features an international "fare with a flare," with imported tequilas, cognacs, and fun martinis; a beautiful pool for guests' enjoyment; seating inside or out (weather permitting); a baby pool—but most of all, really incredible food and view.

**BED-AND-BREAKFAST** When Charles Owens retired from the Civil Service in California, he and his wife, Jeanetta, tried returning to their home in Olympia, Washington, but soon discovered that wouldn't work out. Jeanetta says, "We found that it is really hard to go back. You change, the place you move back to changes, nothing stays the same. What really woke us up was a group of seniors who met every morning in one of the local breakfast restaurants, their conversations on how many pills they took, what their health insurance covered, and what diseases they suffered from. We just knew living the normal U.S.A. lifestyle was not for us."

Having once done a tour of military duty in Panamá, they decided that a tour of Central America might zero in on a country suitable for retirement. Jeanetta's Internet search turned up a small apartment for rent in a large, lovely home near Grecia, not far from San José. They planned on staying just for three months, then moving on to Panamá.

Jeanetta explains: "When we arrived in Grecia, we were delighted to find out the owner was an English-speaking American, yet we worried that she might possibly not like black people. Because you see, Charles and I both are truly black people. In Costa Rica, when someone sees black tourists, they naturally assume you're Costa Rican—from Limón or Cahuita—from anywhere but the U.S.A. Fortunately, the lady who owned the place greeted us warmly and didn't care about our ethnic background and heritage."

They settled into the area and fell in love with the house and surroundings. Suddenly, the owner decided to leave the country for a while and offered to rent them the entire house. Charles and Jeanetta talked it over, and on impulse agreed to a year lease, provided that they could run it as a B&B.

They opened La Terraza Guest House in October 2002. At first they had one customer, who rented the apartment for three months. That paid for the furniture they needed to furnish the rooms. But they didn't worry, because they hadn't seriously considered this a real business. After all, they were both retired.

"We were surprised," Jeanetta said, "when a few months later, the owner contacted us to ask if we would like to purchase La Terraza! We agreed, even though we weren't yet turning a profit. Since Charles and I came here with a comfortable income to back us, that helped with our decision. Too many people move here with not quite enough money, overspend, and expect to have their business begin paying off right away. We've found doing things slowly and steadily has worked out well for us.

"Since we opened we've added three vacation rentals. We stay pretty full, but advertisement is the most difficult part of our business. Our repeat customers are the people who have kept us in business during slow times.

"Our experience as business owners in Costa Rica has been a good one. Establishing a presence has been easy, and we have been able to gain the respect of the people in our community. We've had the same maid and gardener for several years and currently have four full-time employees and one part-time employee. They have good employee benefits, and they are well respected by us.

"Our goal is to add something to the lives of people here in Costa Rica. We have gotten far more of a benefit from our business than just earning a profit. It feels good to see people have a great year and be able to change their lifestyles because they are working in your employ."

La Terraza Guest House maintains a Web site (www.laterrazab-b.com) with pictures of accommodations and landscaping, as well as retirement and relocation packages that include thirty-day accommodations and visits to popular retirement communities in the Central Valley.

**PRIVATE SOCIAL CLUB** Joe and Helena Wygal, from Cambridge, Massachusetts, decided to start one of the most unusual and innovative Costa Rican businesses imaginable. They created an authentic European pub, complete with imported beers, rich wood paneling, custom brews from Costa Rica's draft beer producers, a dartboard, and even a small movie theater. That wouldn't be such an unusual enterprise if the pub were located in a city, but this setting is isolated, at least fifteen minutes from the nearest village. The Black Sheep Pub is situated on a mountainside, surrounded by a tropical forest, with a view of the Pacific in the distance. Howler monkeys and parrots provide background ambience not normally found in Europe or Britain.

Joe says: "My passion for pubs goes back twenty-five years to my first trip to Europe, which covered parts of England, Belgium, the German Rhineland, and the Netherlands. My interest in pubs moved to another level when Helena and I bought a home in Massachusetts, with a large basement that lent itself to becoming a pub. We became acquainted with beer brewers and enthusiasts from all over Europe and the United States, as well as local beer groups. Our parties became renowned throughout the area because we had beer on tap that was not available anywhere else. After a while I began to feel it was time to move our hobby to another level, perhaps a business, though I was not sure what that would be. We did sense that this would not be possible in the Boston area."

Joe and Helena had done considerable traveling in Costa Rica, until they finally decided on the Nosara area for their retirement. However, instead of buying the usual property in the village or Beaches of Nosara development, they decided on a building lot in a new development about a fifteen-minute drive from town. Joe says, "For a while I seriously considered locating the pub in the village of Nosara, but when construction on our home began, we reverted to the idea of having the Black Sheep Pub on our home property. We decided to operate it as a private club, with house rules and free membership."

Joe designed the exterior of the building in a traditional pub style with half-timbering, and the interior in European splendor. The business is actually two pubs, the first of which is a British pub room complete with an English-style bar. The second room is a continental European motif, with German-style long tables and paraphernalia from such countries as

Germany, Belgium, and the Czech republic. (My wife and I have visited there and can attest to the pub's authenticity.)

From the very beginning their target market was the American and European community in the Beaches of Nosara area. They gradually began to attract some of the surfer crowd as well as a group of young and lively *ticos* from San José. As special events were being celebrated, such as a New Year's Eve party, first anniversary bash, and a St. Patrick's Day celebration, the pub attracted more and more people.

Joe said, "From the beginning, I had wondered if a European pub would catch on in tropical Costa Rica, but when the special events became popular, when I could no longer see the bar due to the thirsty mob in the British room, I began to realize that my dream was coming true. A year later at our second New Year's Eve party, with over 200 people mulling around, with a long line forming outside the pub, with young girls wearing high heels and fashionable sexy outfits that would seem more appropriate at the Hotel Hilton, with all assortments of drinker types, with fireworks suddenly cascading over the pub, with the sound of different languages and accents ringing in my ears—I shook my head, shut my eyes, and thought, 'But it was only a hobby—what went wrong?'"

**REVIVING A SMALL HOTEL** In 2004, Ed and Rita Reames, originally from Maryland, decided to take early retirement. Ed was formerly in telecommunications, and Rita worked as a teacher and an airline employee. Too young to qualify for Medicare, and not covered under any group medical plan, they moved to Costa Rica as "medical refugees" to take advantage of the affordable INS medical coverage.

At first, they tried living in Dominical, but they found the year-round summer weather to be a bit too much. So they moved to the San Antonio de Belen area, not too far from the Alajuela Airport. The weather there is year-round spring, much more to their liking. Still too young to adapt to a traditional retirement lifestyle, they began looking around for some kind of business, possibly a bed-and-breakfast—provided it was located in a cool climate. They have found that more opportunities exist in Costa Rica for people not yet ready to fully retire and those with limited capital to invest. In Costa Rica you can start over again, and age is not a deterrent.

They ended their search in Tilarán, renowned for its pleasantly cool and breezy weather. There, Ed and Rita discovered the small La Carreta

Hotel and restaurant, which had been devastated and abandoned by its former managers after they unsuccessfully tried to turn it into a B&B.

Rita tells of their adventure: "We moved into the hotel during the rainy season. It was dark, dreary, and depressing. There were partially finished concrete walls, dust and filth that hadn't been cleaned in years, bathrooms that certainly gave you second thoughts about using them, boxes everywhere, and, most of all, water. One morning we woke up to a flood. Our neighbor's *canoa* [large outside water gutter] had broken in the night. Our garage, which was full of unpacked boxes, was flooded. So was our kitchen. We were concerned that our appliances might be ruined by the water on the floors. We spent the day cleaning up and salvaging our belongings.

"It was not more than two weeks later when a second *canoa* broke. Another flood! This time it took about two weeks for the repairs. We began calling our new home/hotel 'water world.' As we were making our repairs and improvements, we came to know a terrific crew of local workers. They came to our rescue over and over. Now we are known all over the community and have a great circle of friends and resources. Tilarán is a small community, and we have been drawn in to its warmth. This experience has also done wonders for our Spanish!"

Today, the place is immaculate, with walls decorated with fresh and beautiful murals, new furniture, and many extensive (and expensive) changes. They opened for breakfast on November 20, 2007, and a Christmas brunch followed. They offer cozy standard rooms with queen-size bed, private bath, and cable TV, or deluxe rooms that include a queen-size bed and a twin bed, private bath, TV, and excellent balcony views of the garden and surrounding mountains. There is also a rooftop terrace with stunning views and a table and chairs for all to enjoy.

Those planning to visit Monteverde, Lake Arenal, or the volcano will find Hotel La Carreta a convenient base for their travels and adventures. This boutique hotel and art gallery is located in Tilarán between La Fortuna and Monteverde, within driving distance of primary forest and the dramatic Arenal Volcano, and stunning Lake Arenal. The beaches on the Pacific Coast are a short drive. It's ideally located for one-day ecotours, mountain biking (rentals available), bird-watching, world-class sailboarding, hot springs, and freshwater fishing for tilapia. Their Web site is www.lacarretacr.com.

# AGRICULTURE AS **INVESTMENT**

Because of incredibly rich soil and year-round growing seasons, Costa Rica is an agricultural paradise. The country is checker-boarded with crops of all descriptions. Just about anything grows here, with bumper crops the rule rather than the exception. Therefore, agriculture would seem to be one of Costa Rica's best bets for investment. Actually, agriculture can also be one of the biggest investment disasters. Just because crops grow well doesn't guarantee you are going to make money. Furthermore, many native Costa Ricans are abandoning agriculture as a way to earn a living and going into less arduous occupations.

As an example: I have a *tica* friend from a large Costa Rican family—twelve children. Her father was a farmer, and so were all of his nine brothers. (Families of two generations ago were much larger than today.) Yet my friend points out that not a single one of the male descendants went into agriculture as a living. "They sold the land and went into some other occupation or business. Too much hard work for so little money," she explains.

One longtime agriculturist who has struggled to make a living in Costa Rica said, "Farming is a great way to go broke even if you are an experienced agriculturist. There are too many unknowns and too many marketing problems." He added wryly, "If I had invested the same amount in real estate as I spent trying to get an orange grove started, I would be a rich man by now."

Unusual or nontraditional crops that target overseas markets is sometimes a good idea, only if you personally are going to run the operation and you know marketing. You really have to know what you are doing and find a unique market niche. Expatriate farmers who farm successfully here specialize in crops destined for foreign markets or develop a demand overseas for their specialty.

An added incentive for abandoning traditional farming in Costa Rica is the upcoming CAFTA accord, in which North American "factory farms" will be allowed to export U.S.-government-subsidized crops duty-free at prices Costa Rican farmers can't match. This is especially true for crops such as rice and corn, and citrus fruit. Personally, I believe this accord will spell disaster for *tico* agriculture.

**COFFEE FARM** In 1997, Janet Blakeley, her husband, and her daughter, Courtney (age six at the time), decided to make the move to Costa Rica. They found a gorgeous home in the hills above Grecia, with a sweeping view of the city and high mountains on the other side of the Central Valley. (I've visited their home and can attest to the breathtaking layout.)

They discovered that in addition to the house and landscaped grounds, the property included several hectares of coffee trees—the type that produce the highest-quality Arabica beans. Janet's curiosity led her to learn more about coffee, how it should be grown and processed, and how it could be gourmet-roasted on a small scale. She made friends with neighboring coffee growers and soon became fascinated with organic methods of coffee production. She bought processing equipment and began packaging her own brand of gourmet coffee, Tesoros Del Sol.

When her husband left the picture via a divorce, Janet needed to do something with the coffee to supplement her income. She had already been helping neighbors convert to organic coffee growing and looking for ways to help farmers get fair prices, stop losing their land, and to help the environment. Together the group organized a collective of coffee growers.

Janet says, "We are licensed as an organic project, which means my company of Tesoros Del Sol gets them all certified. We make no-interest or low-interest loans for approved fertilizers and such. We train and monitor farms monthly. We pay higher rates to help them during the three years of transition to organic, and much higher rates for their organic beans. We've cut out the middle man."

Farmers who participate in the program are also required to plant tree shade cover, which produces higher-quality coffee beans. They are urged to plant native trees, but planting alternate crop trees such as papaya, bananas, or citrus is also encouraged. Janet grows pineapples between the rows. Being certified organic enables her farmer associates to command a price commensurate with the cost of production.

Janet's marketing strategy: Package only top quality, hand-processed, pure Costa Rican beans (no blends), and market the product directly to consumers in the United States by way of the Internet. Coffee lovers there are delighted to pay a little more for 100 percent Costa Rican coffee that cannot be found elsewhere. It would have to be a low-volume business, Janet decided, but it could be done via the Internet. And it works!

Courtney thoroughly enjoyed her experience of growing up in Costa Rica and loves the *naturaleza* of their Grecia home. She is thoroughly bilingual and finds it easy to make friends with the neighbors. She says she finds them loyal and caring, and she feels as if they are extended family. Janet says, "I appreciate that I don't have to worry about drugs or violence, and that Courtney has grown up with 'people' values."

Janet maintains an exceptionally informative Web site (www.tesdel sol.com) that gives complete information about coffee production in Costa Rica, how it is grown and processed, and the differences between varieties of coffee. The site also provides ordering information for North American consumers who would like to try certified organic coffee.

**TEAK PLANTATIONS** These have been promoted in Costa Rica for years. According to promoters, raising teak trees is a surefire venture that will pay huge dividends. Forestry experts I've interviewed dismiss this as mostly hype. It is true that after an eight-year growth (trees will be from 6 to 10 inches in diameter), they are typically cut into tongue-and-groove boards or into chips to make parquet floors. From what I understand, the profit from this first cutting sometimes just about covers the cost of planting and maintenance. Trees are thinned again every several years, with the last harvest at about twenty-five years, when they finally become high-value lumber. The *Tico Times* once ran an interesting series of investigative feature articles on teak as an investment. The controversy is ongoing, so before you invest, do some investigation on your own. You're likely to find some investors who feel they've made a mistake and others who are pleased.

Years ago, when the teak craze started, *tico* farmers throughout the country planted stands of teak on steep hills where ordinary crops wouldn't do well. It didn't cost much, and over the years, they ignored the trees. But since teak should be planted on flat areas and loses most of its value without early pruning, this teak is not bringing high prices. Today, when you buy tracts of forested land, chances are you'll find some rows of teak trees, some possibly ready for harvesting on a small scale.

I have an expatriate friend who discovered that by using a relatively inexpensive and easily portable sawmill, his workers can turn out stacks of teak tongue-and-groove boards—very much in demand for home building today. Instead of the traditional method of cutting trees, dragging them to a point where they can be loaded on trucks, and selling trees to lumber mills, these entrepreneurs bring the sawmill to the trees. Workers process them on the spot, turning low-value tree trunks into valuable lumber.

This system is much better for ecology, since it doesn't involve cutting roads through the forest or clear-cutting to get at the teak trees. My friend turns a nice profit and feels good about the sensible way the profits are generated.

**REFORESTATION** The traditional way of marketing tree farms is to buy inexpensive, abandoned farms, then plant several thousand teak or pochote trees, then sell the land to investors. There are other ways of doing this: either sell shares in the project, or sell trees to investors rather than land.

Fred Morgan, from western New York, found another approach. Instead of planting hectare after hectare of a single tree crop, his idea is to re-create the original rain forest by interspersing cash-crop trees with varied native and rare species of trees that were originally present before the rain forest or primary forest was destroyed to create pasture for cattle.

Later, when tree crops are harvested, the rain-forest trees are left standing, with a good start for the future. The land will then be withdrawn from further planting, restoring the land to nature. Information about this project can be found at www.fincaleola.com.

When asked his advice for those thinking about going into the reforestation business in Costa Rica, Fred Morgan wrote the following:

"We from the First World perceive that successful businesspeople are usually hard drivers. If you're that way in Costa Rica, you will find that, like walking chest deep in water, you will exhaust yourself by trying to run and not get anywhere much quicker. However, if you move at a reasonable pace (which is a little slower than you're used to), you will find that the water flows around you and even tends to support you when you stumble.

"Work with the characteristics of the culture: Here, community is considered more important than any particular business or enterprise. The labor laws reflect this way of life. You can fight against that for a while, but if your neighbors think it's against the good of the people, you can expect the current to start opposing you and to eventually wear you out. Our goals of re-creating rain forest and creating jobs are considered beneficial to the society, so not only do we rarely find ourselves fighting the culture, we also have been supported and carried by it at times.

"People buy trees from us with the understanding that after their trees are removed, the land will be maintained as perpetual rain forest. For people who want to help without owning trees, we have a program we call the Tree Avalanche that works by using donated trees to create a pioneer forest of valuable wood. Among these trees are also planted the 'succession trees' that will eventually make up the mature rain forest. When the pioneer cash-crop trees are removed, allowing the succession trees to form a forest, the money realized will be used to purchase more land and to plant more pioneer and succession trees.

"Since the money gained from the pioneer trees is more than it costs to plant, care for, and harvest them, the amount going into reforestation keeps multiplying. In the wake of this process, instead of leaving a path of destruction, the Tree Avalanche leaves a swath of new forest." (See the Web site for further details.)

# REAL ESTATE **DEVELOPMENT**

The term "property development" usually stirs negative images in the minds of longtime Costa Rica residents. They picture a group of profit-hungry investors who have one goal: maximizing profits. If primary forest, mangrove wetlands, or wild animals get in their way, no problem. These kinds of developers show no conscience as their projects destroy the environment. The only thing of vital importance to them is getting the highest return for the lowest cost.

Those who live in Costa Rica for any length of time will understand what I'm saying. We've seen foreign companies—Spanish, German, North American—come in with bulldozers and chain saws to clear building sites and construct homes for wealthy foreigners, laying waste to the countryside and invading the beaches. The biggest offenders are those who have the most money and thus have *pata* (connections) with local authorities. Big developers can afford to hire plenty of workers to speed up the process of transferring pristine beaches into gated golf courses and luxury homes. Local authorities are sometimes intimidated by wealthy and powerful corporations, and often are backed down when they try to control development.

**LARGE-SCALE DEVELOPMENT** It doesn't have to be that way, and not all developers are that way. A notable exception is the Bosque Verde development on a low mountain near the Pacific Coast village of Nosara. The developers, Julio and Barbara Batista, are originally from Phoenix, Arizona. Neither Julio nor Barbara had previous experience in land development or anything connected with real estate. Julio was an engineer working for Honeywell on the International Space Station, and Barbara was an educational consultant working with schools in Arizona.

This all changed when the Batistas first visited Costa Rica more than a decade ago (after reading an early edition of *Choose Costa Rica*). They fell in love with the Nosara region. They bought a lovely house with an ocean view and plenty of trees, where bands of howler monkeys, iguanas, and flocks of tropical birds compete for human attention.

By accident, they discovered a *tico* family interested in selling their family farm. It was perched on a low mountaintop with fantastic views of the Pacific Ocean and coastline. Julio and Barbara couldn't resist. Heavily forested and not farmed for many years, the 285-acre property had become a veritable wildlife refuge.

They planned to build a new home on the very summit of the property. When they began looking into the expense of installing electric power lines, digging wells, and building three pumping stations to bring water up to the building site, they realized that they were looking at several times more money than they paid for the land. A natural solution was to subdivide the property into building lots and amortize the cost of the infrastructure among those who bought building sites. Each lot had ocean views yet were out of sight of neighboring lots.

Most developers would, at this point, begin selling lots to buyers, giving flowery promises of future water and electricity—a fast way to raise money to begin development. Julio and Barbara didn't care to do this. They decided not to sell even one building lot until water and electricity were in place, ready to start construction. They didn't want to disappoint buyers in the event that they couldn't come through with the promised utilities. When laying out the building sites, they made sure that each home would have maximum privacy from other homes. Even though it's a gated community, they wanted residents to get the feeling they are the only inhabitants overlooking the Pacific.

They hired a Costa Rican forestry and tropical-plant expert and proceeded to plant thousands of trees, shrubs, and vines. Sixty percent of the land is dedicated as an ecological easement for residents to enjoy, thus protecting the natural ecosystems from further development.

Being an engineer, Julio used his expertise to oversee the construction of the roads, culverts, electrical distribution, and water systems. Finally, after drilling wells, designing and building water-pumping stations, and bringing water to every home site, Bosque Verde was ready to begin selling building sites. All of the above took eight years of intensive (and expensive) work, but it was finally completed in 2005. Julio says, "We feel very good about what we have achieved. We used our retirement money to create an ecologically friendly community where we can live with like-minded adventurers. It has been a creative journey."

Almost the moment the building sites were put on the market, one couple bought two of them—one for their home and one for future investment. An entry with lagoons and gardens for beauty and a gatehouse for security are under construction.

Contact information and Web site: Greg Smith or Susan Loudenslager, 682-0616 or 876-0919 within Costa Rica; 011-506-682-0616 from the United States; www.bosqueverdereserve.com.

**SMALL-SCALE DEVELOPMENT** Property development doesn't have to be done with unlimited funds and investment. A few years ago, José Pelleya, a Cuban American from Florida and owner of a bed-and-breakfast in Alajuela, started looking around for another B&B to complement his business.

José says, "Unexpectedly I ran across a beautiful farm property, rolling hills and good views, on the outskirts of San Ramón. It had a large seven-bedroom, two-bath home (in need of remodeling), sitting on an eight-acre parcel. I loved it and could immediately see possibilities for a unique country bed-and-breakfast."

Formerly an attorney specializing in Florida real estate, José used his skills to negotiate a lease with the option to buy, with seller financing for one year once he exercised the option. José points out that both lease-option and seller financing are practically unheard of in Costa Rica.

So he set about remodeling and modernizing the building. This in itself was no minor project. *Tico* farmhouses are basic to say the least. Being a gregarious person, José realized it could be boring to live on all that property alone. "Why not invite others to share," he thought. So he asked for permission to do a subdivision into building lots (on paper only) and started planning.

"Six months later, I found my first buyer, so I exercised the option," he said. "Then I sold the lot, and away I went!" Divided into seven lots, four sold the first year. Only one lot remains, which José is keeping for himself. Incidentally, one of his clients, a lovely lady named Joanna, bought a lot, built a house, and then married José. He says, "At least she got a good deal on the lot!"

Things were looking good, so José purchased forty-seven acres adjoining his development and created twenty-eight more lots. Almost all of the lots have been purchased, and at least a dozen homes have been constructed. This is creating an interesting community of expatriates, pooling their energy, resources, and creativity. On a roll, José bought a nearby 112-acre tract with incredible mountain, gulf, and ocean views. The Web sites are: www.butterflydance.co.cr and www.rancholobohomes.com.

As if that weren't enough, José's latest project is a business in downtown San Ramón called *Solo Bueno,* "only the best." This is a combination Internet cafe, public mailboxes, used-English-book store, as well as a real estate exchange for rentals and sales in the San Ramón area. Whenever local expats go into town, they naturally drop by for a cup of coffee, check e-mail, pick up a paperback, and catch up on what is happening in the community.

# HIRING **EMPLOYEES**

During World War II the Costa Rican government passed a series of progressive labor laws that remain on the books and are strictly enforced. These laws seek to avoid conflicts between workers and employers by setting out concrete employment rules and a system of wages and benefits. In effect, these laws take the place of union contracts between worker and employer, guaranteeing individual workers benefits they probably couldn't negotiate on their own. If you look at the rules from the viewpoint of the worker, they are basically fair—and certainly not unreasonable from the standpoint of a considerate employer.

However, hiring a maid, a gardener, or an employee in your business involves more than an informal agreement about wages and hours of employment, as is the custom back home. Because we North Americans aren't used to such formal relations with employees, and because we are likely to be hiring workers, even if it's just domestic help around the house and garden, the rules need to be spelled out in some detail. Following the laws to the letter prevents unexpected and serious problems.

Briefly, here are some ground rules: Employers are responsible for making Social Security payments for an employee as well as deducting contributions from the employee's wages. All workers are entitled to paid vacations. After a thirty-day trial period of employment, an employee is entitled to severance pay as well as notice before being laid off. A Christmas bonus is neither a gift nor a nice gesture; it's an obligation mandated by law. The employer is required to give three months of maternity leave at half pay. All these rules are detailed below and should be studied carefully before hiring any help. One other piece of advice: Purchase an accident insurance policy for your employees, even if they are only part-time. Premiums are minimal, but your employees will appreciate the extra coverage. You'll also protect yourself should something horrendous happen to one of your workers.

## GOOD **LABOR RELATIONS**

I once spoke with a woman who was visiting Costa Rica with the intention of starting some kind of business. "When hiring workers," she said, "I understand that the secret is to just hire them for eighty-nine days and then lay them off. That way you aren't responsible for benefits such as severance pay and vacations. Once they work ninety days, you are obligated; so you simply hire new workers every eighty-nine days!"

This upset me, and I told her so. Although her information was incorrect, that wasn't the point. Costa Ricans work very hard for a fraction of the wages employees receive in the United States or Canada, and the law guarantees them certain benefits. It's unfair to try to chisel them out of their rightful benefits. Attitudes like this can do nothing but tarnish the reputations of other North Americans. Those who have lived here for a long time generally realize the wisdom of paying their help more than the law requires. "I try to make it so my maid can't afford to quit," said one woman. "She is wonderful, and I couldn't stand to lose her."

Word quickly gets around the neighborhood if you are a good person to work for (or a difficult one). If you earn a poor reputation as an employer, your job applicants will be those who can't hold a job elsewhere. Then you'll wonder why your employees are lazy, don't show up half the time, or have a tendency to steal!

After I gave the newcomer a piece of my mind about her attitude, she explained that she had heard that if you lay workers off after they've worked more than ninety days, you must pay eight years' salary as severance pay. She heard wrong again. The facts are: For each year worked, an employee is entitled to severance pay of one month's salary—up to a maximum of eight months' pay. That is eight *months'* salary, not eight *years.*

From a worker's point of view, this is only fair. Let's suppose that after eight years of faithful service, it becomes necessary to let your housekeeper go. For eight years the severance pay amounts to about $1,500. Does that sound outrageous for eight years of loyalty and hard work? If it does, then maybe you deserve workers who are lazy, don't show up half the time, or have a tendency to steal.

The owner of a hotel and restaurant in Manuel Antonio told of his experience hiring Costa Rican workers. "It's important to gain their trust," he said. "They don't know anything about you or how you are going to treat them. At first I had trouble attracting the best workers. But I treated people fairly and tried to keep them busy during slack seasons so that I wouldn't have to lay them off. Before long I earned a good reputation. Now I have a waiting list of people who want to join my staff."

## CONDITIONS OF **EMPLOYMENT**

1. **Length of employment.** The first thirty days of employment are a trial period, and either employer or worker can terminate without notice. However, vacation pay and *aguinaldo* (Christmas bonus; described later) must be paid in addition to wages if the employee has worked more than twenty days in that month's time period. Thereafter, for each month worked one day's vacation pay is due, up to two weeks of vacation for a full year's work. Many employees, either by custom or through union contracts, receive three weeks' vacation. My understanding is that an employee may work through his or her

vacation, provided that the employee receives an additional day's pay for each day worked. (I'm not a labor lawyer, however, so you will want to confirm this point if it arises for you.)

2. **Wages.** Just about every employment imaginable in Costa Rica has an official job description with a corresponding minimum wage. From taxi drivers to physicians, from clerk-typists to college professors, all are listed on a biannual list of minimum wages that requires several pages. Laborers who work with machetes are listed separately from those who mend fences or work with shovels. In addition, various regions of the country have different minimum-wage rates.

An interesting facet of the wage structure is that a maid, gardener, or chauffeur who lives in your home is considered to be receiving an additional 50 percent of his or her salary as "payment-in-kind." If, for example, you pay a live-in maid a salary of $150 a month, the actual salary is considered to be $225, or 50 percent more when figuring benefits. This is important, because the gross salary (salary plus payment-in-kind) is used to figure the *aguinaldo*, Social Security payments, and severance pay. A catch here is that an hourly employee who regularly receives a lunch at your home is also considered to be receiving a 50 percent payment-in-kind, so your Christmas bonus, severance pay, and vacation pay have to be based on this. If you feel that you are already paying the hourly employee enough, you can save money by sending them out to lunch! (To be fair, this is a rather extreme example; few employees would ever put in a claim such as this.)

3. **Working hours.** The maximum for domestics is twelve hours a day, although almost nobody expects more than eight. The standard is usually an eight-hour day and a five-day week. For regular employees other than domestics, work on Saturday and Sunday is at double-time rates. Often construction workers work a half day Saturday for a full day's pay. For those working in businesses or industries that traditionally operate seven days a week, the rules are a bit different; check with your local Social Security office. Although the laws are quite specific, *tico* employers often

do not follow the laws to the letter, knowing that employees seldom complain. However, I earnestly advise expatriates to follow the rules; you have a high profile in the community, and cutting corners is really a penny-pinching tactic.

4. **Social Security.** An important obligation for employers, one taken quite seriously by the government, is Social Security. This critical institution pays for health care, sick leave, and disability pensions. You, as an employer, must pay 20 percent of a worker's gross salary and must deduct 9 percent of the worker's wages and pay both portions of the tax to the Caja Costarricanse del Seguro Social. Make sure your workers understand that you are withholding the taxes from their pay. Otherwise their share of taxes could come out of your pocket. Some people pay both sides of the Social Security payments as a bonus for a good employee.

Within eight days of hiring a regular employee, you must notify the local Social Security office. Doing so is vital, because should a worker become ill or injured on the job, you could theoretically be liable for medical bills and 50 percent of the employee's salary for the duration of the sickness. When your employee is covered by Social Security, your liability is limited to the first four days' salary; Social Security takes over from there. To prevent abuse of this law, you, as the employer, are entitled to demand a health certificate from the worker (*carnet de salud*) when the employee is hired and every six months thereafter. This is provided at no cost to the employee by the Seguro Social Hospitals.

Pregnancy is a different situation. Your employee's blessed event will obligate you to some additional employee benefits. Employees are entitled to a month's rest before the baby is born and three additional months afterward— half the salary to be paid by the employer and the other half by the government. By the way, firing a worker for being pregnant is frowned upon, and you might need to validate your reasons for firing other than pregnancy.

5. **Christmas bonus (*aguinaldo*).** Sometime between December 1 and 20, employees are due an *aguinaldo*. For those who

have worked a full year prior to December 1, the bonus is a month's pay. For those who have worked more than the thirty-day trial period but less than a full year, the payment is prorated over the time they have worked. Thus, a person who has worked three months gets three-twelfths of one month's pay. Remember that employees who live in or who regularly receive at least one meal a day get a Christmas bonus based on the payment-in-kind, in addition to their salary, or an additional 50 percent.

6. **Notice and severance pay.** Workers employed more than ninety days and less than a year are entitled to two weeks' notice before being laid off. After a year, one month's notice is required. If you don't or can't give notice, you must pay the employee full wages for the notification period.

Unless an employee quits, you are obligated to pay severance pay dependent on length of employment: up to three months, none; from four to six months, two weeks' pay; between seven months and one year, one month's pay. Then you must pay an additional month's pay for each year or fraction over six months worked. In no case can this payment be more than the equivalent of eight months' salary.

Again, remember that this is based on gross pay (including 50 percent payment-in-kind, if applicable). It doesn't matter if the worker immediately finds a new job; you still have to pay.

A worker can be fired at any time during the first thirty days for any reason, with no obligation other than the *aguinaldo* and wages due. Furthermore, a worker who fails to give notice (*preaviso*) before quitting forfeits the *aguinaldo*.

## EMPLOYEE **OBLIGATIONS**

According to government regulations, workers can be held responsible for damages they have caused, whether intentionally or due to imprudence or "inexcusable neglect." A domestic worker can be discharged without receiving severance if "notorious lack of respect or civil treatment is shown," which should be backed up by witnesses. You had better have good proof, though, because in doubtful cases the Ministry of Labor tends to side with the worker.

When an employee quits or is laid off, it is a good practice to make things crystal clear by having him or her sign a statement (in Spanish) to the effect that all benefits have been paid. Include the severance pay, vacation pay, Christmas bonus, and any salary due up to the time of separation. Have the employee sign the document in front of a witness. Should the employee be quitting voluntarily, be sure to note that in the document.

## SALARIES AND **WAGE RATES**

*Tico* employers tend to be reluctant to pay higher wages than the law requires, but they are often forced to if they want good help. At times construction workers are in very short supply, so they can demand more than minimum rates. In some parts of the country, workers could earn double what they could make in more depressed areas. Nicaraguan workers (most of them illegal) will usually accept the minimum or less and are resented by *ticos* who have to compete with them for jobs. North Americans who successfully operate their own businesses usually agree that paying decent salaries means happy employees who are loyal and hardworking.

We always pay a little more than our neighbors for two reasons. First of all, we don't want to feel like cheapskates. Secondly, wages are so low in the first place that we feel somewhat embarrassed on payday, as though we're exploiting our employees. Yes, we risk the ire of those who accuse us of "ruining it for everyone," but I can easily dismiss that. I reject the idea that paying our gardener an extra 60 cents an hour will "ruin it" for anyone. Nor can I believe that all this extra money will go to our workers' heads and cause labor unrest among our neighbors' domestic help. We try to be friends with our employees, not bosses. Our maid always gives us both a hug and a kiss on the cheek when we see each other on the village street, just as we do with our good expat friends when we meet.

Unlike the United States, Costa Rica stipulates an individual wage rate for each and every possible job classification and profession, not simply a basic minimum salary no matter what the job. The government's Web page (see below) posts specific wage scales for more than 250 occupations; for example: cook's helper, captain of a boat, and bus drivers (there is a different wage scale for a bus driver who also collects fares). The wage rates listed below are accurate only until July 1, 2008, when the new schedule will be posted.

Not only does just about every job classification have a specified minimum wage, but the level of education is considered, having its own minimum wage. For example, minimum wages range from 107,883 colones ($207) a month for domestic workers to 383,359 colones ($737) a month for someone holding a master's degree from a university. Our local librarian went to night school at the university for several years. Once she received her degree in library science, she was entitled to almost double her salary.

Among the highest-paid jobs on the list is journalism, which pays 487,500 colones ($975) a month, compared with a university professor's salary of 395,000 colones ($790) per month. My impression is that because legislators are sensitive to press criticism, by awarding newswriters the top pay rates, they hope to receive special consideration. Since this is my profession, I feel top pay is perfectly fair. (My publishers might quarrel with that belief.) However, most journalists in the United States earn more money than that every week.

## Sample Minimum Wages

| Workers | (colones) | (dollars) |
|---|---|---|
| Housemaid | 107,883 | $207* |
| Field hand | 138,715 | $267 |
| Unskilled | 171,265 | $329 |
| Semiskilled | 185,653 | $357 |
| Skilled | 198,976 | $383 |
| Technicians | 213,897 | $411 |
| University graduates | 320,477 | $616 |
| With graduate degree | 383,359 | $737 |

*Actual wages vary, depending on whether domestics are live-in workers, how many hours they work, and other variables.

In addition to the official minimum wages, there are other costs. The employer is obligated to pay 13 percent Social Security taxes, plus withhold 9 percent from the paycheck on behalf of the employee. (Many employers pay the whole tax as a special benefit.) Then there is 3 percent for retirement and 2 percent for workmen's compensation insurance. It's important that these payments are made and that these obligations are met, either by yourself or by a professional manager. Again, accident insurance is also a very good idea.

# WORKING IN **COSTA RICA**

A question often asked is, "How can I get a job in Costa Rica?" The answer is, "It can be done, but it's not easy." The Costa Rican government discourages foreigners from competing with citizens for work. In order to work legally, you'll need a special permit, which involves proving that you are uniquely qualified for a job that can't be done by a *tico*. Foreign companies are entitled to a limited percentage of noncitizen employees, but in practice they seldom fill this quota. The reason is simple: They can hire all the qualified *tico* employees they need, and most foreigners don't want to work for *tico* wages. Twenty dollars a day is considered a generous wage. A bartender earns $12 a day, a skilled carpenter about $3 an hour.

Since the collapse of high-tech employment and the dot-com meltdown, many highly qualified and skilled software engineers, technicians, and Web specialists are "at liberty," and many are eager to begin life anew in an interesting setting such as Costa Rica. They are aware that the country's computer technology is riding a wave of expansion as business, industry, and government become computerized and enter the Web universe. It's only natural that those recently unemployed and soon-to-be-downsized high-tech people who love Costa Rica will be looking in this direction.

Are there jobs for these highly qualified people? Probably not. You have to realize that Costa Ricans also see the future opportunities in the world of digital employment. Seems as if every other high school student you meet plans to major in computer science. At every one of the many satellite campuses of the universities, the most popular classes involve computers. Students come from miles around to take night classes in *computación*. The good news is that many high-tech jobs have been created through foreign investment. The bad news is that Intel and other corporations are limited to 10 percent of their workforce being foreigners on work permits, and they are committed to hiring as many *ticos* as they can. One exception is in the field of teaching English. Qualified teachers can often find employment, although, again, for minimal salaries. More on this subject can be found in chapter 15, "Costa Rican Schools."

## POSSIBLE **WORK-IMMIGRATION CHANGES**

This is not to say that a large number of foreigners aren't working illegally in the country. A large number are. Most work in real estate sales, property management, and tourism. You'll find them employed as waitresses, bartenders, tour guides, and hotel employees. Most are young and willing to take whatever pay they can get, just to live in Costa Rica. Many work as English teachers, tolerated by the government, ostensibly because they aren't taking work from *ticos*. A few with special skills find work in construction. Often, foreigners working as building contractors don't get hassled by local officials, probably because they hire workers and provide jobs, but basically because they are supervising rather than laboring. Unless foreigners are obviously taking work from *ticos*, their activities are often overlooked. But at the other end of the scale are an estimated 500,000 Nicaraguans working as coffee pickers, laborers, etc., which obviously is a large immigration issue, like in the United States. If that figure is true (and I doubt that it is), that's a lot of illegal workers in a country of around four million inhabitants!

Let me emphasize: Over the years of updating this book, I've never recommended that people work illegally; I am simply reporting what is the case. The fact is, the Costa Rican government hasn't been overly zealous in enforcing existing laws.

After the last national election (2006), the National Assembly passed a law that has the potential to radically change past immigration policies. The intent of the law was to crack down on foreigners living and working illegally in Costa Rica. Principally it was aimed at the flood of illegal immigrants from Nicaragua, Panama, and other Central American countries, but the law could logically have been applied to North Americans as well. Those working without work permits could face fines and possible deportation. Permanent residents without legal residency papers could be hassled. The law also specified fines for employers who hire illegal aliens and provides deportation for those who cannot prove they are in the country legally.

However, the new immigration rules also give the Policía de Migración (immigration police) broader powers to inspect documents and to detain and deport any person who cannot demonstrate his or her legal right to be in the country, including visitors who overstay their tourist visas. If this law is upheld, many "permanent tourists" who have been living in Costa Rica for years, going out of the country every ninety days to renew their visas, could be affected.

When Oscar Arias, the Costa Rican president, took office in 2006, he declared the new immigration laws "draconian" and requested that some of the laws be held in abeyance while the new government studied the laws and made reasonable changes in the rules and regulations. The courts ruled that since the laws were on the books, they could not be postponed. But the official in charge of administering the law, the Ministero de Seguridad (Security Minister), pointed out that no funds or immigration agents were provided to enforce the new regulations. He confirmed that it is an impossibility for the immigration service to apply the new regulations, saying that "no one is obligated to do the impossible."

However, the Arias government still seems determined to delay the more negative effects of the law while legislators take time to make changes to the existing legislation for a more "practical" law. Needless to say, strict enforcement of these laws could affect many people living and working in Costa Rica more or less illegally. People who could be technically in violation of immigration laws should be aware of what is happening.

This is the state of affairs at the time of this writing (fall 2008), when this book is about to go to press. My personal opinion (and it's only an opinion) is that the government is not going to do anything drastic that might affect the status quo for most of those who are technically in violation of immigration rules. Nevertheless, it would be prudent to keep abreast of events should there be any question in your mind. You can do this by watching the online newspapers and reading the *Tico Times* and local Costa Rican daily papers. You can also follow my Costa Rica update Web site at: www.discoverypress.com/update.

# GETTING TO **COSTA RICA**

The quickest and easiest way to get to Costa Rica is by air, of course, but this restricts the amount of belongings you can take—items you may need for a long-term stay. Those who live here full- or part-time always enter with as much luggage as we're allowed. With rising costs of fuel, weight limits on baggage are going down while fares are going up. Our bags are usually packed with items difficult to find in Costa Rica, such as tools, home fixtures, and items from the "wish lists" of our friends in Costa Rica. We bring everything from paperbacks and videotapes to bedding and automobile parts. Customs tend to be rather casual about this, as long as one doesn't go overboard. (Remember, there's only a $500-per-passenger duty exemption.)

A growing number of airlines schedule regular service to Costa Rica—including American Airlines, United, American, Continental, and others—and inexpensive Canadian charter flights fly from Vancouver and Montreal. Foreign lines, such as Mexicana, TACA, Aviateca, COPA, and others, fly from Miami, New Orleans, Houston, San Francisco, and Los Angeles. Some start-up airlines, usually flying out of Miami, occasionally offer "get-acquainted" fares for as little as $16 round-trip from Florida to San José!

## COSTA RICA'S **AIRPORTS**

Costa Rica's main air facility—totally renovated and ultramodern—the Juan Santamaría Airport, near San José, has streamlined its arrival and departure procedures and is almost a pleasure to use. Customs inspections are relaxed yet professional. Airport taxis to downtown San José are plentiful, and prices are controlled. The standard price to downtown San José is around $15. Cab drivers readily accept dollars. A real improvement in the taxi situation is that you no longer have to haggle over the fare. As you exit customs, you'll see some windows on your left where you can buy a ticket to wherever your destination. You hand the ticket to a waiting taxi driver, and your fare is paid! You probably will leave a tip, but that's up to you. By the way, some airport taxis aren't supposed to go to more than one hotel or address per trip, so if you share a cab with someone, make a deal with the driver, if necessary, perhaps a tip for the extra stop. Also, a bus stops on the main road in front of the terminal, with inexpensive fares of less than a dollar to go to downtown San José or to nearby Alajuela. Buses pass by every few minutes.

When returning from Costa Rica, you must pay a departure tax of $26. You'll find two lines in the terminal for paying this tax, and you must pay before going to the ticket counter. You can use colones, dollars, or a combination of either. If you use a credit card, they have to add about $4 to the bill. You'll hear travelers complaining about this tax, but consider that U.S. airports also have hefty charges, which customers often aren't aware of—they simply add it to the price of your ticket.

An additional international airport—Daniel Oduber International, near the northwestern city of Liberia—opened not too long ago. Many of the major airlines, as well as charter flights from the United States and Canada, are making Liberia a major destination for air travelers. For those tourists and residents headed for the popular Guanacaste coast, this means avoiding an overnight stay in San José, coming and going. Of course hotels and tourist facilities in the San José area fiercely resisted the new airport. But travelers to the Pacific beaches love it!

The economy of this region is already healthy, but increased airline traffic is boosting it even higher. A friend flew in from Miami, with about two and a half hours' flight time and two and a quarter hours' drive time from Liberia to a Pacific beach resort—a total travel time of less than it

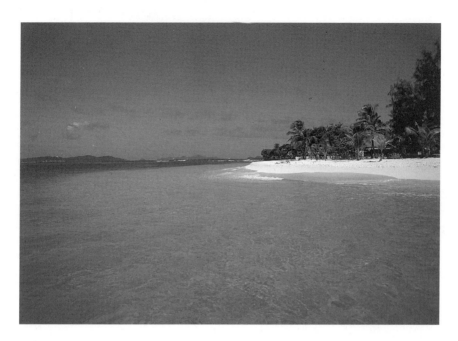

used to take just to drive from the San José airport to his destination in Tamarindo!

# DRIVING TO **COSTA RICA**

For a while, civil war in Guatemala, El Salvador, and Nicaragua brought tourist automobile travel through these countries to a virtual standstill. But even then some intrepid tourists insisted on driving, merely changing the route somewhat. They traveled the Pacific coastal route through Guatemala, avoided El Salvador by detouring through Honduras, and then carefully skirted trouble spots in Nicaragua. We tried to drive through Guatemala in the 1980s but returned to Mexico after facing gauntlets of gun barrels being pointed at our foreheads at every military stop. Today, with the return of peace to the region, automobile travel is once again routine.

Our last adventure took place in 1999, and I understand that conditions haven't much changed since then. The actual driving time from the Arizona border at Nogales was around eight days of no more than eight to ten hours of relaxed driving per day. But not being in a hurry, we spread the trip over a full month. We stopped to visit friends in Lake Chapala and Guatemala City. We also detoured to spend some time at the marvelous Mayan ruins in Copán, Honduras.

Not everyone would have enjoyed the trip as much as we did, but we had done it before, and for us it was a pleasant adventure. From the time we entered Mexico until we reached our home in Costa Rica, we encountered not one military stop, saw no military presence, and were halted only a few times for routine checks of the car—presumably to make sure it wasn't stolen. At none of the borders did they inspect our luggage or do anything other than glance in the back of our station wagon. Also, we were careful not to do anything stupid, like driving after dark.

Please don't think I'm suggesting that everybody will have a breeze. It's a long trip, with bad roads as well as good ones. Sometimes the accommodations are awful; sometimes they're delightful. If you can speak some Spanish, it would be helpful, but we met many travelers who spoke very little Spanish yet were making out just fine. Some people will enjoy traveling through Mexico and Central America, others will not. Those who won't enjoy this kind of journey are those who probably wouldn't think about going in the first place. You'll know into which category you fall.

I've interviewed more than a dozen travelers who made the trip between 1995 and 2007; all shrugged off these inconveniences. Most described their trip as an adventure they wouldn't have missed for anything. The secret to stress-free traveling in Central America is to "hang loose" at the customs stops—try to laugh at the process. A smile will do a lot to smooth your path across borders. A smile and a $5 bill will do even more. With the exception of the excellent and efficient toll roads through Mexico, the Central American portion of the Inter-American Highway today consists of low-speed pavement—sometimes pockmarked, occasionally smooth—with dual lanes.

Every day on the road was a new adventure, a new challenge, full of photo opportunities and stimulating encounters with other travelers and local people. The most annoying part of the journey was the delay and inconvenience while crossing borders. Sour-faced officials examine your papers with suspicious eyes, then hand out a sheaf of forms to be filled out in triplicate. Then they rubber-stamp everything in sight. (Oh, how they love rubber stamps!) You go from one official to another for what seems an eternity. Finally, you are allowed to leave the country, only to drive 50 feet into the next country and start the process all over again at the next customs office.

Even if you speak Spanish well, I highly recommend that you hire a *tramitador*, someone to help you through customs, at the busy crossings. (You can generally tell when you need one: when the lines are long and not moving.) You'll usually find kids hanging around who, for a fee, will run your passport and car papers around to the places where they will be rubber-stamped, have stamps affixed, and have signatures scrawled upon them. Which of the kids to hire? I always pick one who appears to be the most aggressive. He will not be shy about elbowing other tourists aside to shove his way to the front of the line so that the officials can look at your papers first. The cost is usually $10, but it's worth it. Get the price fixed before you start. If things appear to be moving smoothly, you may not need to hire a helper.

We didn't drive through El Salvador this last trip, though not because we wanted to avoid it; our visit to Copán, Honduras, just happened to route us around El Salvador. The border crossing from Guatemala to Honduras at that point is exceptionally easy and painless. So few cars cross there that the border guards seemed delighted to have someone to chat with.

**ON THE ROAD** From the U.S. border at Brownsville, Texas, to Costa Rica, the drive is 2,300 miles. From Mexicali the distance is 3,700 miles. Your car should be in good condition, with new tires, a spare, an emergency tool kit, road flares, and flashlights with extra batteries.

Always get out of the car and supervise the gas station attendant while he services the car. Attendants have been known to accidentally put diesel fuel or leaded gas into a car requiring no-lead fuel. And make sure they turn the pump back to zero before they start so that you don't end up paying for gas you don't get. (I've never had this happen in Costa Rica.) You might carry a hand calculator to make sure you are paying the correct amount and getting the right change. Even if you don't know what you are doing, the attendant will think you do, and he won't cheat. A trick that station attendants in Mexico might try to pull on you: When you hand them a 100-peso bill, they quickly switch it for a 50-peso note, to make you think you made a mistake. The cure for this is to carefully hand them the note and say, "*Billete de cien pesos*" ("hundred-peso bill").

Don't forget car insurance. Your U.S. or Canadian policy isn't recognized south of the border, but carry it with you anyway as proof that you have a valid policy, just in case. You can buy a special insurance policy for Central America. Before you cross into Mexico, contact Sanborn's Insurance at (210) 686-0711 (fax 210-686-0732), or write to P.O. Box 310, McAllen, TX 78505-0310. The Web site is www.sanbornsinsurance.com. This company can write Central American policies by telephone and will take credit cards. Most people purchase a fifteen-day policy, which should be more than ample time to drive all the way to Costa Rica. Ask for a *Travelog* with detailed directions, maps, and hotel/restaurant listings for Central America (free with insurance).

# TOURING **COSTA RICA**

Every nook and cranny of Costa Rica has something special to offer, something to dazzle the eyes or gratify the other senses. Newcomers are never satisfied until they have seen it all; longtime residents tend to repeat their travels, to see everything again and again. Fortunately, getting around the country is easy. Within a few hours you can visit just about any section of Costa Rica you choose, and you usually have several modes of transportation available to you.

The quickest way to travel about the country is by SANSA, Nature Air, or charter flights. Planes fly regularly, serving San José, Quepos, Golfito, Palmar Sur, Barra del Colorado, Nosara, Tamarindo, and Sámara. Ticket prices used to be inexpensive, but in the past few years, they have become costly, and service often leaves much to be desired. Charter flights cost only a few dollars more than scheduled flights. SANSA offers a 50 percent discount for residents with *cédulas* (permanent residents), but it's still five to ten times as expensive as bus travel. Flights to anywhere in the country take far less than an hour, including stopovers. Check with travel agents or Web sites for schedules. They can change overnight or be canceled entirely.

Because flights are popular and the planes are small, they are frequently booked solid. Make reservations well in advance. And since regular service can be crowded, "air taxi" or charter flights are popular. Small five-passenger planes will take you anyplace in the country with an airstrip. What's nice is that you can have a driver awaiting your arrival, who rushes directly to your charter flight, and you don't need to overnight in San José. (Pause for cheers and whistles.)

What if you are a pilot and would like to rent a plane and fly yourself? Not so easy. Even if you are a certified pilot with a license from another country, you can't rent a Costa Rican plane until you've earned a Costa Rican license. You need to show proof of your total air hours logged in your country as well as log a certain amount of time in Costa Rica. To import an airplane, see chapter 16.

## TRAINS AND **BUSES**

Guidebooks used to rave about the scenic wonders of the country's train system. Especially tempting were descriptions of the spectacular railroad trip from San José to the Caribbean city of Limón. However, since the earthquake of 1991, passenger trains no longer journey to Limón, or anywhere else for that matter. Sad, but true. Some roadbeds and a few ancient bridges slipped downhill—common occurrences during Costa Rica earthquakes—but this time the government decided not to rebuild. The lines were losing money anyway.

It's possible that service to the Pacific port of Puntarenas could be resumed sometime in the future, with a private company taking over the operations. In early 2000 a test run to Puntarenas had people sleeping in line overnight to get tickets. Two hundred disappointed would-be passengers watched the train roll away without them. The train to the Caribbean Coast, however, definitely appears to be history. The cost of repairing the bridges and tracks would be prohibitive.

Buses are another story. In addition to excellent city bus service, eight intercity bus companies provide frequent service to just about anyplace you'd care to go. Unlike the situation in the United States, where monopolistic intercity bus fares sometimes border on extortion, tickets between Costa Rican cities are downright cheap. A four-hour ride from San José to Limón, for example, costs little more than $6.

San José has no central bus station; bus lines depart from separate terminals, ranging from a new, full-service terminal to a curbside parking place in front of a small ticket office. For example, to go to Quepos and Manuel Antonio, you take the buses that leave from the "Coca Cola" terminal. (The Coca Cola terminal gains its name in a typical *tico* fashion: There used to be a Coca-Cola bottling plant in the neighborhood.) Buses for Limón, Cahuita, Puerto Viejo, and other Caribbean destinations have their own terminal on Calle Central, 6 blocks north of the Metropolitan Cathedral. Often reservations need to be made a day or two in advance. The better tourist guidebooks list the bus terminals, destinations, and travel times.

A number of smaller bus companies (often with only one or two buses in the fleet) carry passengers to all imaginable sectors of the country. Few towns or villages in the republic lack bus transportation of some sort. Often while I was negotiating impossible backcountry roads, bouncing through deep potholes, skirting boulders in the trail, and wondering whether my rental car could ever make it back in one piece, a passenger-laden bus would appear from out of nowhere, sound its horn impatiently to move me aside, and then rumble past as it hurried on its way.

These country buses tend to be of an older, rattletrap variety, often secondhand school buses bought at surplus in the United States. Sometimes the owner-drivers don't bother to change the paint, and the bus finishes its transportation career bouncing along dusty trails in Costa Rica with MAPLEWOOD UNIFIED SCHOOL DISTRICT still painted on its side. Occasionally you'll be pleasantly surprised by an air-conditioned vehicle of late manufacture, which makes the backcountry surprisingly luxurious. Of course, there's nothing to guarantee the driver will actually turn on the air-conditioning, which draws power from the engine and consumes more diesel fuel. And since *ticos* open the windows from force of habit, the air-conditioning is redundant.

Since the distance between San José and any destination in the country is not very far, bus trips don't take too long. From San José to Quepos, a popular tourist destination, bus travel time is less than four hours. By air it is only twenty minutes or so, but by the time you get out to the airport an hour early, wait for the plane to leave (often a half hour to an hour late), and then wait for a bus to take you from the airstrip to town, you haven't saved all that much time. Plus you've missed a lot of interesting scenery.

However, be aware that different bus lines have varying schedules. For example, travel from San José to Puntarenas takes two hours on one bus line but four hours on another.

I knew Costa Rica had a lot of competing bus companies, but for a while I was astounded at how many different bus lines there appeared to be serving the public. It seemed that the bus lines' names were very creative. Then I discovered that the name painted on a bus's side or on the back wasn't the name of a bus company at all, but rather an imaginative name given to the bus by its driver as an expression of his individuality.

The *Tico Times* once ran a feature article on these names, at which point I realized that the Papa Lolo bus that passed by my house every morning as I waited for my ride was not owned by Papa Lolo Bus Lines but driven by a driver with the nickname "Papa Lolo." Some buses were named after family members; other names were exercises in imagination. Additional names the article noted were Desert Storm, Krakatoa, *El Principe Azul* (the Blue Prince), *Mil Amores* (Thousand Loves), the Dancing Queen, and *El Guerrero del Camino* (the Road Warrior). Having mentioned this (one of my favorite stories about buses in Costa Rica), I have to admit that the major bus lines are becoming much more professional, and fewer of them give the driver the autonomy to personalize his vehicle.

## A MULTITUDE OF **TAXICABS**

Costa Rica enjoys an excellent system of taxis, with more than 7,000 cabs zipping along the streets of San José and the suburbs—double what there were a decade ago. Almost all taxis are late-model Japanese imports, usually Toyotas or Nissans. Occasionally you'll see a Volkswagen or a Volvo. By law taxicabs are painted bright red. You can't miss them. In San José you can go practically anywhere in the city from downtown for between $1 and $5. Between 10:00 p.m. and 5:00 a.m., drivers are permitted to charge an additional 20 percent. Drivers don't expect tips, but I always round the bill up to the next 200 colones, and they drive away happy.

All San José taxis are supposed to have meters, and except for the "pirate" cabs, most do. (A "pirate" cab is one without a legal permit, described later.) *Ticos* refer to a taxi meter as a *maría*. Why *maría*? Some years ago Costa Rica's president decided that taxis should have meters

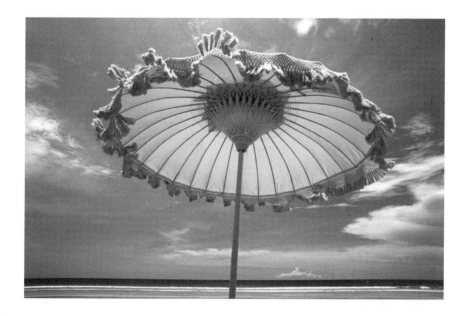

rather than have drivers and clients haggling over the price of each ride. So he ordered a batch of taximeters from a company in Argentina for a trial run. The company's name contained the words Santa-María-something-or-other. But with typical Costa Rican bureaucracy, customs officials in Limón refused to allow the contraptions into the country until all the proper papers and forms were filled out in triplicate and stamped. By the time all the red tape and tax stamps had been glued to quadrupli-cate copies and signatures affixed, the meters—which were mechanical, as opposed to the electronic ones they use today—had rusted in Limón's damp climate and had to be trashed. *Ticos* thought this so funny that they adopted the word *maría* for a taximeter.

Avoid cabs parked in front of hotels or discos. The drivers will tell you that they don't have to use meters because they pay more insurance or some other baloney. The truth is, they charge from two to four times the normal rate. When in doubt, ask, "*¿Hay una maría?*" If the driver claims the meter isn't working, don't enter the cab until you've established a price (provided, of course, that you know about what the price should be). If the driver quotes a ridiculous price or if you haven't any idea of the correct fare, take another cab with a meter. At certain times of the day, especially when it's pouring down rain, drivers are reluctant to turn on the meters because they know they can get all the customers they want and don't want the cab's owner to know exactly how much was taken in.

Often you'll find cabs without meters, known as *piratas*, or "pirates," which are private autos illegally operating as taxis. Usually the fares quoted by these nonmetered cabs are about the same as you'd pay in a legally operated vehicle. The problem with *piratas* is that some of them aren't in safe operating condition. And unless you know what the fare should be and you know enough Spanish to negotiate, I'd recommend waiting for a cab with a meter. All in all, I think Costa Rican taxi drivers are fairly honest. Rarely have I been overcharged, and that was during times of heavy rains or rush hours, when the extra cost was worth it to me.

Although the law says that taxicabs must use meters, bear in mind that any trip over 12 kilometers (7.5 miles) is exempt. A trip from the airport to San José, for example, should cost between $15 and $20, depending on what part of the city you are going to.

Why are most cabs new? Because one side benefit of owning a taxi is that it can be purchased free of import duties, as long as it is used for three years before selling it as a used car. This means that after three years of generating income, the vehicle can be sold for almost as much as it cost in the first place.

Up to this point we've been discussing taxicabs around the Central Valley. Taxis aren't only for city folk: You'll find them all over the country, sometimes in places so isolated that they would seem implausible. Not all villages will have a taxi, but most have access to one from a neighboring village. Today, with the cell phone explosion, you know the village cab driver will be available anytime his cell phone rings. Away from the city's paved roads, four-wheel-drive taxis are common—and in the rainy season, a must. Four-wheel-drive trucks sometimes serve as taxis, with the truck bed used to transport furniture, appliances, or more passengers. In rural areas, where buses and taxis are rare or nonexistent, private autos and trucks often provide free rides to local people walking from one village to another. I do the same and find that locals appreciate rides—the hospitality enhances their opinion of foreigners.

**TAXI CHAUFFEURS** Driving a car around San José or through the narrow roads in the immediate countryside isn't exactly a relaxing pastime. I sometimes find myself so involved with traffic and confusion that I see very little. My passengers see even less, since they spend a great deal of their time praying, cursing, or shouting at me: "Watch where you're going, you dummy!" For that reason I rarely drive in downtown San José, even though I have my own car. It used to take me ten minutes of sweating and cursing to get from our condo to the center of town, whereas it takes only five minutes of sweating and praying in the average taxi. (My idea of hell would be driving a taxi in San José through eternity!)

There is a better way to explore the Central Valley: Rent a cab! Taxi drivers much prefer the idea of one fare for the entire day, instead of wandering all over town waiting for someone to flag them down. One fare isn't nearly as hard on the cab, since passengers always want to stop, get out, and spend time looking around, giving the taxi and driver a deserved rest.

Not only is it convenient to let someone else drive (someone who knows what he's doing), but renting a cab costs not much more than renting a car for the day. A competent, English-speaking cabdriver will chauffeur you around the Central Valley for five or six hours for about $100. A rental car for one day, with insurance and gasoline, would cost at least $75—and $1 million worth of tension. In other words, after you buy the driver's lunch and give a small tip, you're about even. Most any cabdriver will rent for about $15 per hour, but you're better off making prior arrangements with an English-speaking driver.

Taxicab rental will also save you hours of time and frustration when checking out neighborhoods for real estate. The driver can whisk you to a half dozen suburbs in less time than you can stumble onto one. This is also a great idea for sightseeing trips around the Central Valley. Instead of four people paying $30 to $50 per person for a five-hour commercial tour, a cabdriver can show you the same sights, with individual attention, for much less. Some drivers will even take you on longer trips, anyplace in the country you care to go—Monteverde or Manuel Antonio, for example— as long as you also take care of their hotel and meal expenses.

Not all drivers are willing to rent by the hour, and not all can speak English well enough to explain what you are seeing. To find one who does, check with your hotel clerk or a travel agency. Many English-speaking drivers are available and eager to show you around the Central Valley.

## COSTA RICA **RENTAL CARS**

Renting a car is by far the most convenient way of touring the country. When you get serious about looking for a place to live for a few months or for the rest of your life, renting a car for a week or two allows you to travel about freely in search of your dream location. You don't have to bother with bus schedules; you can check out side streets or country lanes, and you can stop whenever you find a particularly interesting view. With a car, you needn't worry about hotel reservations; chances are, if one hotel is full, another will have room. You can drive around, checking out FOR SALE or FOR RENT signs. You can investigate for yourself instead of being under the control of a salesperson, a rental agent, or others with a vested interest in showing you only their own properties.

At present, automobile insurance is a government monopoly, and it's mandatory that your rental-car insurance be purchased through the government agency. This could change soon, bringing much-needed competition to the field. The way it is now, there's usually a hefty $750 deductible in case of an accident with a rental car. Should the car be totaled or stolen, the deductible is $1,500. Since auto theft of rental cars is common, this calls for keeping your rental car in a safe place at night. Nowadays you can pay extra and have full collision insurance, and pay a little more and insure against theft. The insurance isn't cheap, but if you have a gold or platinum credit card (such as Visa or American Express), it should cover the deductible in case of an accident. Check with your credit-card provider to be certain. Be sure to report a mishap to the credit-card company within twenty days, even if the rental agent assures you that the other driver's insurance covers the repairs (from sad experience).

Accessories such as antennas, radios, tires, and mirrors aren't covered by rental insurance; if they are stolen, you are liable. The answer to the insurance problem is to keep your car in a guarded parking lot overnight when in the vicinity of San José. Auto-accessory theft is not as common in smaller towns, but in San José and other large cities, be aware.

Important: Unless you purchase full-coverage insurance, before you accept a rental car, check the car for dents, scratches, and blemishes! Make sure the rental-car employee notes each of them on your contract. Unscrupulous employees in some car-rental agencies have been known to work a scam by charging for the same damage over and over. If the damage is there but not duly noted, you could be blamed and may have to pay. Generally, this only happens with smaller rental companies. Discuss the issue before you sign a contract.

Finally, insist on good tires. A sharp rock can penetrate a tire if the tread is thin and the sidewalls weak. If the tire is destroyed, you're liable for that, too. Insist on another car if the tires are not in good shape. If the car-rental agency gives you trouble about this, consider finding another agency.

# DRIVING **COSTA RICA ROADS**

Your regular driver's license is perfectly legal in Costa Rica for ninety days from the time you enter the country. After that you need a Costa Rican license. For residents or for those awaiting *residente* status, a license is relatively easy to get: Simply apply at the local office of the Ministry of Public Works ("MOPT" for us gringos; ask a friend to help you find one locally) and present a certificate of health from one of the doctors' offices nearby. The license is issued while you wait.

As a tourist, you are permitted to drive with your home country's license as long as your passport indicates you are in the country legally— that is, if your passport shows you haven't been here more than ninety days. If you leave the country long enough to get a fresh stamp on your passport, you'll be okay for another ninety days. Take this warning seriously. Some MOPT offices issue driver's licenses to nonresidents; some will not. However, the advantages of having a driver's license are nebulous unless you are a resident or have made application for residency.

Some people believe that with a Costa Rica driver's license, you needn't have to carry a passport. Not so. If you can't show either a passport or a resident's *cédula* to prove you are in the country legally, you could have a problem. A photocopy of the passport is acceptable, provided you have a copy of the page showing the date you entered. The original passport is much preferred. Photocopies of your driver's license are not acceptable. In fact, without your original driver's license, car-rental agencies won't even rent you a car.

The first rule of driving in Costa Rica is one that should be followed in any country: Do not leave anything valuable in the car, even out of sight. They say that a favorite trick of thieves is to monitor the car-rental desks at the airport and watch who rents a car and fills the trunk with interesting luggage. They then follow the car to the hotel, and while the passengers are inside at the registration desk, the thieves open the trunk and help themselves to the luggage, extra money, cameras, and so on. Frankly, I've never known anyone who has had this happen, and I think this is a bit far-fetched, but why take chances? If possible, leave someone in the car during that crucial first stop. Once you are outside of San José, the chance of something like this happening is almost nil.

Driving through the Costa Rican countryside isn't difficult, it's just slower. With all that gorgeous scenery, who wants to travel fast? Be especially careful when passing. Make sure you have time to get around safely, and be cautious near hills and curves. Always drive as though you expect trouble. That's just common sense in any country, but particularly so in Costa Rica. Too many drivers have a daring attitude that urges them to pass on hills and curves. For this reason accident rates in Costa Rica are unusually high. Drive defensively, and keep an eye on the speedometer.

Americans, used to high-speed, paved highways, sometimes have difficulty keeping their speed under 65 miles per hour; it doesn't seem normal to drive slower. But you must realize that 65 miles per hour is about 110 kilometers per hour, an illegal speed anywhere in the country. Most Costa Rican highways have an 80-kilometer-per-hour speed limit. That's only 48 miles an hour—not a normal speed for North American drivers, who are used to 65-mile-per-hour limits with most everyone driving 10 miles an hour faster. Depending on the quality of a Costa Rica highway, an 80-, 90-, or an occasional 100-kilometer-per-hour speed might be permissible.

Watch for oncoming drivers who flash their headlights off and on. That means trouble ahead, usually a radar speed trap or occasionally an accident. Another sign of danger is a tree branch or piece of shrubbery lying across one lane of the pavement. That signifies that an accident, a washout, or some other nasty surprise could await you ahead.

Driving in city traffic anywhere around San José can be frustrating. As you get the knack of it and learn the system, it gets easier, but never easy. Theoretically, finding your way around San José should be simple, because downtown city streets are logically organized on a north-south, east-west grid. *Calles* (streets) run north to south, and *avenidas* (avenues) run east to west.

However, nothing in Costa Rica is as simple as it sounds. For one thing, street signs are usually missing. Sometimes they'll be posted on the corner of a building or sometimes on a signpost, but just when you need to know exactly where you are, you'll not find a clue. Furthermore, most downtown streets are one-way, sometimes without arrows to indicate which way! You are expected to know. Okay, so you know that Avenida 9 is a one-way street going west, but how do you know the street you are looking at is Avenida 9 when there are neither street signs nor one-way signs? All you can do is watch to see which way traffic is flowing. If no cars are coming either way, you don't dare take a chance.

In the surrounding towns of the Central Valley, traffic is lighter than in San José, but the problem of missing street signs becomes even worse. Some streets are one-way and others two-way, but often there aren't any signs to clue you in as to which is which. An arrow painted on the pavement should indicate which direction is permissible, but often the arrow has faded into history. It's especially disconcerting to be driving along what you believe to be a two-way street and suddenly notice that all the cars parked on both sides of the street are pointing in your direction. Since parking on either side of the street is okay in Costa Rica, you have no way of knowing if they just happen to be facing your direction or if you are traveling the wrong way again.

Away from the cities and major highways, you find bumpy roads that demand slow driving. Going too fast over rocks can cut tires, marooning you several kilometers from a repair shop. You may have to change a tire yourself! When this last happened to me, I stood around looking perplexed until two young men stopped to change the spare for me. They refused to accept money. Next I drove to a sort of auto-repair place where two kids fixed my tire in a jiffy using strips of an old inner tube, some kind of glue, and what appeared to be a steel crochet needle. They didn't even have to take the tire off the rim, as I expected. They charged the equivalent of $1.50; that included putting the repaired wheel on the car and stashing the spare in the trunk.

Eventually, if you drive very much in Costa Rica, you are guaranteed to find yourself stalled in an unmoving string of traffic that seems as if it will never start going again. Chances are this is caused by an automobile accident somewhere ahead on the road. It doesn't have to be a horrendous crash; it could just be a fender bender. Then what's the holdup? In case of a collision, no matter how minor, the vehicles mustn't be moved until the police arrive. That really backs up traffic!

What do you do if you are involved in an accident? Call 911 if possible and wait for the police get there. Take some notes, make sketches of what happened, and wait for the police to give a direct order to move your car. This is important, especially when damages are significant, because there could be issues with insurance claims. Supposedly the cops can't make a clear judgment of what happened if they can't observe the position of the vehicles involved.

## MAPS AND **DIRECTIONS**

Maps of Costa Rica are notoriously inaccurate. I've only seen a couple that are up to date. Many of them show roads that haven't been traveled in years, having been abandoned long ago. New roads take forever to show up on most maps. The one map I am familiar with and in which I have faith is published by a company called Berndtson & Berndtson. It's rather expensive, but it's printed on a plastic-coated fiber that ought to last forever.

One of my favorite Costa Rica map incidents occurred while I was trying to find my way from Zancudo back to the Panamerican Highway. I had been there several times before, but I was forever getting lost. This time it seemed hopeless. I knew I was about two hours away from the pavement up north, but how to get there? I saw a truck approaching and flagged it down. With my three maps, I approached the driver and asked him to give me a clue as to how to find the sandy trail that headed north.

He puzzled over the maps, shaking his head in despair. "This map is wrong, *Señor,*" he said. "This town is not here, it is way over here, and this road has not been used for years." He took a pencil and began tracing what he thought might be the road I wanted. Finally, with a flourish, he marked the last portion of the horrible road that connected with the pavement near Golfito. He explained once again how to find the correct turning points and, as an afterthought, he asked, "But *Señor,* I don't understand why you don't return to San José on the paved road instead of such a bad road?"

"Paved road?" I interjected. "These maps don't show a paved road!"

"Of course not. This is a new road and not yet on the maps. Just go 2 kilometers in the opposite direction and you'll reach the pavement!" (Actually, the road had been there for several years, but mapmakers are notoriously slow updating Costa Rica maps.) A few minutes later we were cruising along the road that follows the Panamanian border, with Panamá on one side and Costa Rica on the other, headed for the Panamerican Highway!

# TRAFFIC COPS AND **SPEED TRAPS**

I often hear reports of tourists being harassed by Costa Rican traffic cops. No doubt these things happen, as is the case anywhere else in the world. A few bad guys can get on the force. Yet after driving many thousands of miles and receiving numerous traffic tickets (all deserved), I have found the overwhelming majority of Costa Rican traffic police to be courteous and rarely stop someone without due cause. With all the crazy drivers in this country, cops have little reason to stop somebody for "nothing at all." Let's face it: Issuing a ticket for speeding, illegal passing, or no safety belt is not police harassment. In the United States it's known as "law enforcement." Tourists aren't exempt from traffic laws, even if they don't thoroughly understand them. Why should they be?

Yet you'll continually hear gringos complain that "the cops only stop rental cars. Why not *tico* cars?" This is partly true, because *ticos* know a little secret: When they see a speed-limit sign of 60 kilometers per hour (38 miles per hour), they slow down because they know there's a good chance that there's a radar gun ahead. Tourists, used to 65-mile-per-hour highways back home, blissfully pass the slowpoke *ticos* in front of them. And guess what happens?

Paved Costa Rican highways usually are posted at 80 kilometers per hour. This may seem ridiculously slow (49 miles per hour), but you can avoid being stopped if you simply relax and drive the speed limit. *Ticos* know that those occasional long, straight stretches of good pavement are also favorite places for radar guns. Maybe it seems sneaky, but when 80 kilometers per hour is the maximum, you're asking for trouble by going any faster. I've come to love those speed traps; if it weren't for them, all *ticos* would be traveling 80 miles an hour! The fine for speeding is about $40 for ordinary violations, or $100 for *velocidad temerario*. That means "frightful and reckless" driving, defined as 120 kilometers per hour (75 miles an hour) and above.

As is the custom in Mexico and all Central American countries, motorists cooperate with each other by giving a flashing headlight warning of a speed trap ahead. So when you see an oncoming vehicle flicking headlights on and off, bring your speedometer down to the proper range, and you'll avoid being "stopped for no reason."

Allow me to offer some advice for when you're stopped by traffic police (I've had lots of firsthand experience in this department):

1. **Be calm, cool, and courteous.** After all, a ticket is no big deal. Until you're officially a resident, a traffic ticket cannot affect your driving record or insurance. Stay cool. I've escaped several well-earned tickets simply by joking with the officers.
2. **Do not get belligerent or raise your voice.** Shouting won't help; it only makes things worse. When a cop feels he's being harassed for doing his job, don't be surprised if he retaliates in kind. I suspect this is where many cases of true police harassment originate: A tourist isn't aware that he's done anything wrong and becomes angry and abusive. The cop loses his temper, too.

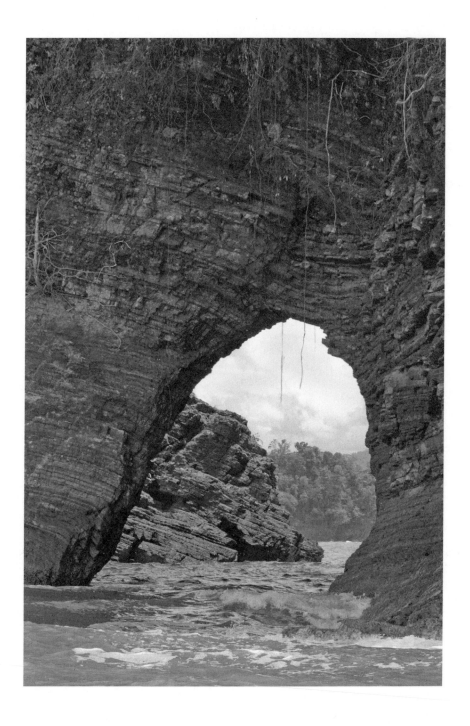

3. **Never offer a bribe.** Even the best cops will accept money if you force it on them. This encourages a bad practice that undermines the department's continual efforts to enforce standards of professionalism. Wages are routinely increased, crooked cops are being dismissed, and intensive training programs are under way.

If the cop suggests that it would be easier to pay him than have to go to some distant place to pay your ticket, just politely decline and calmly wait for the ticket. Don't even discuss it with him. Sometimes, when the cop realizes you aren't going to give him a bribe, he figures it isn't worth his while, and he'll let you off with a warning. Example: One day while driving up the Inter-American Highway toward Liberia, I happened to pass another car on a long bridge. On the other side of the bridge, I was flagged down by a waiting traffic cop. He asked in Spanish if I knew why I was being stopped.

When I replied, "Of course," the cop was surprised, and asked: "Well, why did I stop you?"

My reply: "Because I passed on a bridge."

"But, don't you know that's against the law?"

I shrugged and said, "Of course."

The policeman looked puzzled as he said, "Then why did you pass on the bridge?"

"Because I didn't know you were here."

Knowing he stood no chance of collecting a "tip" for not issuing a ticket, the cop laughed and motioned for me to get out of his life. It doesn't always work that way, but I feel that's better than apologizing and pleading, and then getting a ticket anyway.

If a cop tries to insist on a bribe, make a good mental image of him, including his badge number, and report the incident to the Ministry of Public Works (MOPT) at 2-227-2188 or at the MOPT office on Calle 9 between Avenidas 22 and 23.

Again, traffic tickets are no big deal; you can pay at any national bank or simply give them to the auto-rental company when you return your rental car. The agency adds the fine to your credit card and pays it for you. *Ticos* and expat residents routinely save their tickets and pay them once a year, just before it's time to renew their auto license plates.

I might add that since I've grown accustomed to watching the speedometer, I haven't received a speeding ticket in more than seven years, even though I make frequent round-trips to the Nicoya Peninsula—past a dozen speed traps—sometimes with California plates, sometimes in a rental car, usually with my *tico* plates. Having no speeding tickets in seven years is a lifetime Central America record for me.

# FINDING **HOTELS AND LODGING**

The tourist bonanza over the past few years made the hotel situation somewhat tight at times. To compensate, new hotels have been constructed, and *tico* families converted their homes into bed-and-breakfasts as quickly as they could. Some North Americans have joined this bed-and-breakfast boom, partly financing their retirement by renting out spare bedrooms. In smaller communities, hotels and ecotourism facilities raced to accommodate demand. Today you can often find a room for rent in isolated places where camping was the only choice before. This trend has caught up with demand, at least temporarily, because now there seems to be a slight oversupply of rooms.

The tightest hotel-room market in Costa Rica is during the Christmas–New Year's weeks. Not impossible, just tight. Easter week and spring break are other busy times. During the rush seasons, making reservations before you leave for Costa Rica, even if only for the first couple of nights, is a good insurance policy. After you arrive, you can check around and locate something to suit your taste and/or the size of your pocketbook.

Around San José, hotels come in all sizes and flavors, with expensive rooms costing $100 a night and up and cheap rooms around $20. I looked at one room for under $15 recently, but shivers ran down my spine when I peered into the gloomy-looking room, with dirty linens on the bed, housed in a ramshackle wooden building that looked like a firetrap. For my personal tastes a $35 room would be my bottom choice (of course, I am easily satisfied—even though I do insist on wall-to-wall ceilings). My wife's preferences fall into the $60 range or above. For medium-priced hotel rooms, expect to pay from $45 to $75 a night during the tourist season.

If you're on a budget—as long-term travelers usually are—don't expect too much in the way of luxury. You may find an affordable rate for a room with a private bath, only to discover that the shower is plumbed for cold water only. When a hotel advertises hot water, you'll often find one of those rinky-dink electric heaters attached to the showerhead. This contraption, known as a "suicide shower," has a lever that can be set to one of three positions: hot, warm, and off. The position that says "off" is often the only setting that works all the time. This encourages short but exhilarating showers (ideal for anyone considering celibacy). The secret is allowing the water to flow at its lowest possible volume, in the hope of coaxing warmth from the heating element. You'll usually get a satisfactory warm stream of water.

Should you be stranded out in the country, unable to find a place to stay, your ace in the hole is the local *pulpería*. This is the Costa Rican equivalent of a country "general store." It also serves as the social center of the community. Drinks and snacks are sold, as neighbors congregate to exchange news and tidbits of gossip as well as purchase necessary items ranging from matches to machetes. The proprietor of the *pulpería* can sometimes find you a room with a local family. This is a unique opportunity to see how country folk live in Costa Rica, but don't expect luxury. A *pulpería* is also an excellent place to inquire about real estate. If anything is for sale or rent in the neighborhood, the proprietor will know, and she might even know the bottom-line price as well as the asking price.

# COSTA RICAN **SCHOOLS**

Because of Costa Rica's high literacy rate and extensive education system, a higher percentage of people speak English here than in any other Latin American country. English is a required course in grade school and high school. However, don't expect every *tico* you meet to understand your English. *Ticos* forget high school English just as quickly as you forgot your high school Spanish. The fact that most Costa Ricans know at least a smattering of English makes it easier for those newcomers who are struggling with Spanish conversation. When a certain word eludes you, you simply toss in the English word and forge ahead with your discourse, knowing there's a good chance the listener will understand either the word or its context. Fluency and learning are greatly enhanced when you don't have the tension of pausing and searching your memory for the proper word. Tension is an enemy of language acquisition.

I'm continually surprised at the number of North Americans who live in Costa Rica for years and never bother to learn any more Spanish words than those needed to deal with the gardener or the gas-station attendant. Learning a language isn't easy, but those who do take the trouble to at least try to learn Spanish find that they are highly respected by their *tico* friends and neighbors. This opens the door to interaction with a whole new set of friends and acquaintances.

## SPANISH-LANGUAGE **SCHOOLS**

An excellent way to study Spanish and to learn about Costa Rica at the same time is to enroll in one of the country's many Spanish-language schools. Language acquisition is big business here. There are at least twenty schools just in San José offering intensive Spanish classes. Throughout the country you'll find schools and individuals who are eager to give you private, one-on-one Spanish lessons. Some schools keep the class size to three or four students, ensuring each person maximum attention from the teacher.

Most schools offer programs that include homestay living arrangements with a Costa Rican family. By interacting with a local household, you might learn how Costa Ricans cook, where and how they shop, and how to deal with servants, as well as other everyday routines of life that can be so different from back home. Combining classroom study and a homestay with a Costa Rican family puts you in a round-the-clock Spanish-speaking environment, speeding up the learning process. Some schools include tours of farms, factories, archaeological sites, museums, conservation projects, national parks, and other places of ecological and cultural importance as part of the curriculum. Some schools will pick you up at your door every morning and return you to your family homestay in the afternoon.

An important observation about homestays comes from a former student, who says: "It's best to find a situation where you are the only guest in the home. When three or four students stay in the same house, you'll find yourselves talking to one another in English instead of to your hosts in Spanish."

No matter where you are in Costa Rica, there'll be a language school nearby. You can study Spanish in downtown San José, on the beach in Quepos, in the cloud forest at Monteverde, or even in a typical rural village. The sheer number of schools makes it impractical to list them here. Also, the varying quality of instruction makes it impossible for this book to make recommendations; we just don't know enough about them to vouch for their quality. The *Tico Times,* various tourist publications, and the Internet are full of information about *tico* language schools. Your best source for recommendations are from those who have attended a language school in Costa Rica.

## YOUR CHILDREN IN **COSTA RICAN SCHOOLS**

A remarkable difference between Latin American children and their North American counterparts is their behavior toward one another and toward authority. Gringo kids are typically boisterous, full of energy, and extremely competitive. On the other hand, Latin American children, especially *ticos,* tend to be polite, calm, and well behaved. Bullying other students is all but unknown. Both in the family and in school, cooperation is approved and competition discouraged. Classroom discipline is no problem for the teachers, which makes *tico* kids a delight to work with. (I can say this from experience, as one who has taught language classes both in the United States and in Costa Rica.)

Your children can select from three types of Costa Rican schools: 1) private English-only schools, 2) private bilingual schools, or 3) free public schools. The farther you live from the Central Valley, the more limited your choices. When you live in an area where private schools are too far away to commute, your choices could be a public school or homeschooling.

Most foreign residents I've interviewed about their children's progress in private schools heartily endorse the educational and cultural experience their kids were enjoying. Tuition costs vary from the most expensive private school, with tuition and fees of about $7,500 per year (plus bus transportation), to some of the more inexpensive bilingual schools that offer tuition as low as $100 a month, last time I checked. Again, it's way beyond my scope of expertise to even try to make recommendations. You'll need to interview your neighbors and interview the school personnel.

## PRIVATE **SCHOOLS**

Most North American parents prefer an American-accredited school with a curriculum equal to that offered stateside. Around the San José area, you'll find a choice of twenty or thirty English-only or bilingual private schools. Some present classes half in Spanish, half in English; others are basically English-language schools. Some offer classes from prekindergarten through high school, others just the first three to seven grades. English-only schools are popular with Costa Rican families who can afford the tuition. They want their children to learn English, and these schools are essential for those preparing for U.S. universities.

At the end of this chapter, you'll find a partial list of well-known private schools that cater to North American students. Tuition varies from moderate to expensive, and selections will depend on the location of the school facility and the distance from your new home.

## PUBLIC **SCHOOLS**

For the most part, Costa Rica's public schools are patronized by expatriate children living too far from the larger population centers to attend a conventional private school. Despite the fact that Costa Rica spends an inordinate amount of money on education, schoolrooms and facilities can be crude and rustic when compared with the average U.S. or Canadian classroom. Often library books are scarce or nonexistent, and the quality of the teachers varies widely.

The daily hours of a public school day are usually shorter than those at private schools. Also, when a teacher is absent, classes are canceled and children are sent home early. This is partly due to an irrational government policy of assigning teachers to schools based on need, without considering where a teacher's home is located. Schools provide housing for teachers during the week, and they go home every weekend. Of course,

teachers look for any possible excuse to cancel Friday-afternoon classes so that they can get an early start on the trip to their hometowns.

Depending on where you live, your only alternatives could be homeschooling or a Spanish-only public school (sometimes both). Parents of kids enrolled in public schools give mixed reviews. Some children are immediately befriended and accepted by the other children and love their teachers. Others feel lonely and ignored. None reported their kids being mistreated, bullied, or teased because they are different—these things are often a problem in U.S. schools. Much depends on a combination of the individual child's ability to adjust and the particular situation in the school (the attitude of the teachers, the friendliness of the other students, etc.).

I knew a couple from Holland whose three children attended an all-Spanish classroom located in a small village on the Guanacaste coast. The youngest (in second grade) absolutely adored the school, the teacher, and her classmates. The next oldest (fourth grade) hated school as much as her sister loved it. The older brother, who has Downs syndrome, enjoyed school so much that his parents had trouble making him come home after classes. The students his size encouraged him to play soccer (which he loves), and they treated him with extraordinary kindness and respect.

The bottom line is that not all children can adapt to a public-school setting in Costa Rica, and some could do poorly. It seems to be an either/or situation that becomes apparent rather quickly. They either love it or they hate it. Whatever you do, don't force the issue if the child is not happy with public school.

## COSTA RICA **HOMESCHOOLING**

Some families choose homeschooling as an alternative to expensive private schools or to supplement the public school curriculum. To be honest, while children benefit immeasurably from immersion in the Spanish language and Costa Rican culture, a public school can't provide the background needed to be accepted at a North American university. Homeschooling can be crucial here. Also some children will not like public schools; homeschooling could be their only alternative. A poll among parents with school-age children indicated that 30 percent of the parents responding described themselves as homeschoolers. Those attending conventional schools were divided between 25 percent in public schools and 75 percent attending private schools.

Sharon Wallace, from Ciudad Colón, has homeschooled three children over the years and sent them away to be accepted at universities in the United States and France. She has this to say about homeschooling in Costa Rica: "The nitty gritty is that homeschooling isn't recognized as a legal entity, yet the government takes a typical laissez-faire attitude. The official word is that kids must be in an educational program until age sixteen, but this is not enforced. In fact, local schools are delighted to not have the burden of more students in an already crowded environment. So, like almost everything here, it's considered tacky to butt into someone else's business.

"We've been homeschoolers in Costa Rica for more than thirty-five years. Parents all use a wide range of techniques. Among them are: online classes, standard curriculum, various mixed media courses, supplementary classes, mentor situations, and none of the above (aka: 'unschoolers.') My husband and I are unschoolers, meaning no prescribed course of study; instead we facilitate the kids' interests. And it's worked out beautifully for us. It's interesting that many of us who are totally sold on homeschooling also work as volunteers in local public schools, teaching English, helping set up computer access, teaching CPR (I did that), and whatever is needed."

One common objection to homeschooling is that children miss the social interaction of being in a traditional classroom. However, homeschooling parents in Costa Rica typically get together on a regular basis, bringing the children into social groups, doing ad hoc classes in creative writing, book reviews, science, drama, art, and other subjects. Since the Costa Rican school day is a half day, at any given time half the school kids are available for an out-of-the-classroom social life.

## CHILDREN LEARNING **SPANISH**

Whether your children go to public or private schools, you will be astounded at how quickly they become fluent in Spanish (while you struggle and can't seem to get anywhere). It's nothing short of miraculous how kids can absorb a language simply by sitting in a classroom and listening to strange words and mixing with children using these same words. With most adults, it's too late to simply "pick up" the language; you're going to have to work at it.

My favorite example of this instant-learning process comes from Hilary Aeschliman, originally from Kansas City. Her daughter Stephanie had been placed in a very rustic village school on Costa Rica's Guanacaste coast. She started class not knowing a word of Spanish. After a few weeks, they needed to purchase Stephanie another school uniform. Hilary says, "We went to this little village store, but despite my Spanish lessons, I couldn't understand a thing the owner was saying. We were just talking in circles—my husband and I in English, the lady who was running the shop spoke only Spanish. We exchanged plenty of smiles and *lo siento*'s, but neither had a clue to what the other was saying. After about fifteen minutes we gave up.

"As we were leaving, I said, 'Well that wasn't very productive. I have no idea what she was trying to tell us.'

"At that point, Stef piped up and explained, 'She said that the lady who makes the uniforms is in Nicoya today and for us to come back next week. She'll be here Monday and Tuesday.'

"I could have strangled her!"

## ATTENDING THE **UNIVERSITY**

Students from abroad are welcome at Costa Rica's many universities. There are four public universities and nine listings for private institutions. The largest school is the University of Costa Rica (UCR), with about 35,000 students, located in San Pedro, on San José's northeastern edge. Tuition for *tico* students is about $70 a semester; foreign students are charged considerably more, with rates available on request. The other large school is Universidad Nacional. It has about 13,000 students and has several campuses scattered about the country, as does UCR.

Most satellite campuses are rather basic, with instruction geared to *ticos* who can't afford to take time off from work to study in the San José area. Most classes are held in the evening and offer studies in computers or bookkeeping or preparatory classes for entering a full university setting. I doubt that many gringos could benefit from attending one of these schools.

Private universities offer programs ranging from MBAs to degrees in theology, tropical agriculture, and conservation. Most accept and welcome foreign students, charging tuition of about $100 per class and $5,600 for an MBA degree.

# EXCHANGE-STUDENT **OPTION**

If you're convinced that you'd like to relocate to Costa Rica but just aren't ready for it right now, an interesting idea is to send your offspring here for a school term as an exchange student—or maybe just for a class during summer vacation. This gives the youth a head start in learning the language as well as a great cultural experience. And you will have an interpreter when you do decide to make the move. You can contact the Iberoamerican Cultural Exchange Program and inquire about their various exchange-student programs in Costa Rica. The address is 13920 Ninety-third Avenue NE, Kirkland, WA 98034; (206) 821-1463; fax (206) 821-1849.

Christen Kemp, at the time a Spanish and international business major at the University of Tennessee at Knoxville, tells of her experience as an exchange student in a Costa Rican university where she studied Spanish under ISEP (International Student Exchange Program) for a year. The Universidad Nacional is one of few schools offering an optional fee-paid ISEP Spanish program outside the United States and is designed to provide study opportunities beyond those offered typically only through reciprocal exchange.

Christen says, "I studied at the university's campus in Heredia, and, though it's not the nicest school in Costa Rica, it was better than I had expected. Some foreign students who studied at other universities claim their schools are better. Apparently Universidad Nacional enrolls many *ticos* who can't afford the tuition to attend the better schools. I spoke to one who told me the tuition for a *tico* at the school was only about $30 a semester. (I can't help but wonder what happened to the thousands I paid.)

"Technology at this university is not up to U.S. standards. There are only a few computers in the library, and students line up to use them. I found it easier to go to one of the many Internet cafes around town. An hour's Internet connection costs only a dollar. And then there's McDonald's, where you can use the Internet if you buy a Value Meal.

"Registering for classes was quite confusing. They don't use a computer system, so you end up making several trips to classes and the registrar's office. Another big difference is that the teachers are on *tico* time. In my first class the teacher was always about forty-five minutes late. The students told me that teachers can be up to an hour late, and, unlike the United States, where a class meets for an hour three days a week, at this school a class was held once a week for three to four hours. It's hard to

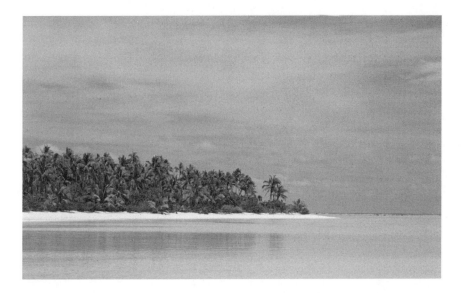

keep focused for that long, but the teachers were actually pretty good. I had an excellent literature teacher from Chile. You do not buy books for your classes. Instead your teacher places a packet of photocopies at a designated copy shop and you go there each week and make copies. They are really cheap, like 10 colones each.

"Living with a *tico* host family is awesome. This was probably the best part of my education in Costa Rica. Being introduced to and actually accepted into a traditional family and being part of their religious-holiday celebrations was an unexpected gift.

"There are many advertisements for families looking for students. The exchange program from the University of Tennessee paid my family $300 a month. For this I received a nice room, three full meals a day, and all my clothes and linens washed and ironed (sheets, pajamas—everything was ironed!). The family had a maid from Nicaragua whom they paid $100 a month to cook and clean five days a week."

## TEACHING **ENGLISH**

If you look on the Internet, you'll find a dozen or so Costa Rica forums and bulletin boards where folks exchange information about living or retiring in Costa Rica. Very common on these forums are requests for job information from young people who want to live in Costa Rica so bad they'll work for any amount of money. The most frequent question is, "How can I get a job teaching English in Costa Rica?" Many queries come from those who assume that just because they speak English, they are competent to teach English. This obviously can't be true, or else people wouldn't waste time in universities earning teaching credentials and studying classroom techniques or the latest ESL (English as a Second Language) methods. Believe me, as a credentialed ESL teacher myself and one who passed courses in these techniques, I can vouch for the awesome magnitude of facing a class of eager faces and hoping they will learn more from today's lesson than I will. (Even though I have university training in ESL, have taken all the requisite classes, and have even coauthored textbooks in language acquisition, I am the first to admit that I am not a very good teacher. I have neither the temperament nor the patience.)

That's not to say that you can't find a teaching position without an ESL degree. Mike Curls, who teaches ESL at two schools in the San José area, points out that it's not essential to be an experienced English teacher. But you should have some teaching background, he says. "Myself, I have a degree in business administration (accounting major) and teaching experience from the Air Force. I was a classroom instructor in resource management school with extensive background training." By the way, many local colleges offer classes in teaching English to foreigners. It will go a long way toward your finding a job if you have some experience before you move to Costa Rica.

How to find one of these jobs? Something that ought to be obvious is that you won't find a teaching position while in the United States or Canada. You'll have to apply in person, in Costa Rica, ready to go to work. Every day schools receive job queries from people 6,000 miles away; the schools routinely ignore them. Why waste time corresponding with someone who may or may not ever come to Costa Rica—who is very likely just daydreaming about an adventure that will never happen? You'll have to be on the ground, ready to go to work.

Claudia Jenkins taught ESL in Costa Rica and points out an exception to the rule of applying in Costa Rica. "One way for an experienced ESL teacher—or one with a master's degree or at least an ESL certificate—to get a job with a Costa Rican language school might be to go to the annual springtime TESOL conference, which is held in different parts of the United States and sometimes other countries. While there, I showed copies of my résumé to two school administrators from the Centro Cultural Costarricense-Norteamericano. They wanted me to start teaching in ten days! I couldn't do it because I was a full-time teacher and only looking for something during my summer vacation. Later I did teach at that school for a ten-week bi-semester."

Claudia also points out an enormous drawback to teaching English in Costa Rica: the pay. She says, "At that time [in 1990] my net pay in Costa Rica was $2 per hour. My hourly pay in California at the same time was more than ten times that amount! Fifteen years later, the school was paying $4 an hour. And it's mostly part-time work." Today Claudia is a volunteer ESL teacher for an expatriate-sponsored library in Nosara and does teacher training of volunteer college students who come to Nosara every winter to teach classes for university credit.

Mike Curls reports on today's salaries, saying, "The pay is not adequate if someone needs to live on the salary. The Pro English school where I work pays $5.75 per hour, but most classes are two hours a day, two days a week ($23 a week). Where I teach in Cartago, they pay by class size. For example, a class of six to nine students pays $114 a month; twelve or more students pays $142 per month."

Why such low wages? Obviously because of the excess of applicants for the jobs. This is one of the few jobs foreigners can obtain without a work permit being absolutely necessary. Technically, one would think that schools would demand work papers, but they get around this by hiring their teachers as *servicios profesionales* (independent contractors). Technically, they aren't really working for the school. Mike Curls says he is aware of a couple of schools requiring working papers at the moment.

Claudia Jenkins says, "Teaching adults at a private school in Costa Rica is simply a wonderful experience. The students pay a lot of money, by local standards, for the classes, so they are motivated to learn. Since *ticos* like to *quedar bien,* even the most disinterested adult student would never be disruptive in class!"

A few Americans and Canadians earn extra money by tutoring in English in their homes. Sometimes a lack of formal training isn't that much of a handicap because the students merely want an opportunity to practice their fluency in one-on-one conversations.

# LIST OF **PRIVATE SCHOOLS**

A full list of private schools is far too long for this book, and I have no way of evaluating them. Below are a few of the more popular and prestigious schools that have come to my attention. As in any educational situation, you'll need to ask other parents for recommendations and personally interview school personnel before making any decisions.

- Country Day School is a prestigious institution in Escazú, with classes from prekindergarten through the twelfth grade. It is Costa Rican accredited and has 650 students, with classes all in English. There is also a Country Day School in Flamingo. Tuition is moderately expensive. Phone (506) 2-289-8406; fax (506) 2-228-2076; Web site www.cds.ed.cr.

- Costa Rica Academy is another popular school and charges similar tuition. It is accredited by Costa Rica and in the United States by the Southern Association of Colleges and Schools. It's located in Ciudad Carrari, west of San José, on the way to the airport. Phone (506) 2-253-1231; fax (506) 2-225-9762.

- Lincoln School in Moravia is the largest, on the northeast side of San José, with 1,600 students. Tuition is somewhat less than the above-mentioned schools. Phone (506) 2-247-0800; fax (506) 2-247-0900; Web site www.lincoln.ed.cr.

- Escuela Britanica teaches half in English and half in Spanish, kindergarten through eleventh grade. It's located in Santa Catalina on San José's west side and has 800 students. Tuition is very affordable. Phone (506) 2-220-0719.

- American International School is located in Cariari. This is a coeducational day school and college-preparatory school, with classes from prekindergarten through twelfth grade. Phone (506) 2-239-0376.

- Marian Baker School in San Ramón de Tres Rios offers a U.S.- and Costa Rican–based curriculum to prepare students for colleges and universities in the United States and Costa Rica. Phone (506) 2-273-3426; fax (506) 2-273-4609; Web site www.mbs.ed.cr.

# IMPORTING YOUR
# **BELONGINGS**

Importing an automobile is one of the first things newcomers consider. Public transportation in Costa Rica is more than adequate, and many folks here do perfectly well without an automobile, yet having your own wheels is a luxury some refuse to forgo. Since car rentals cost between $800 and $1,200 a month, before long the savings involved in owning your own car will become quite evident. The equivalent of a year's car rental would purchase a nifty used, four-wheel-drive vehicle.

There are places in Costa Rica where it just isn't practical to visit without a vehicle. True, buses make it just about anywhere you can imagine—some places I'd hesitate to take a four-wheel-drive vehicle—but after you get there, then what do you do? If you have to walk 3 kilometers (2 miles) to the nearest store or restaurant, you are stuck. Without a set of wheels, your choice of hotel accommodations is governed by where the bus stops—if there is a bus. With your own transportation you can shop around for the best place to stay, and then use your wheels to select the best restaurants or hunt out the nicest beaches (which are usually a long way from a bus stop).

# BUY OR IMPORT **YOUR VEHICLE?**

Chapter 13 gives details on driving your vehicle down from the United States. That's an option for the hardy, one not to be undertaken lightly, but it can be fun, too. If you choose not to drive, you are left with the alternatives of buying a vehicle in Costa Rica or shipping one down from the north. There are advantages to both options. Which option is better depends on several conditions in effect at the time you need a vehicle.

There are two schools of thought about buying vehicles in Costa Rica. One claims that cars here are maintained in excellent shape because they are so expensive; folks protect their investments with loving care. The other school of thought is that Costa Rican roads are so full of bumps that cars age quickly beyond their years.

No matter which school of thought you favor, take my advice: Never buy a refurbished taxicab! Taxis in Costa Rica go through absolute hell, driving all day and all night, cruising over rough streets—stop and go, stop and go—the worst kind of wear. I know a mechanic in San José who restores taxicabs for a living. He has a great body-and-paint man and has a skilled upholsterer on his staff. I've seen vehicles limp in looking hopeless and strut out looking brand new. I've studied these cars in minute detail, and I swear, each looks showroom fresh! How can you tell if a car is a rebuilt taxi? You need to find an expert mechanic you trust and have him inspect the vehicle.

This is sometimes easier said than done. I happen to have a good friend who is also a great *tico* mechanic, and several years ago I asked him to find a trustworthy four-wheel drive for me. He had a mechanic search Heredia and Alajuela for reliable vehicles and found five to recommend. I bought the first one I looked at, which was his first choice, too.

**IMPORT TAXES ON AUTOS** Customs duties are responsible for the sky-high prices of new and used cars in Costa Rica. At one time taxes were more than 100 percent of the vehicle's value. They are a bit lower now but are still about 60 percent (sometimes more) of the appraised value, depending on age. Tax rates keep changing as the Congress and Ministry of Customs vacillate on how to apply customs duties. Decisions change every year or so.

I know, this sounds like highway robbery (excuse the metaphor), but the government presents two arguments for high customs duties. One, of course: They need the money. *Ticos* dodge as many taxes as they can, but they can't avoid customs on that new Mercedes because it's collected before they get their hands on the steering wheel. The other justification is that high prices discourage people from adding more vehicles to already overcrowded streets and highways. This strategy doesn't seem to be working, at least not the last time I tried to drive along Paseo Colón.

It doesn't do any good to argue about the value of your vehicle with the customs people, because they go by a printed list of market values. If your vehicle is in bad shape, they may deduct for that. But you wouldn't be bringing a piece of junk here in the first place. My recommendation is to contact a customs agent who knows how to get things done and can tell you exactly what you'll need to pay in taxes. Note: At press time there was an announcement that starting in 2009 the government will restrict importation of older vehicles. The plan is to slowly prohibit importation of old vehicles with a strict measure that will first be applied to vehicles older than five years. The decree setting the guidelines is supposed to be announced in the fall of 2008.

## SHIPPING YOUR **VEHICLE**

Cars can be shipped from either Atlantic or Pacific ports to Costa Rica. But the cheapest and fastest way is from Florida or New Orleans. Most people say they paid $400 to $800, depending on the shipping line and availability of space. From California, costs are higher: I paid $1,300 from San Francisco. From Florida, the destination port is Limón; from California it's Puerto Caldera (near Puntarenas). The shipping line will prepare the documents stateside and take care of details once you deliver the car. Don't fail to ask for full-coverage insurance; it's not terribly expensive. You will also need to obtain a smog certificate from the state of origin of the car before shipping it to Costa Rica.

Once the car arrives at the port, you have the option of picking it up at the port or waiting until it arrives at the main customs house in San José. In either event, you then have the decision of taking possession and going through customs yourself or hiring a Costa Rican customs agent to handle the paperwork for you. If you speak a bit of Spanish, you can do it yourself, but I'd advise asking a *tico* friend to walk you through the hurdles of red tape and forms in triplicate. The friend needn't be an expert, just someone who speaks good Spanish and who can ask which line you must stand in—and which line after that.

## SHIPPING YOUR **HOUSEHOLD GOODS**

Although many will disagree, I wouldn't bother shipping household goods and belongings to Costa Rica, unless they were items I couldn't replace or couldn't live without. Just about anything you can think of to import into Costa Rica can be purchased for less than what you would pay in the United States or Canada, including import duties and shipping.

Another idea is that you can make a trip to Golfito or to the Panamanian border and buy your appliances—duty-free in Golfito and $500 per person duty-free at the border (a couple gets $1,000, and they can do this every six months). I've been told that the government decided that automatic washers and dryers are no longer luxury goods; they've reduced, if not eliminated, import taxes on them. This brings prices down to U.S. levels.

Many of you will go ahead and import everything but the proverbial kitchen sink. If so, you will need a shipper in the United States to make sure things are packed properly and stowed away on a ship. When your cargo arrives, you will need a customs broker to handle things on this end. You can get your personal items out of customs yourself, but I'm convinced that an experienced hand, someone who knows whom, when, and where to schmooze, will save you aggravation.

Some people I know have shipped by air, as long as it wasn't too much weight, because the cost is about a dollar a pound. The cost is much less by cargo ship, and unless you have an inordinate amount of stuff, your things will share a container with other merchandise. Shipping from Florida or New Orleans is much less expensive than from the West Coast.

A problem with cargo ships is they are seldom on schedule. This makes it difficult to arrange a definite date to meet the ship and usher your belongings through customs. You'll have to wait until the unpredictable day when the ship finally docks in Costa Rica. When we shipped our car from San Francisco, we were told it would arrive within a three-day spread. Would it surprise anyone that the ship was fifteen days late? We called every day, and they promised it would be there within two more days, God willing. (God was most unwilling during those two weeks.) By the way, shipping from San Francisco was three times more expensive than it would have been from Tampa.

Packing your goods correctly will save them from damage when tossed around in the loading process. Labeling them properly will help keep duty down. Marking boxes "used household goods" and "not for sale" will also help. Some people take grease pens and mark *usado* on the items themselves to make it clear that they aren't going to be sold.

Duty assessed can be rather erratic, depending on the mood of the customs official, so this is where your suave customs representative can earn his pay. I will say that I've always been treated with respect when dealing with customs, with one exception: I was bringing in a computer that the customs official wanted to mark on my passport as my exempted duty. After a shouting match (which I won), we both apologized.

You are entitled to import a certain amount of items for personal use tax-free (as well as $500 per person of normally taxable goods). The amount of duty you pay on additional items can be minimal or very high according to a highly involved and subjective combination of import duty, consumption tax, sales tax, and other miscellaneous charges. These are multiplied by the value of the item (a combination of estimated cost plus freight plus insurance). Depending on the article, there could be a 37 percent tax or, sometimes, no tax at all.

I've heard about different experiences from people who've brought a lot of belongings into the country by automobile, and they've been mostly favorable. My own experience is that when entering Costa Rica from Nicaragua with the back of our station wagon stuffed to the max with household goods, power tools, and who knows what, the only inspection we got was from a Costa Rican guard, who asked whether we had electronic items such as TVs or VCRs. When we said no, he waved us on without even looking. Maybe we were lucky. By the way, two things you don't want to get caught bringing in without proper papers are arms and munitions!

# BRINGING AN **AIRCRAFT TO COSTA RICA**

(*The following information was supplied by Peter Todd, manager of Helicorp S.A. Maintenance at Tobias Bolanos Airport in Pavas.*)

There are two options the private owner has regarding bringing an aircraft to Costa Rica.

**As a tourist:** You have the same privileges as the local aircraft do for three months. No duties, no taxes, no local insurance required. At the end of three months, you will have to take the aircraft out of the country for at least three months. You may then bring it back again for another three months.

**Import the aircraft into Costa Rica:** To do this, you will need the following: Either here or in the United States you will need to get a DAR (Designated Airworthiness Representative) to issue an Export Airworthiness Certificate naming Costa Rica as the importing country. For the DAR to do this, the aircraft will need to have had an "Annual Type" inspection within the last thirty days and be airworthy.

When this is done you will have to de-register the aircraft from the United States This can be done from Costa Rica, and the FAA will issue a letter confirming this. The AOPA can assist with this function. Once this is done you may start the registration proceedings in Costa Rica. This is fairly simple and should only take about two weeks if you have your ducks lined up. The DGAC will inspect your aircraft, review the documents, and issue you a TI number and local certificates.

You will also have to pay the import taxes, which are about 20 percent based on market value. I have been told that the taxes are in reality pretty reasonable, but things can change! You will also have to purchase the local liability insurance from the government insurance agency, INS.

Some other items for aviators coming to Costa Rica: There is no night VFR here, and you have to file a flight plan no matter where you go. There are four international airports in Costa Rica: the main ones in Alajuela and Liberia, and two smaller ones in Pavas and Limón. Your FAA private license will get you a *tico* private license just by showing it. For a commercial license you will have to take the test. I have heard conflicting stories about it being available in English and Spanish.

## BRINGING PETS TO **COSTA RICA**

Those of you who refuse to relocate anywhere without your faithful furry companions will be pleased to know that there is no legal problem bringing them to Costa Rica. You will, of course, have a certain amount of paperwork.

You begin the process with a visit to your local veterinarian for a complete examination of your pet to make sure that your companion is free of all infectious and/or contagious diseases and that all vaccinations are up to date against rabies, distemper, hepatitis, parvovirus, and leptospirosis. The rabies shots should be at least thirty days but less than one year old at time of departure. The examination report will identify the pet's name, breed, sex, and color, as well as the owner's name and address. This health certificate must be signed by a licensed veterinarian. The papers are supposed to be good for ten days after issue by the consulate, but customs people say thirty days is okay. Many travelers report that they weren't even asked for papers when they arrived in Costa Rica, but it makes sense to shoot for the ten-day deadline if possible.

I have a friend who doesn't bother with papers going in either direction; she just tucks her toy poodle into her large handbag and marches aboard the airplane. That's taking a chance, but she claims that if there's a problem, she has a thirty-day grace period to straighten things out. (Presumably, little Fifi could be incarcerated in a doggy jail in the meantime.) I highly recommend getting all the proper documents, with precisely crossed *i*'s and correctly dotted *t*'s—or whatever.

Some unusual animals, especially endangered species, require special papers, from both the U.S. and Costa Rican governments. Another friend's son insisted on bringing his pet Tasmanian monitor lizard (or some such thing), and although she had the proper papers, the freaked-out customs inspectors at the San José airport refused to allow the large reptile to enter until a veterinarian certified that it wasn't venomous.

Yet another friend, Pam, wanted to bring Oliver, her daughter's blue and gold macaw, into the country (akin to carrying coal to Newcastle). After three months of paperwork in both the United States and Costa Rica, paying fees and duty and such, Pam made a special trip back to the States, only to spend a lot more time cutting through red tape. "The only hassles I ran into were in the States!" she said. "When I arrived in Costa Rica, the customs guy peeked into the large carrier, glanced at my paperwork, and sent me on my merry way, never asking to see the health certificate or declaration papers that cost me so much time, effort, and worry!"

Once you have your pet's papers, you still have to figure out how to get the animal to Costa Rica. I find it difficult to give advice in this area because airlines keep changing their policies. Some airlines (and maybe all) are currently refusing to carry pets in the cargo holds in summer

because of possible heat danger to the animals. Some airlines are refusing to accept animals, period; others are more pet-friendly. The last I heard, Delta was the most friendly, still allowing small animals to be carried into the passenger cabins (although they could balk at accepting a large Tasmanian reptile). With the current uncertainty about rules and regulations, you'll need to check individual airlines to find the right carrier. I'll try to post current info on my Web page for the book update (www.discovery press.com/update).

To leave the country, your pet needs an exit permit, just like human *residentes*. For this you'll need a health certificate from a Costa Rican veterinarian (well, actually, *you* don't need it, your pet does). The vet usually accepts your original papers as valid and fills out the proper Costa Rican exit permit without having to personally inspect the animal. The vet can do all the paperwork, obtain the proper stamps, and pay fees. Some people arrange this by fax; the vet or an assistant then meets them at the airport with the necessary permits. Call your vet or contact the Departamento de Zoonosis, Ministerio de Salud, Apartado 10123, San José; (506) 2-223-0333, ext. 331.

Contrary to the situation in some Latin American countries, pet food is readily available at most Costa Rican supermarkets and sometimes in the local *pulpería*. Veterinarians are numerous, with at least a dozen practicing in the San José area. Some will even make house calls. Actually, a few villages are without a small-animal veterinarian because most vets specialize in treating large animals such as horses and cattle. They have little experience taking care of pets, and some don't like to be bothered with them. Those vets with small-animal practices are often reluctant to travel 30 or 40 kilometers (19 or 25 miles) to your beach-village home just to give a distemper shot to Fido or to neuter Miss Pussycat. Expats sometimes bring their pets together and have a "veterinarian party." They'll have a dozen animals ready for the vet to work on when he arrives for his monthly visit. The party guests enjoy themselves, eating *bocas* and sipping cocktails, while the unfortunate *animalitos* are experiencing the business end of needles—and possibly losing some precious parts of their anatomy.

## IMPORTING **FIREARMS**

Over the years, I've had numerous inquiries about bringing handguns into the country. Technically, it can be done. However, the government strongly discourages the practice and erects legal and red tape barriers that make it highly impractical. This doesn't mean you cannot legally purchase a handgun in Costa Rica. Under certain circumstances you can even obtain a permit to carry one. The following is some information from the *Tico Times*.

First of all, you must be a legal resident to own a handgun and/or apply for a concealed carry permit. Nonresidents can own a gun when it's registered in the name of their corporation, but nonresidents cannot get a concealed weapons permit.

To buy a new gun, you'll need to fill out a form, giving the name of the gun shop, the serial number, and other descriptions of the purchase. (For some reason you can buy a used gun and take it with you, provided you report it to the Armament Administration within ten days.) Next you take a written test, and a firearms practice test that requires you to hit a target seven out of ten shots. You must pass a psychological exam given by a government-certified psychologist and undergo a criminal background check by the OIJ (Judicial Investigation Police), and then you must provide two photographs of yourself. Finally, you receive papers and official seals that entitle you to purchase your handgun.

All of this sounds very reasonable, but my impression is that many people skip the formal application and simply buy a used gun and never follow through with the official process.

I urge you to consider the philosophy of handguns in Costa Rica; that is, carrying concealed weapons is not part of Costa Rica's peaceful *pura vida* culture. Because burglaries while residents are home are rare, few *ticos* even bother to keep weapons in their homes. Furthermore, in instances of disputes involving a handgun, the law often comes down against the shooter, even though a U.S. court would consider justified self-defense in similar circumstances. Just carrying a weapon raises a suspicion of aggressive intent.

Commonly, in many sections of the United States, juries of your peers will listen to your plea of self-defense with sympathetic ears, taking the word of the survivor over the silence of the deceased. In Costa Rica, you plead your case in front of three judges who take a dim view of foreigners packing guns and shooting each other. A few years ago, when an American bar owner in Playas del Coco was attacked by a belligerent customer with a knife, he fired a gun in obvious self-defense. Yet the bar owner was held in prison for almost two years before a decision of self-defense was reluctantly rendered. In the meantime, his business deteriorated and his finances were devastated, and, if I'm not mistaken, he was forced to return to the United States after his release.

# BECOMING **A RESIDENT**

Because the rules for entering Costa Rica are so liberal, most people who live in the country for six months or less at a time do not feel it is worth the effort of applying for residency. My wife and I fall into this category. We seldom live in our Costa Rica home more than three months at a time, and when we do, we leave the country for a seventy-two-hour stay in Nicaragua or Panamá before returning and receiving another visa.

Although the laws seem clear—you are entitled to one visa extension—many people have spent years in Costa Rica, leaving every ninety days and "renewing" their visas at the border. For years, many haven't even bothered doing that, since the fine for having an expired visa used to be a ridiculous amount, about $6 a month. However, several years ago the government did away with the fines and began cracking down on those overstaying their visas. Several persons have been picked up and deported for having expired visas. So far, the seventy-two hours outside the country seems to be acceptable. Generally tourists who do get deported are those who are somewhat undesirable in the first place.

But be aware that at some point, the Ministry of Immigration could become serious and begin enforcing regulations. Once your application is in, you don't have to worry about leaving while your residency is being processed. I must emphasize that I am in no way encouraging people to do this "ninety-day turnaround" to get around the rules. I am merely reporting the situation at the time of this writing. If you are going to stay in Costa Rica year-round, you would be well advised to consider applying for residency. (This is discussed in detail in chapter 12.)

Even though Costa Rica's rules have tightened somewhat, they are still exceedingly liberal compared with those in most other countries. In the United States, for example, if you stay even one day over your visa, you might never be permitted to return!

It's embarrassing to contrast the openness of Costa Rica's immigration with the way the United States treats Costa Ricans when they want to vacation in Disneyland or Las Vegas, or visit friends and relatives who have immigrated to the States. To receive a temporary visa, a Costa Rican must visit the embassy, hat in hand, pay a nonrefundable application fee, and prove beyond the shadow of a doubt that he or she has every intention of returning to Costa Rica and has no possible motive for staying in the United States. It must be a humiliating experience to be denied a visa because your job doesn't pay a salary high enough to convince an embassy employee that you're sufficiently trustworthy to visit Hollywood and return. A large percentage of those requests are turned down with no explanation. Supposedly, a daughter of a Costa Rican vice president was once rejected because a clerk doubted her character, assuming her to be a prostitute looking for employment abroad.

Compared with U.S. immigration rules, Costa Rica's are very liberal. To become a legal resident, all you need to do is prove you have either $600 or $1,000 a month income and do not have a serious criminal record. From time to time the Costa Rican congress considers raising income requirements, thinking that they may be unrealistically low. In my opinion, it is unlikely they will take any action. If they do, I will report it on my *Choose Costa Rica* update Web site at www.discoverypress.com/update.

Also, from time to time the government declares an amnesty; those who've been in the country illegally for a certain amount of time—say, two years or longer—can apply for permanent residence. (However, this has not happened recently.) And people who are operating successful businesses are sometimes permitted to apply for residence papers. Those who qualify under amnesty rules are particularly lucky because they don't have to certify that they won't work for a living and therefore aren't restricted from holding jobs.

Again, I'm not recommending that anyone overstay his or her visa or try to ignore Costa Rican laws. I'm simply reporting how the laws are being enforced at this time and how they are being applied toward foreigners who have the wherewithal to support themselves, who may invest much-needed capital in the country, and who won't be taking jobs from Costa Rican citizens. Those who are indigent or who get into trouble may not find the laws applied quite so gently. Having said this, I again bring your attention to chapter 12, under the heading "Possible Work-Immigration Changes." There you will find a discussion of recent legal changes that could make a big difference in the lives of those who repeatedly renew visas and more or less live here permanently without legal residency. For those who contemplate staying in Costa Rica more than six months at a stretch, it isn't very difficult to obtain legal residency, so why not bite the bullet and make it legal?

## COSTA RICAN **RESIDENCY**

The government fully recognizes the economic value of foreign residents living in Costa Rica, bringing dollars to spend and deposit in banks. People from North America and Europe create jobs by investing money, building homes, starting businesses, and hiring Costa Rican employees.

For people like my wife and I, who can be satisfied with living half the year in Costa Rica and the other half in my home country, there's no clear advantage to becoming a legal resident. We can own property or a business and can travel about the country with nothing more than a tourist visa. On the other hand, there are restrictions and obligations on *pensionados* and *rentistas*—not ponderous ones, but they involve a certain amount of red tape. For example, you must prove that a certain amount of monthly income has been deposited in a Costa Rican bank. On a regular basis, you must provide police certification of good conduct, and you must live in Costa Rica for at least four (nonconsecutive) months of the year in order to hold on to your *residente* status.

For those who will be staying pretty much full-time in Costa Rica or who plan on entering business and working as a manager in the business, the resident option is no doubt the best way to go. Once you have the papers and fulfill the residency obligations, you are completely legal and can enjoy all the rights of a Costa Rican, except voting. Becoming a legal resident of Costa Rica doesn't affect your U.S. or Canadian citizenship in any way.

**CATEGORIES OF RESIDENTS** Immigration and applications for residency are handled by the Costa Rican Immigration Department. There are dozens of types of residency, but most North Americans use three classes of legal immigrant residents: Residente Pensionado, Pensionado Rentista, and Rentista Inversionista. After a stipulated number of years of residency under one of these categories, you may apply for permanent residency, and then you have fewer restrictions; for example, you can work without permission from the government.

**Residente Pensionado.** This category pertains to retired people with guaranteed pensions of $600 or more per month. Social Security is usually sufficient to qualify for this status. A total of at least $7,200 a year must be converted from dollars to colones in a Costa Rican bank and proof of this shown to the government every year. No law says that you can't take the money out of the bank right away and change it to a dollar account or that you have to spend all of it; you have only to prove that you've brought that amount of dollars into the country. Some people deposit the full amount at the beginning of the year to get the requirement out of the way, although Migracion may not like this much.

For a married couple the person without retirement income is considered a dependent, and no extra income is required (that is, only one pension per family). Children under the age of eighteen (or under twenty-five if in school) are also considered dependents. Social Security is sufficient proof of income. This is the option most retired people go for.

**Pensionado Rentista.** This category is for those who are not old enough to retire or who do not have a pension, yet who want residency in Costa Rica. Applicants must prove $1,000 a month income. The way to acquire this residency status is to deposit $60,000 in an interest-bearing dollar account in a Costa Rican bank. The bank then pays you $1,000 a month, or $12,000 a year (plus interest), from this account for a period of five years; this is often done by means of a Term Deposit. A recent change in the rules requires that the spouse of the applicant must also prove $1,000 a month income and has to make a similar deposit, plus $500 per child. Deposits in state-owned banks are government guaranteed without limit, and most bank interest in Costa Rica is not taxed by the Costa Rica government. Younger people and those who want to go into business often choose this option.

**Rentista Inversionista.** People who are serious about going into business prefer this category. It requires a $50,000 investment with an approved tourism or export business, $100,000 in a reforestation project, or $150,000 to $200,000 in any other type of business. If the investment is in an existing company, you need to submit the firm's latest balance sheet and a statement indicating its profit-and-loss situation, and there must be a (unspecified) number of legal employees. This status has become much more difficult to obtain.

You understand, of course, that you needn't become a resident to own or operate a business in Costa Rica: You can do so on a tourist visa. Many foreigners invest far less and don't bother with residency. However, they are ostensibly restricted to management duties and not permitted to work at ordinary tasks in the business. This is not usually enforced, especially if the person working isn't displacing a Costa Rican worker.

When it comes to investment in a business or a reforestation project, please exercise extreme caution. As mentioned elsewhere in this book, Costa Rica is teeming with sharks just waiting for fish like you and me. Reforestation investments are highly promoted as lucrative investments. You should be cautious of overly optimistic claims; teak promoters have poor track records in fulfilling their promises. Consult a good lawyer first.

**What Do You Get with Residency?** As a resident with any of the aforementioned three statuses, you have the following benefits and requirements:

1. You have all the rights of citizenship except voting.
2. You can own and manage businesses, but you cannot earn a salary from a Costa Rican employer. You can pay yourself dividends, however. Once your residency is permanent, you can work for anyone.
3. You must reside in Costa Rica the equivalent of at least four months a year, not necessarily contiguous months. Once you have permanent residency, you are expected to visit Costa Rica once a year for at least one day.
4. You must renew proof of stable and permanent income annually until you have full residency.

**RED TAPE** The question of whether to become a legal resident or to visit using a tourist visa varies with the individual. Some feel that four or five months is all they want to stay, so why bother with the red tape of papers? Others plan on making Costa Rica their primary home and therefore see benefits in becoming residents. It all depends on your circumstances. One benefit is that residents receive a 50 percent discount on in-country airline flights as well as certain other breaks, such as reduced entrance fees to parks.

To make an application, you can either do it yourself or hire someone to go through the red tape for you. The process requires a deposit of about $100 and about $30 for fees, stamps, and forms. It could take from a few months to a year before approval comes through, depending on the thoroughness of your preparation and who is assisting you. Meanwhile your residency status is legal and won't be challenged.

Ask around the North American community for recommendations of a good lawyer or an experienced *tramitador* (a person who knows which lines to stand in and knows whom to see to get your papers processed promptly). Some people I've talked to have had good experiences with *tramitadores* they located through classified ads in the *Tico Times*. But be careful: Hiring someone who doesn't know what he or she is doing not only takes a lot more time but could be a waste of money if the person does not or cannot follow through.

**ASSOCIATION OF RESIDENTS OF COSTA RICA** Personally, I am convinced that one of the most important moves you can make toward obtaining residency is joining ARCR (Association of Residents of Costa Rica) and letting them handle the red tape. Yes, some individuals have done the paperwork on their own, but you'll hear sad tales of woe from those who have tried it without knowing what they were doing or who chose a lawyer with little experience in maneuvering through the maze of bureaucracy. A provisional ARCR membership is $100, entitling you to apply for residency through the group, attend social events and meetings, and other benefits. Regular membership is $50 a year, and spouses are only $10 additional.

Further benefits are as follows: The association can make sure your annual papers are up to date, translate and notarize your documents, renew the required Costa Rican ID card, help you get a driver's license and other special permits, and assist you in many other ways before your move. The organization will also do English-to-Spanish translations and authenticate a photocopy of your resident's *carnét* so that you can leave your original at home.

Members with residency are eligible to receive doctor and hospital care in the National Health Services System, under terms of a special contract. This relieves you of the obligation of standing in line each month to make your payments. The organization pays it on a three-month basis and sends you proof of payment for the current month, which entitles you to medical service. You can also obtain all other types of insurance, a Miami P.O. box to receive your mail, and many other services. The association also publishes a newsletter six times a year. For more information write ARCR, Apdo. 1191–1007, Centro Colón, San José, or call (506) 2-233-8068. The ARCR has a comprehensive Web site at www.arcr.net.

**PAPERWORK** In any event, the process of getting your resident papers is best started by you, right in your home country. It's much easier to get these at home than by mail from Costa Rica. The four main items you need are listed below, and in all cases processing must be done through your local Costa Rican consulate. They charge about $40 per document.

1. **Income certification.** This is the first and most important step; it's often complicated and difficult. Rules and proof of income differ

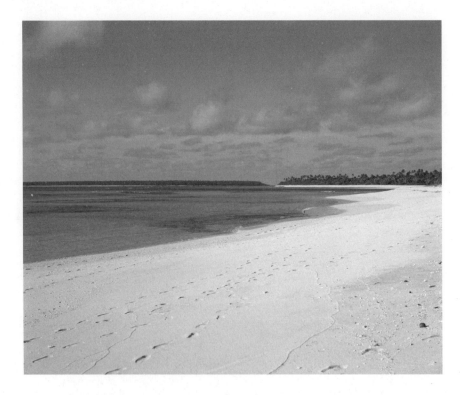

between Residente Pensionados and Pensionado Rentistas. Social Security or other government pension money is the easiest to prove. Ask for a statement from the pension source confirming that you have at least $600 a month pension, and have that notarized at a Costa Rican consulate in your country. If the pension is nongovernmental, you'll need notarized letters that the pension is for life and two letters from bank officials testifying to the soundness of the company's pension plan.

The guarantee of income for *rentistas* is $1,000 in interest and dividends from banks or investment houses. The decision on whether your income qualifies is made on a case-by-case basis. You'll need statements establishing that this income is guaranteed for at least five years, and you'll need to renew these guarantees every succeeding five years. The Costa Rican consulate can help you with this. Again, it's important to have the notary certification and authentication of the documents done by a consulate in your home country.

2. **Birth certificate.** This is needed for you and each of your dependents.
3. **Marriage certificate.** Proof of previous divorce is not necessary.
4. **Police certificate of good conduct.** Obtain this at your last place of residence, and make it the last document you receive. Have the police certify a set of fingerprints as well; ask the Costa Rican consulate for the necessary forms. Make the good-conduct verification your last step because it's only valid for six months from the time of certification. If you get this document first and then spend a lot of time with the other papers, it could expire before your application gets under way. I know of people who've had to return to the United States to get another conduct certification because theirs was more than six months old. You'll also need certificates of good conduct for dependents over eighteen.

Note, too, that if you are traveling with children, some special rules apply. Apparently, these rules apply more for Costa Rican citizens than for tourists, and even though they don't seem to be strictly enforced, it's important that you be aware of them. When a child traveling without both parents stays beyond thirty days, the child falls under the jurisdiction of the Patronato Nacional de la Infancia, a children's welfare organization. In order for a child to leave the country without both parents, it might be necessary to have a permit notarized by the Patronato offices on Nineteenth Street and Sixth Avenue in San José. I've never heard of any tourist being hassled for this, but if just one parent is traveling with a child for long periods, it might be a good idea to have a notarized statement of permission from the other parent. And remember, just having your documents notarized is not enough.

The documents must be taken to the Costa Rican consulate in your country to verify the notary's validity and certification. The notary isn't merely verifying your signature but also that the documents are valid and that they belong to you. Not following each step correctly is responsible for the many delays and obstacles you often hear people complain about.

Other details can be taken care of in Costa Rica at the time you make a formal request for residency. Several certified copies of your passport are required, and you'll fill out a questionnaire of personal information.

As a retiree, you'll have to sign a statement that you won't work for pay while in Costa Rica (without authorization) and that you'll spend at least four months a year in Costa Rica. (As stated earlier, the months needn't be consecutive.)

From here on, it's filling out forms, standing in line, waiting for stamps and signatures, standing in more lines to put a deposit in the bank, going hither and yon to stand in still more lines—most of which can be done by your surrogate, the *tramitador.*

# LEGAL **MATTERS**

In chapter 10 we discussed the pros and cons of buying real estate in Costa Rica. The nice thing is that property ownership is open to anyone, no matter what citizenship; it's fairly easy to gain a clear title, and you can feel absolutely confident about your ownership. The nasty part is that a lot of charlatans and swindlers are out there ready to take advantage of your trusting nature. Don't worry: They haven't a chance if you do things correctly and don't skip any steps in the process.

The following information comes to us courtesy of my friend Carlos Umaña of Tacsan & Umaña law offices in San José. For those of you with connections to the Internet, another source of Costa Rica legal information can be found at www.discoverypress.com/crinet. Another connection for understanding Costa Rica rules and regulations is the Association of Residents of Costa Rica (ARCR) Web site at www.casa canada.net/rulesandregulations.html.

Your first step is to cultivate a relationship with a lawyer who knows what the score is. In Costa Rica it's much easier to become an attorney than it is in the United States or Canada, so just because someone can legally assume the title *licenciado* doesn't guarantee he knows what he's doing, or even that he's ever practiced law. You'll find many *ticos*

who are entitled to call themselves attorneys but actually practice law as an occasional sideline. A poor attorney isn't necessarily crooked; he could be lazy, inefficient, or incompetent, which is just as bad.

A second important point, mentioned earlier: Make certain the lawyer is working for you, and exclusively for you. If you use the other party's attorney to represent both interests, you're facing the probability that the lawyer is primarily working for his first client and isn't on your side at all. Unlike the situation in the United States, this is how it can work in Costa Rica. So insist on having your attorney handle your part of the sale, buying or selling.

## PURCHASING **REAL ESTATE**

To make it easy to check on land ownership, all property, with a few exceptions, must be registered at the Property Department of the Public Record Office, known as the Registro Nacional. This office is located in Zapote and is open to the public. You can access the records on the Internet also. It's a rather easy system to research; however, it's best to have your attorney do the checking because he knows what to look for and where.

The first step, before you hand over any money, is to run a thorough title search of the public records to see whether the property really belongs to the seller, whether the seller is who he claims to be, and whether any mortgages, liens, encumbrances, or easements come attached to the property. Mortgages and liens must be properly registered to have any effect on the buyer. So if the title is clear, you needn't worry about outstanding debts. If a lender didn't register a second deed of trust, he's out of luck. A title search should cost less than $50, and it is well worth it. If the seller was untruthful, you won't waste any more time. Actually, to get started you can research a title or plot of land yourself in the Registro Nacional, simply by going to the Web site and filling in a form. If you find nothing wrong with the title, you can authorize your attorney to investigate further. (For details see the end of this chapter.)

You'll remember that all property is registered, with some exceptions. These exceptions are important. Let's review the three basic categories of Costa Rican properties:

1. **Recorded land.** This includes all properties you'll find registered at the Public Record Office. The vast majority of properties for sale today fall into this category.
2. **Nonrecorded land.** This is property that could be registered at the Public Record Office but has not yet been recorded. This applies to farmland, *fincas* (ranches), and homesteads—places that haven't legally changed hands for many decades or perhaps have been changed through a private contract. Nonrecorded land requires an attorney familiar with the procedure. It takes a judicial procedure to register land for the first time into public records. This kind of sale lacks the security granted by the Public Record Office.
3. **Nonregisterable land.** This is property that cannot be legally recorded at the Public Registry. This is the case with most beach-front property. In some instances beach properties can be possessed legally by individuals or corporations through a concession granted by the government. The lease is always through the government, but you must acquire possession from the previous possessor, if there is one.

# TRANSFERRING **RECORDED LAND**

Any individual or company, national or foreign, may legally own land sheltered by the Registro Nacional Public Record Office system. But for legal and economic reasons, you should consider placing your property in the name of a Costa Rican corporation, or *sociedad anónima* (more about this later in this chapter).

Recorded land transfers must be granted through a public deed. That is, buyer and seller must appear before a Costa Rican lawyer, or to be more precise, a notary public (to be chosen by the purchaser), who will insert the title transfer in his protocol. (A notary public is a licensed attorney who is endowed with "public trust" and the right to validate and legalize all contracts and deeds. Again, to protect your investment, you should insist on having your own attorney to perform as your notary public in the transaction.)

The purchase deed, as well as any liens or mortgages agreed to by the buyer, are then presented to the Public Record Office to be registered.

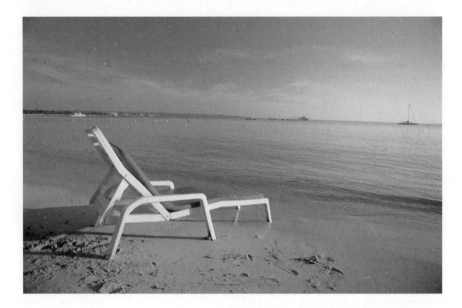

It's also the notary's duty to complete all recording procedures necessary to provide the title transfer with full efficacy. (This is another reason to have a good attorney working for you, someone who knows what the word *efficacy* means.)

Expenses and legal fees involved can range from 6 to 7 percent of the total amount of the transaction and on the assessed price of the property. These costs are customarily shared by buyer and seller on a fifty-fifty basis, unless agreed otherwise. My attorney recommends not to agree otherwise. Any deal you make should be on a fifty-fifty basis, with your lawyer involved to watch out for your interests.

## BEACHFRONT **PROPERTY**

Because of special regulations, some areas are not subject to private ownership. This is the case with most beachfront property, which is leased through concessions granted by the government. This is where things become complicated. Public Law No. 6043 of March 1977 established a restricted coastal zone called the Zona Marítimo/Terrestre. This law covers a strip of land, 200 meters (656 feet) deep, along both the Pacific Coast and the Atlantic Coast. The restricted zone is divided into two sections:

**1.** The Public Zone (*Zona Publica*), that first 50-meter strip of land starting at the mean high-tide line. This is public property; the public has full access to the Public Zone.
**2.** The next 150-meter strip of land is called the Restricted Zone (*Zona Restringida*).

The law states that no private individual or corporation is allowed to build on or use for private purposes "any portion whatsoever" of the Public Zone. However, it's sometimes possible to obtain a lease/concession on Restricted Zone properties for private or business use. Understand that when this happens, it isn't a deed, it's a "lease concession." At first the lease is with the local municipality; later on, after a procedure, the lease is with the Costa Rica Tourism Institute. Beneficiaries of lease concessions can be granted the use, occupation, and possession of the land, including the right to build. But the municipality can withhold building permits under certain circumstances.

Now comes a sticky point. The law says, "No lease concessions are granted to non–Costa Ricans who have resided in the country less than five years, nor to foreign companies, nor to national companies of which 50 percent or more of its stock is owned by non–Costa Ricans."

While that may be the law, the fact is that many if not most of the desirable Zona Restringida properties are held by Costa Rican corporations that are owned entirely by foreigners. This is, of course, difficult to verify, because ownership of a Costa Rican corporation is impossible to substantiate. (Tips on how to start a corporation are found later in this chapter.)

These lease concessions can be transferred from one person or company to another, subject to the approval of the municipality and the Costa Rican Tourism Institute. Leases are generally granted for periods that range from five to twenty years. The local municipality is entitled to charge a small leasing fee. At the end of the leasing period, the lessee can apply for an extension of the lease concession, and extensions are normally granted with the previous approval of the Tourism Institute.

Beachfront land not regulated by this law can be found, but it's extremely unusual to find titled property in areas within the restricted 200-meter zone. True, some beachfront land isn't regulated because it was in use before the beach laws were passed. These exempt parcels are so-called grandfathered properties. However, be cautious: Many people think that their property is grandfathered when it really is not. Some sellers claim that their property is grandfathered when they know it is not. The danger is that somewhere down the road, the government can decide that your lovely beach house is illegally constructed on property you do not own. All the more reason to have a good attorney, to protect your investment.

## OFFSHORE **CORPORATIONS**

For a variety of reasons, banking-secrecy laws such as those in Switzerland attract a great deal of interest among certain folks who have motives for hiding assets. As far as I know, there is no law against this as long as these accounts aren't used to defraud creditors or to evade paying taxes. Like Switzerland, Costa Rica has strict rules on nondisclosure of bank accounts. Having said this, I must point out that recent pressure from the U.S. government seems to be forcing U.S.-owned banks to reveal information about accounts held by U.S. citizens. The IRS wants the banks to fill out W-9 forms (Request for Taxpayer Identification Number and Certification), which contain depositors' Social Security numbers. As far as I know, this does not yet apply to Costa Rican government-owned institutions. That could be a matter of time.

An interesting angle of financial secrecy is the use of Costa Rican "offshore" corporations. Corporations can be started by anyone—citizen, resident, or tourist. Since there's no way of knowing precisely whose names are on the corporation books, it's almost impossible for others to discover who actually controls these corporations. In fact, the legal term *sociedad anónima* means "anonymous society." That's why Costa Rican corporation names are appended with "S.A." instead of "Inc." or "Ltd."

One common example of a legitimate use of a corporation is when buying or selling real estate. If the property belongs to a corporation, transfer of ownership is simple. You merely transfer the corporation's stock; the property belongs to whoever holds this stock. The ownership of the property hasn't changed hands, only the corporation shares, and the owners of the shares are now in control of the property.

Having stressed all of this about secrecy, I have to say that I feel uneasy about the extent of the anonymous nature of any corporation. Some feel that the U.S. government, using the pretext of "containing terrorism," has been pressuring countries that allow offshore corporations to relax their rules on financial secrecy. It stands to reason that Washington has pressured Costa Rica as well. A few years ago, the Costa Rican government insisted that every *sociadad anónima* (corporation) file a special one-time, year-end tax form that requested details about the officers of the corporation and how much income, if any, the corporation made. Whether any of this information will be surrendered to outsiders is questionable. For those who use their corporations for the usual legal purposes, such as property ownership, there is no problem. For those who have something to worry about, I would suggest a serious talk with your attorney.

Before we go any further, you need to understand a few crucial points. First, I am not an attorney, and even if I were, you would be foolish to accept legal advice from a book, particularly when it comes to activities as complicated as offshore corporations or foreign banking practices. Second, while most corporations and bank accounts in Costa Rica are legal, used for perfectly legitimate purposes, the ones used for illegal schemes are frequently toppled, sending overly creative schemers to jail. I suspect that what happens is that the corporation originally starts off with legal goals in mind and then branches out into a small tax fraud, which grows until it gets out of hand. Some schemes are so obvious that the IRS has little trouble spotting the smoke and flames. My final point is a reiteration of the first: I am not a lawyer, nor am I in any way urging readers to get involved in offshore corporations or secret bank accounts. I am merely reporting what Costa Rican residents and attorneys have passed along to me: Controlling real estate through a Costa Rican corporation is perfectly legal.

## YOUR COSTA RICAN **CORPORATION**

Costa Rica's corporate structure allows any person or persons (Costa Rican or not) to control a company without his or her name appearing in the public records. A Costa Rican lawyer (who must be a specialist in this) sets up a corporation without the real owners' names ever appearing in the record. It is termed a *sociedad anónima con acciones al portador,* or "anonymous society with all stock owned by the bearer." This means that although there is a legal president, secretary, and treasurer (often simply employees of the attorney), the actual ownership of the corporation is invested in whoever physically has the stock certificates in his or her pocket or safe-deposit box. Even the attorney has no way of knowing whether the original clients still own the shares. This arrangement is prohibited in the United States but is perfectly legal in Costa Rica.

This corporation is free to engage in many types of business activities, both in Costa Rica and in other countries. Theoretically, because it is considered a "foreign corporation" as far as the IRS is concerned, it pays no taxes in the United States. (There's talk about changing this.) Because it's a Costa Rican corporation, it pays nothing on what it earns outside Costa Rica. This doesn't relieve the individual of the responsibility of reporting income and paying income taxes in his or her home country. Recent laws now require that a yearly report of a corporation must be filed with the Costa Rican government; should there be no income to report, there are no tax consequences, but not filing the report makes the corporation liable for a fine. So if you already have a corporation in Costa Rica and haven't been filing reports, see your lawyer.

Be aware that from time to time there can be arbitrary changes in tax rules for corporations. No matter that your corporation does not make money. For example, if the corporation's only asset is a house or an automobile, there could be an extra form to fill out to report that there is no income. To avoid any fines for not filing, you should have someone in Costa Rica monitoring the situation and notify you when something new comes up. I have my lawyer take care of things like this for me—it's done automatically. If you prefer to do it yourself, you should watch the *Tico Times* or one of the online newspapers, such as *A.M. Costa Rica* or *La Nación*, or at least have a friend in Costa Rica give you a heads-up on the rare occasion some special law change happens.

**ADVANTAGES OF A CORPORATION** Again, it's always advisable for both foreigners and Costa Ricans to own land through a corporation. Among the advantages is a reduction of personal liabilities and taxes. The ownership of assets, such as real estate, boats, and automobiles, is the main purpose of most registered corporations in Costa Rica.

A corporation can be owned by a group of shareholders or fully owned by one shareholder. This way a single individual or a small group of people can operate the company in a relatively simple and inexpensive manner. The asset (your house or your car) can be sold or transferred simply by handing over the shares of the corporation, because it is owned by the corporation, not the individual, even though he or she may own all the shares. Your attorney will show you the best ways to ensure control of the company and the overall handling of corporate power.

An important point about corporations is to make sure you are getting a full-fledged corporation; there are shortened versions that have some serious drawbacks. Don't go for a cut-rate, partial incorporation, because you'll not get all the required services, and it could expire at the end of a brief period. Later you'll find you have to go back and spend more money to put the company on a par with other corporations. Most attorneys will charge from $350 to $900 to form a complete corporation.

**LEGAL DETAILS** There are four main stages in the process of forming a Costa Rican corporation. (The details herewith were supplied by my attorney, who knows what he is doing, so I merely present them here, without any attempt to explain or even understand them!)

1. A document called the Articles of Incorporation or Constitutive Charter of the company will need to be prepared. This document will be drawn up by your attorney. The Constitutive Charter determines the organization, administration, and bylaws of the

company. This is signed by all the shareholders, the appointed members of the board of directors, the controller, and the *agente residente*.

2. Before registration in the Public Record Office, your attorney will announce the company's constitution in Costa Rica's official newspaper, *La Gaceta*. This takes about two weeks. Also, you must make a deposit of the amount of the capital stock indicated in the Constitutive Charter—usually 1,000 colones—in a national bank. The amount of shares in the corporation and their denomination are determined by the founders. All shares must have equal value and must be worth at least 1 colón, but there's no top limit to a share's value. The money deposited can be withdrawn once the company has been duly recorded.

3. The company must be registered in the Public Record Office. This registration is essential to legally constitute a corporation in Costa Rica. The registration process is performed by the notary public (your lawyer). The whole process takes from one to three months, depending on the time it takes for the Public Registry to approve the company's bylaws, including the books.

4. You'll receive a set of three accounting books (*Diario, Mayor, and Inventario y Balances*) and three "legal" books (Shareholders' Record, Shareholders' Assemblies, and Board of Directors' Meetings). Your attorney will present the books to the Ministerio de Hacienda for their initial authorization. Once duly legalized, these books should register all internal affairs of the company (as well as stock transfers) and are kept privately by the shareholders. You can leave them with your attorney or place them in a secure place, such as a safe-deposit box. Remember, whoever has the books in hand also has control of the assets.

To form a Costa Rican corporation, you need a minimum of two initial shareholders. Once the company is formed and properly inscribed in the Public Record Office, the shares can be transferred to a single person, who becomes the sole shareholder of the company.

The name of the company must be in Spanish, Latin, or any native dialect. Of course, a name can't be identical or equivalent to that of an existing corporation. And names with a meaning in a foreign language (such as English or German) are not allowed without special exceptions. Your attorney in charge of preparing the Articles of Incorporation will ask you for a list of names (in Spanish), and he'll research them and determine whether they will be accepted by the Public Record Office.

There must be a board of directors with at least the following officers: president, secretary, and treasurer. The president must be the principal representative of the company. Other members of the board can also be made representatives of the corporation, depending on how the founders of the company decide to do the Articles of Incorporation. (The attorney who sets up the corporation takes care of this.) The members of the board may or may not be shareholders. The directors must be present when the company is legally formed, to personally accept their designation and sign the Corporation Charter along with the shareholders or power of attorney.

The controller cannot be a shareholder or a member of the board of directors. The person appointed as controller has to sign the Articles of Incorporation. Usually this will be someone on your lawyer's office staff.

Every Costa Rican company must designate an *agente residente*. The *agente residente* will probably be your Costa Rican attorney, who will be a formal representative for official matters. He has no powers to act on the company's behalf. The fee for this service is usually $100 a year.

# CHECKING PROPERTY **ON THE INTERNET**

Costa Rica may be somewhat backward in some aspects, as are most developing countries, but we must admire the way the government has utilized the Internet to open the Registro Nacional to the public. What used to be a time-consuming and bewildering process of investigating the legal status of a piece of real estate or ownership of an automobile has now become a simple matter of calling up a Web page and entering a few numbers. Within a few seconds, you can find out if that beautiful house with a view of the valley actually belongs to the person who is try-ing to sell it to you. Does he have a mortgage on the property that he neglected to mention? Are there any liens against the house because of an automobile accident or a liable judgment? You can discover who the previous owners were, in case you would like to talk with them to see if they have any information for you. In some instances you can find out who the neighbors are. Before you decide to buy that bargain four-wheel-drive Toyota, you might be interested to know that it hasn't been reported stolen, or that the title is not held encumbered by a bank loan. The previous owners are also listed.

Having described the benefits of using the Registro Web site, I have to make a disclaimer: Within the past few months, some significant changes have been made in the site layout and how to work the system. Instructions published in the eighth edition of *Choose Costa Rica* are now out of date. It may require some practice in order to locate the documents you need, yet navigating the site on your own is entirely possible as long as you understand what data needs to be entered where. You might ask a *tico* friend to walk you through the procedure until you get the hang of it. Your attorney can also help you out. A Spanish dictionary will help you understand some of the legal terms. Even the Internet address has changed. It is now www.registronacional.go.cr.

# UNITED STATES **INCOME TAX**

U.S. citizens living abroad must file income taxes. You can file through the U.S. embassy, and you have until June 15 (instead of April 15). The general rule is: U.S. citizens are taxed on their worldwide income and must file and pay U.S. income taxes regardless of where they live. In 2007 more than four million Americans living outside the country filed income tax returns. However, most taxes assessed by a foreign country are deductible from U.S. taxes.

With the general rule comes an exception that could be valuable for some workers. That is, qualified taxpayers can exclude from gross income as much as $80,000 in income earned while living abroad. To qualify, this income has to be earned at a job with wages received in the foreign country. Money earned from rentals, investments, bonuses, or pensions in the United States do not fall under this provision.

The tax-free foreign-earned income includes foreign-source wages, salaries, bonuses, commissions, cost-of-living differential, home leave, tips, professional fees, and any other form of compensation for personal services rendered. It even includes noncash income, such as the use of a car. To be eligible, you must have a job that's expected to last for not less than one year, and you are expected to spend at least 330 full days

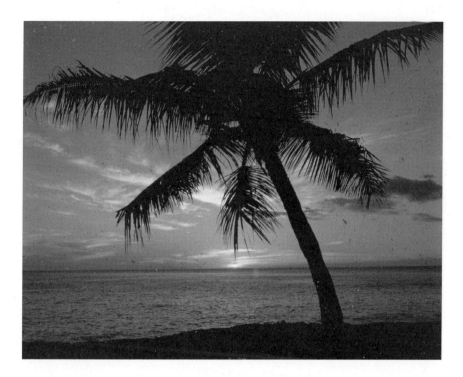

out of any twelve consecutive months outside of the United States. This is generous of the IRS; however, I can't imagine many expatriates earning enough wages in Costa Rica to make it worth their while to file an exemption. Since work permits are so difficult to come by, there are very few U.S. taxpayers who are working legally in the country in the first place.

You are required to file with the Costa Rican government on all income earned within the country. Your attorney can file these tax forms. You're also required to file a tax statement for any corporation that owns property, even if there's no income. If you own a house or land, chances are it is held in the name of your personal corporation. If the house has earned no income, you won't pay taxes, but there is a fine for not filing.

Until recently, income earned in the United States and Canada was totally exempt from Costa Rican income taxes. However, in 2005 the National Assembly passed a law to the effect that certain foreign income will be taxable. The problem is, at this point in time, nobody knows what this means, just what income will be taxable, at what rate, and what deductions will be allowed. Furthermore, it is unclear how the government will know how much taxable income an expatriate receives in his home country. These details could take some time to figure out, and in the meantime, most foreign taxes are deductible from your U.S. taxes. I'll try to keep folks informed via my Web site: www.discoverypress.com/update.

A caveat here: I am not a tax expert. Please check with a tax professional before making any major tax decisions.

# APPENDIX

## EMBASSY OF COSTA RICA **IN THE UNITED STATES**

2112 S Street NW, Washington, DC 20008; (202) 234-2945; fax (202) 265-4795. Tomas Dueñas, ambassador.

## COSTA RICAN CONSULATES **IN THE UNITED STATES**

### ARIZONA

**Phoenix** (area of coverage: Arizona): Andrew P. Burke, Honorary Consul, 7373 E Doubletree Ranch Road, Suite 200, Scottsdale, AZ 85258; (480) 951-2264; fax (480) 991-6606

### CALIFORNIA

**Los Angeles** (areas of coverage: Arizona, Hawaii, Nevada, Southern California, and Utah): Percy Calvo Cartín, Consul, 1605 West Olympic Boulevard, Suite 400, Los Angeles, CA 90015; (213) 380-7915; fax (213) 380-5639

**San Francisco** (areas of coverage: Alaska, Idaho, Montana, Northern California, Oregon, and Washington): Manuel Escoto, Honorary Consul, P.O. Box 7643, Fremont, CA 94537; (510) 790-0785; fax (510) 792-5249

### COLORADO

**Denver** (area of coverage: Colorado): Tito Chaverri, Honorary Consul, 3356 South Xenia Street, Denver, CO 80231-4542; (303) 696-8211; fax (303) 696-1110

### DISTRICT OF COLUMBIA

(Areas of coverage: all U.S. territory): Alejandro Cendeño, Consul General, 2112 S Street NW, Washington, DC 20008; (202) 328-6628; fax (202) 265-4795

## FLORIDA

**Miami** (area of coverage: Florida): Oscar Camacho, Consul General, 1600 NW Forty-second Avenue, Miami, FL 33126; (305) 871-7485

**Tampa** (area of coverage: Florida): Erica Salgado, Consul General, 14502 North Dale Mabry Highway, Suite 200, Tampa, FL 33618; (813) 969-3837; fax (813) 969-3357

## GEORGIA

**Atlanta** (area of coverage: Georgia): Emilia Trejos, Consul General, 1870 The Exchange, Suite 100, Atlanta, GA 30339; (770) 951-7025; fax (770) 951-7073

## ILLINOIS

**Chicago** (areas of coverage: Illinois, Indiana, Iowa, Kentucky, Michigan, Minnesota, Missouri, North Dakota, Ohio, South Dakota, and Wisconsin): Juan Salas Araya, Consul, 185 North Wabash Avenue, Suite 1123, Chicago, IL 60601; (312) 263-2772; fax (312) 263-5807

## LOUISIANA

**New Orleans Temporary** (areas of coverage: Alabama, Arkansas, Louisiana, Mississippi, New Mexico, Oklahoma, and Tennessee): 1514 Martens Drive, Suite 210, Hammond, LA 70401; (504) 581-6400 or (985) 549-5454

## MASSACHUSETTS

**Boston** (area of coverage: Massachusetts): 175 McClellan Highway, East Boston, MA 02134; (617) 561-2444; fax (617) 561-2461

## MINNESOTA

**St. Paul** (area of coverage: Minnesota): Anthony L. Andersen, Honorary Consul, 2424 Territorial Road, St. Paul, MN 55114; (651) 481-3616; fax (651) 645-4684

## NEW YORK

**New York City** (areas of coverage: Connecticut, Maine, Massachusetts, New York, New Jersey, Pennsylvania, and Rhode Island): 80 Wall Street, Suite 718, New York, NY 10005; (212) 509-3066; fax (212) 509-3068

## PUERTO RICO

**San Juan** (area of coverage: Puerto Rico): Avenida Ponce de Leon, Edificio 1510, Oficina P1, Esquina Calle Pelaval, San Juan, Puerto Rico 00909; (787) 723-6227; fax (787) 723-6226

## TEXAS

**Houston** (area of coverage: Texas): Sergio Valverde, Consul General, 3000 Wilcrest, Suite 112, Houston, TX 77042; (713) 266-0484; fax (713) 266-1527

**San Antonio** (area of coverage: Texas): Marta Rojas, Consul, 6836 San Pedro, Suite 116, San Antonio, TX 78216; (210) 824-8474; fax (210) 824-8489

## COSTA RICAN CONSULATES **IN CANADA**

### BRITISH COLUMBIA

**Vancouver:** Antonio Arreaga, Honorary Consul, Suite 430–789, West Pender Street, Vancouver, BC V6C 1H2 Canada; (604) 681-2152; fax (604) 688-2152

### ONTARIO

**Ottawa** (areas of coverage: all Canadian territory): 325 Dalhouise Street, Suite 407, Ottawa, ON K1N 7G2 Canada; (613) 562-2855; fax: (613) 562-2582

**Embassy of Costa Rica,** 135 York Street, Suite 208, Ottawa, ON K1N 5TA Canada; (613) 562-2855; fax (613) 562-2582

**Toronto:** Peter Alexander Kircher, Honorary Consul, 164 Avenue Road, Toronto, ON M5R 2H9 Canada; (416) 961-6773; fax (416) 961-6771

### QUEBEC

**Montreal:** Roy Thompson, Consul General, 1425 René Levexque-West, Suite 602, Montreal, QC H3G 1T7 Canada; (514) 393-1057; fax (514) 393-1624

# INDEX

## ABOUT THE **AUTHOR**

John Howells and his wife, Sherry, know Latin America well. John lived with his family in Mexico as a youth and has traveled extensively throughout Central and South America, Spain, and Portugal, publishing several guidebooks about living, retiring, and investing in these foreign locations. His thirty-three-year love affair with Costa Rica and Central America uniquely qualifies him as an expert on what it is like to be an expatriate in this charming little country known as "the Switzerland of the Americas." John and Sherry divide their time between Costa Rica and California.